PRAISE FOR *MUSIC TO MY YEARS*

"If Chance the Rapper and Cristela the Comedian had a baby, it would be this book. Cristela's memoir is an emotional journey that will make you laugh, cry, and everything in between. As the first Latina woman to create, produce, write, and star in her own prime-time show and who found success despite all the challenges she faced, Cristela will have you continually rooting for her. Also, all the songs she name-drops are real bops."

—Wanda Sykes

"Cristela's real life evolved into her comedy and her comedy informed her sense of right and wrong—but more than anything, Cristela has remained real and funny. Read the book. You'll understand."

—Whoopi Goldberg

"Cristela brings her signature humor to bear as she offers a brilliant and touching reflection on how the personal is political. It is no coincidence that after ruminating on themes that include identity, representation, and inequality, she caps off the book with a fierce defense of our democracy and the people whom it is meant to serve. I was inspired by her story of political awakening and hope others will read this and deepen their own political activism."

—Julián Castro

"*I loved the book.* Cristela vividly enlightens, educates, and entertains us on her hard journey from the poverty and culture of the Mexico–Texas border to stardom, honestly sharing her life lessons and the music that sustained her. [This is] a story that will guide us to want to be as strong, compassionate, and visionary as she is for family, friends, and country. Music is such a big part of one's life. When we stood on the picket lines, we sang 'We Shall Overcome' and 'This Little Light of Mine' a thousand times from the early morning till the strikebreakers left the fields. There is so much to say about the book, it affirmed my life in many ways, as I am sure it will for so many Latinas. We are alike."

—Dolores Huerta

"Alonzo crafts a humorous writing style that feels like an intimate conversation with readers. The jokes jump off the page and provide an emotional relief to the harsh realities of hardship and poverty she experienced. Alonzo's memoir is a timely reminder that regardless of economic status, race, or gender, love is the connection that ties together all humanity."

—*Booklist*

"A lovely reflection on comedy, pop culture, and community—one that will make you want to revisit the soundtrack of your own life."

—*Bookriot*

MUSIC

TO MY YEARS

A Mixtape Memoir of Growing Up and Standing Up

●

CRISTELA ALONZO

ATRIA PAPERBACK

New York   London   Toronto   Sydney   New Delhi

ATRIA
PAPERBACK

An Imprint of Simon & Schuster, LLC
1230 Avenue of the Americas
New York, NY 10020

First Atria Paperback edition May 2024

ATRIA PAPERBACK and colophon are trademarks of Simon & Schuster, LLC

Simon & Schuster: Celebrating 100 years of publishing in 2024

For information about special discounts for bulk purchases, please contact Simon &
Schuster Special Sales at 1-866-506-1949 or business@simonandschuster.com.

The Simon & Schuster Speakers Bureau can bring authors to your live event. For
more information or to book an event, contact the Simon & Schuster Speakers
Bureau at 1-866-248-3049 or visit our website at www.simonspeakers.com.

Interior design by A. Kathryn Barrett

Manufactured in the United States of America

1   3   5   7   9   10   8   6   4   2

Library of Congress Cataloging-in-Publication Data

Names: Alonzo, Cristela, author.
Title: Music to my years : a mixtape memoir of growing up
and standing up / Cristela Alonzo.
Description: First Atria Books hardcover edition. | New York : Atria Books, 2019.
Identifiers: LCCN 2019019265 (print) | LCCN 2019980326 (ebook) |
ISBN 9781501189203 (hardcover) | ISBN 9781501189210 (paperback) |
ISBN 9781501189227 (ebook other)
Subjects: LCSH: Alonzo, Cristela. | Women comedians—United States—
Biography. | Hispanic American comedians—Biography. | Children of
immigrants—United States—Biography.
Classification: LCC PN2287.A544 A3 2019 (print) | LCC PN2287.A544 (ebook)
| DDC 792.702/8092 [B]—dc23
LC record available at https://lccn.loc.gov/2019019265
LC ebook record available at https://lccn.loc.gov/2019980326

ISBN 978-1-5011-8920-3
ISBN 978-1-5011-8921-0 (pbk)
ISBN 978-1-5011-8922-7 (ebook)

This book is dedicated to the people who have worked in the fields, picking the food we eat. The people who clean houses, take care of children, and work in restaurants. To every person who has worked in a job that sometimes makes them feel invisible, I want you to know that not only do I see you, but I am a child who comes from someone just like you.

People like me get to live out their dream because of people like you who have sacrificed their own dreams in order to let their future generations have a chance at life.

Gracias.
Thank you.

TRACK LISTING

INTRODUCTION
IN THE BEGINNING . . .

I'm sitting in my living room, having just finished a bag of Flamin' Hot Cheetos that I dipped into melted nacho cheese. My fingers are stained from that weird (yet delicious) red coating that makes me look like I just murdered someone with my bare hands. And I can't help but think, *Cristela, this is NOT how you write a book. Unless it's a guide to murder.*

I have to be honest, if you had told me when I was a kid that I would ever attempt to write a book, I would've said, "Get away from me, stranger. I don't know you." And the truth is that this is not really a book, per se, but a brand spanking New Testament. You read that right. I've decided to write a new Bible. I figured since we seem to be remaking old TV shows and movies, why not reboot the Bible and update it for what people are into nowadays? Let's add more explosions; maybe a car chase?

I'm kidding. I was raised very Catholic: I don't know anything about the Bible.

So why am I writing a book? It was inevitable. I'm one of the few Latina stand-up comedians that get to travel the country and live their dream. I made TV history by becoming the first Mexican

American woman to create, produce, and star in her own network TV sitcom, *Cristela* (named after me, of course—not some other Cristela). I was also the first Latina lead in a Disney-Pixar release when I got the opportunity to voice the character of Cruz Ramirez in a little movie called *Cars 3*. My life is now filled with mansions and limos. I'm living the life of a Brown Barbie. Isn't that exciting? I know, I am SO successful!

Kidding again. The closest I get to living in a mansion is being able to afford all the brand-name cereal I want—and that is EXACTLY where I am happy being. I consider my journey a success story because I chased after my dream and accomplished it. And how many people can say that? People ask me how I've been able to do what I've done, and the answer is always the same: "I have no clue." I mean it. There is no map I can give people to show them my path. I am not Dora the Explorer, even though if you saw childhood pictures of me, you would think otherwise.

I was raised in a tiny town in south Texas, on the US–Mexico border, by a Mexican immigrant woman who had a second-grade education and a PhD in spankings.

Life wasn't easy. I grew up really poor. I know a lot of people say they grew up poor, but my family lived well below the poverty line for decades. You know how some kids would play "The floor is lava"? I would play "The floor is a real floor that doesn't have holes!" I used to watch extreme home makeover shows and wish my family could one day live in a house that looked like the before picture.

For most of my childhood, I was a latchkey kid. It was vital I get home immediately after classes. I wasn't allowed to go outside and play because my mom didn't think it was safe. I couldn't spend time with my friends after school and had to spend my life indoors. I had to create my own world filled with friendships that would fit the constraints I had been given. Little did I know I would find the best friend I was yearning for inside my house.

This friend was perfect for me because I could pick whenever I wanted to spend time with it and ours was the kind of friendship my mom approved of. I didn't have to leave the house to spend time with it, and it protected me from the outside world. It was pop culture—my intense love of music and TV, to be specific. It was enabled by the amount of time I would spend by myself as a latchkey kid in search of life lessons and friendship. I forged friendships with characters from my favorite TV shows, connecting with them as if they were real people. I would listen to my music on a little red AM/FM plastic radio from RadioShack.

My love of music and television became not only my best friend but my teacher as well. It taught me to love art. It taught me to speak English (Spanish was my first language). It taught me how to "be American." I didn't know that was a lesson I would even have to learn, since I was American myself, but I had been born in Texas and my mother hadn't. I had to figure out a lot of stuff on my own because my mother was unfamiliar with certain things, like how important college was or what a casserole was. I still don't know what a casserole is, but I imagine it's a lasagna that's not Italian. Am I even close?

She came from a culture that was different from the one I was being raised in. Some of her thinking didn't coincide with ideals I was discovering in Texas, like in regards to what she had been taught about gender roles. She had been raised to believe women were meant to serve men and didn't have a voice. The men could do whatever they wanted to women because the women were seen as property. Men could pick the women they'd marry and the women (and young girls) had no say. Yet what I learned by watching TV shows in America was that women had their own minds, their own thoughts. They could make their own decisions, and if that meant being single, then so be it. That is a lesson I learned from watching *The Mary Tyler Moore Show*. The character Mary was a single woman in her thirties: she had a career, no man, and she was happy. Watching TV shows like that made me feel like I had hope. I didn't have to follow in the footsteps of women who came before me in my family. Here, I had a choice.

While television taught me about American culture, music taught me a more abstract lesson: it taught me how to feel. A good song entertains you. A great song takes you on a journey you'll never forget. When I look back and think of some of the purest moments of joy I had with my family, music was usually involved. These moments were unplanned and at times came from some kind of struggle, but there was such a beauty to them because they made me feel as if everything was going to be okay. Even if for a minute, I would forget about the bad times because I was feeling such happiness.

Sometimes we'd have our electricity turned off because there was no money to pay the bill. It usually wasn't that big of a deal during the day, but at night, when it was pitch-black, we sat around, limited in what we could do because we couldn't see anything.

I remember a lot of those nights when my mom would come home from work because we would end up outside, lying on the trunk of our car, looking up at the sky. The moon and the stars served as our electricity. Some of the best moments of those stargazing nights were when someone would grab the keys and turn on the car radio to have music playing in the background. Most of those times, we would listen to a soft rock radio station we could pick up from across the border in Reynosa, Tamaulipas. A lot of times, the songs that played would inspire our conversations. If a Vicente Fernández song played (for those of you who don't know, he is like Mexican Elvis but possibly bigger), it would inspire my mom to tell stories about her difficult childhood living in Mexico, having no food to eat, no shoes or education. Even though we had no electricity and at times no food ourselves, I knew I had it better than she had as a child. Then there were other instances when a song like Prince's "Kiss" would come on and we'd all sing along as my mother tried to hilariously re-create the music video, which would make us laugh for what seemed to be an eternity. Looking back, I realize music was like another member of my family; it always has been.

I'm a first-generation Mexican American woman with not much of a sense of who she really is. I've straddled two cultures that at times make me question if I'm "enough" for either one. I feel as if there are other people who feel like I do. I'm not sure where I come from or where I belong, and I mean that literally. My mother came from a little village in Mexico that didn't keep a lot of records. She wasn't even sure when her birthday was. She thought it was anywhere from December 13 to 15. She wasn't even sure about the year she had been born. It was either 1943 or 1944. She ended up figuring out that the best guess for her birthday was December 15, 1944.

One of the reasons I wanted to write about my life is because I want people to know about my history, the part I do know about. I have struggled to figure out my own sense of identity, due in part to constantly having to defend it to people. A recurring theme in my life has been me telling people stories about my hard upbringing and them finding those stories completely unbelievable, at times asking me if I'm exaggerating the poverty. I've heard the tired "But you speak so well . . ." line from people more times than I can count. I've never understood this idea, that if you are able to speak in complete sentences, you must come from money. Poor people can be smart too. We don't learn different math; we don't read a different version of books than rich people do. Money doesn't dictate your future; you do. I am proof of that. I started with absolutely nothing but an insane love of pop culture that led me to where I am now. I forged my own way and became the black sheep in the family by following my dreams, taking a leap into the unknown, and not listening to people when they said I couldn't reach them. I'm so glad I didn't. I can't imagine my life if I hadn't tried to follow my dreams. People need to know that it doesn't matter where your source of inspiration and ambition comes from. It's how you use it that counts.

My book is a collection of stories, ranging from the ridiculous—like the time the theme song of *The Golden Girls* taught me about friendship but also ironically got me sent to the principal's office—to more devastating times, like when I was in the hospital room as my mother took her last breath and left me an orphan at the age of twenty-three. It's a mixtape or playlist I've curated of some of the most important songs and TV shows of my life.

We all have songs that come into our lives to remind us of specific moments. We might think about our first love, our first loss . . . sometimes you remember the person you hooked up with that you wish you could forget about . . . but you can't because of that stupid song! "Don't Speak" from No Doubt is one of those songs for me. I half like it, half can't stand it because when I was in high school, this guy I had a huge crush on (but would never be allowed to date) gave me the *Tragic Kingdom* CD and told me to listen to that specific song. When I first heard it, I was so in love with it. I couldn't believe that he had picked a song for me. Then he started ignoring me. After a week, I realized that giving me that CD was his way of saying he didn't want to talk to me anymore. I was seventeen when that happened, but cut to decades later: even though I can sing along to that song now, there's still a part of me that gets taken to that moment when he put that CD in my hand, and it bums me out. That's usually the point where I'll go online and look him up to see how he's doing now. (Unfortunately, he's doing well.)

So maybe you picked up this book because you're dying to know how to become a successful Latina in Hollywood. Here's your answer: Google "Sofía Vergara" and read how she did it because she is killing it. Maybe you picked up this book because it's the perfect size to hold up a piece of furniture missing a leg, or maybe you just want to read my version of the Bible, which includes my pitch for making Vicks into a saint so that when we get sick, we can light a candle and stand over a jar of it to let the vapors clear up our sinuses.

Either way, thank you for buying this book. *Music to My Years* is the mixtape of my life and all proceeds go to Charity.*

---

*That's what I call my bank account.

Three-year-old me, barefoot outside the diner where my family squatted on Nebraska Street in San Juan, Texas.

"MORE THAN A FEELING"
BOSTON

It was the best of times, it was the worst of times. (By now you might have guessed this is a Latino reboot of *A Tale of Two Cities*. I wanted to make sure the chapter started out strong.)

I'm joking, of course, but that first line does apply to where I grew up. It was the best and worst times for me in south Texas, and in a way, it *was* a tale of two cities: San Juan, Texas, and Reynosa, Tamaulipas. I was born and raised in a tiny border town named San Juan, and when I was a little kid, I was convinced we were Puerto Ricans (which as a child, I thought was a different way of saying Mexican). It turns out we weren't. I lived in an area called the Rio Grande Valley, the southernmost part of the state of Texas. I loved growing up in my little neck of the woods. Most of the area was flat, sometimes with palm trees lining streets or with the occasional water tower looming over a town in an empty field. Musician Freddy Fender was from one of the towns in the Rio Grande Valley—San Benito, Texas—and had the distinction of getting his face painted on one of those water towers. I've always said that, in my area, getting your face on a water tower is like getting a spot on the Hollywood Walk of Fame.

I like the idea of starting my story with a reference to Freddy Fender because it's a nod to some of the music I grew up listening to as a kid, but looking back now, I see that I have spent my entire life putting together this amazing quilt of melodies from different genres. A blanket of old songs, friends that wrap around me when I feel happy or sad. "More Than a Feeling" from Boston was one of those songs for me. For those who are unfamiliar, Boston was a band out of Des Moines, Iowa.

I'm joking, can you imagine?

Boston is a band from, well, Boston that was huge in the seventies. They had a number of hits, but "More Than a Feeling" is probably the one for which they're best known. It was more than just a song to me because it reminded me of the beginning of a dream.

This is the part where one might wonder how on earth a song like "More Than a Feeling" is tied to the life of this little faux Puerto Rican girl (that obviously had an identity crisis for the first part of her life), but go with me on this. First things first, let me break down the song for those that might not be familiar with it. It is considered classic rock, which means that when it plays, parents get excited and kids make fun of them for liking it. One of the surest ways to feel old is the moment you start seeing TV shows and listening to music you grew up with being called "classic."

When I first heard this song, I was seven years old. It was nighttime, and I was sitting in the family car outside of my godmother's house while my mom was inside paying for some Avon products she had ordered. I didn't feel like joining her because my godmother, Martha, and my mom would get into talking about family gossip and I didn't know anyone they were talking about. You'd hear them say, "Did you hear about Jose? No, not Big Jose, Little Jose." It was summer and the windows had to be rolled down because our car didn't have air conditioning. (In fact, I didn't even know cars had air conditioning until I was way older.)

I also wanted to be outside because, at night, I planned to wish on a star. I would do this every night. The sun would set, and I would look for the first star I could find, close my eyes, and say the kids' poem "Twinkle, twinkle, little star . . ." Then I'd make a wish.

That specific night, my sister, Julie, had driven my mom to my godmother's house because my mom didn't drive. Julie went in with my mom because she liked hearing them talk and had left the keys in the ignition for me so I could turn the key and listen to music. Then "More Than a Feeling" started playing. It started out so quietly that, for a couple of seconds, I wondered if the song was actually even playing. But it was. Its slow introduction as the guitar faded in caught me by surprise. I remember thinking, *What was that? Why is it so cool?* The drums kicked in and the lyrics began as the singer, Brad Delp, started talking about playing music to start his day. I remember being so overwhelmed by this line because I did that same thing. As a kid, I would wake up every day and listen to music immediately. No day of mine officially began without a song. I used to own a red plastic radio from RadioShack that used AAA batteries. I'd pull out the antenna to pick up reception and would listen to the local radio stations. Back then, they would play the same small group of songs over and over again, so you'd get to learn the lyrics pretty quickly. The first song I would hear in the day would dictate the energy I would have. I used to play this game where I would ask the radio a question and then I'd turn it on and the first song I heard was the answer to the question I asked it. The questions ranged from the silly, like "Will I get that red Menudo lunch box I want?" to "Will I ever have my own bed?"

I always wanted to leave my hometown to explore the world. Maybe it was because I loved staring up at the sky, and the never-ending stars in a small-town sky make you realize there is so much out there you don't know about. As I sat in the car listening to this song, I remember looking up and finding the star for my nightly wish. I closed my eyes and the chorus of the song started playing. *More than a feeling* . . .

The chorus collided with my wish, and I smiled as if it were the first time I had ever wished on a star. I felt as if I were in a music video, with the lyrics fitting my thoughts perfectly. My wish that night was to leave San Juan, Texas—to explore the world and take my family with me. That song made me feel like I could do just that. I made my wish and, afterward, even told myself, "Cris, you have to remember this wish for the rest of your life . . . This is the most important wish ever!" And to this day I do. I remind myself of that night all the time. And I think about how I often started my day (with the radio) and ended my day (with the star) in a state of hope.

You might wonder how a child so young was capable of thinking like this. Well, my family didn't have money. We were poor. Most of the time, I was too busy to notice this because I had a happy childhood. But there were times where the brutal truth was too hard to ignore. Indeed, if I were a superhero, you might say this was my origin story—a story that began in the 78589 zip code . . .

My hometown looked like a lot of the small towns I've come across on the road doing stand-up. It was in the middle of what felt like nowhere, a place that might seem to others like a forgotten blip on a map. But to me, it was the best place on earth. It was the kind of town where families would drive out of town in a caravan if a high school football team made it to playoffs. A town where (before the days of Kickstarter) the main fundraising effort was to sell chicken plates in the parking lot of a school on a Saturday. They would come with a piece of chicken, a couple sides, and the infamous Texas toast. If you are not familiar with what Texas toast is, let me explain. It's a thick slice of bread that looks like it would normally be two slices of bread. We call it Texas toast because it's bigger than other bread, and if there's one thing I've learned from growing up Texan, it's that if something is bigger than what you're normally used to seeing, just call it the Texas version of that thing. Because damn straight it is!

If you have never visited Texas, you might think the state is overrun by cows and white men and women dressed up in cowboy gear because that's a lot of the footage you see on TV shows set in Texas. But I'd like to take a minute to correct you. In Texas, the cows wear cowboy hats too. Yes, I grew up with friends going to rodeos, and yes, there were men that walked around wearing cowboy hats every day as if the hats were permanently attached to their heads, but there's so much more to the state, specifically to my hometown area. It was a side of Texas that I didn't see on TV very often, if at all. The Texas I grew up with was so different. It was a hybrid of Texas and Mexico. It was a place where walking back and forth between the two countries was common for many. A place where you'd hear the word *Tejano* used over and over again—a term to describe people of Mexican descent who lived in south Texas and also to describe a style of music that was Mexican with German and polka influences.

When I say I grew up in south Texas, I really mean SOUTH Texas. When I tell people this, many of them ask, "So, San Antonio?"

I always tell them I'm from about a four-hour drive south of that. That's when they ask, "Corpus Christi?" Then I tell them, "I grew up about two hours away from there." That's when they get tired of me and walk away thinking I'm from San Antonio.

I spend a lot of time educating people about this whole other world that exists in the tip of the state, but I don't mind. I love to do it because I believe it's such a special place. I guess I should begin by saying that, because it's a border town, everyone who lives there works for the cartel. My high school mascot was the Fighting Drug Mule.

I am completely lying, of course, but wanted to start off with the cartoonish depiction that so many mistakenly attribute to the place that made me. We are not all drug dealers. We are not all criminals. The people I grew up with were hardworking, wanted the best for their families, and sacrificed so much to ensure that future generations would have it a little easier than the ones that came before them. Many of the families I knew were migrant farmworkers, meaning they worked in the fields, picking crops for little money. They would move up north for part of the year; sometimes they'd come back; sometimes they wouldn't. I knew as a kid that every time I would have to say goodbye to one of my migrant farmworker friends, I might not see them again. I got used to that.

The one thing I don't miss about growing up in San Juan is the weather. The summers felt like hell. I hated summer, especially because once we could afford a car, it came with vinyl seats, so we'd have to place towels on the seats before we sat down to not have them burn our skin. If you forgot your towel, the red marks on your skin from the sun hitting the seats would remind you to never do that again. Not only did we not have air conditioning in the car, we didn't have air conditioning at home either. I didn't know houses even had air conditioning. I thought air conditioning was something that only businesses had because when we went to stores and school, it always felt nice and cool. In order to beat the heat, my family would fill a spray bottle up with water and we'd spray it all over ourselves. Then we'd stand in front of an oscillating fan (yes, we had the kind of money to get a fan that would move) and wait until it cooled us as much as it could.

The winters were harsh for us because the only source of warmth we had for years was a small space heater. The temperature would drop so low at night that, during the winter, we would sleep under two or three blankets to help offset the lack of heat. Aside from sweltering summers and cold winters, we also had hurricane season because the Rio Grande Valley was near the Gulf of Mexico. Every time a hurricane or tropical storm would get near us, we had to prepare, which meant my family had to go to the grocery store and buy batteries, a loaf of bread, a gallon of water, and peanut butter. While that combo might not make any sense, it was what we could afford. That's what I find interesting about preparing for catastrophes: your level of preparedness depends on your economic status. If you're wealthy, the sky's the limit. If you're poor, you do as much as you can possibly afford to do and hope for the best. We would put duct tape strips in an X-formation on windows so that if they broke, they would break in bigger shards and be easier to clean up (people are now being dissuaded from doing this). We would even board up the windows if it seemed like we were in imminent danger of getting hit. My family tried to protect ourselves from hurricanes as much as we could, but we were still left pretty vulnerable because we never left our house and it wasn't sturdy enough to withstand the power of Mother Nature. We didn't go to shelters because, back then, we didn't really know where to look for information about where to go (this was years before the internet would be a thing). I remember we sought shelter one time. I can't remember how old I was, but I was at an age where I finally understood how devastating a hurricane could be. We went to our neighbor's bakery because, that one specific time, the storm was so bad that my mother was scared something would happen to our little house. We grabbed our loaf of bread, the gallon of water, and left.

I remember being holed up in the bakery with my family during that hurricane. My brother Eloy played the guitar and had brought it with him because it was his prized possession; his guitar was like another sibling in the family. He used to teach me songs so I could sing them while he played the guitar. That day, we did U2's entire *The Joshua Tree* album. In reality, I think he was trying to distract me in case things got bad with the storm. I remember not being able to look out the windows because I wasn't allowed to get near them. Then everything got silent. I thought the storm was over, but none of us could be sure. That's when the adults told me that the storm might not be over; there was a chance we were in the eye of the hurricane, meaning we were in the intermission portion and it would soon start back up again. In that moment, I kept thinking about everything my family owned, which wasn't much. I wondered if we would have a house to go back to. I also wondered if I was allowed to eat some of my neighbor's *pan dulce*.

The little house we lived in was a shack. It was made of wood, some of it rotting. It had a front door, a back door, and a bathroom door; the rest of the house was open. The inside had a living room, a kitchen, a bathroom, and two other little rooms that were separated by walls, but there were no doors to separate the rooms, so we all lived among one another with absolutely no privacy. Our bathroom had a shower, but the toilet didn't work. We made it work by filling up buckets of water and throwing them into the toilet, which would make the sewage go away. The bathroom had no light, so if we had to shower after the sun had set, it had to happen in complete darkness. I liked showering in the daylight, but chose the nighttime because we had cockroaches running around everywhere, and I preferred not to see them if I could help it. They were like another family with whom we were sharing the house. They were big, dark cockroaches, and sometimes I would get in the shower and see a bunch of them crawling around on the walls. I would get terrified and cry, but I had no choice but to shower with them.

The kitchen was small. We had a stove that kind of worked, as well as a refrigerator. The plumbing under the kitchen sink was faulty and ended up causing a drip we couldn't afford to fix, so with time, we had to put a big plastic tub underneath the sink that we'd have to take outside and empty about once or twice a day. The drip eventually rotted the wood underneath the sink and we had a gaping hole in the kitchen where occasionally mice would enter and become our housemates along with the roaches.

We had two beds: a twin bed that my mother and I would share until I graduated from high school and a queen bed my brothers shared. Our twin bed was pressed up against a window that for a long time didn't have a screen on it. We couldn't close the window in the summer because the nights were so warm; any gust of wind would help cool us down. I was the one that slept right at the window, sometimes scared that someone could come and pull me out of the house in an instant because it was open and the neighborhood wasn't great.

I lived in that house from the age of about eight to eighteen and then again for a couple of years in my twenties. I am aware that to most people this house doesn't sound great, but it was my first real "house" and I was so grateful to have it. It was an upgrade from where my life had begun because, up until then, my family and I had been living two blocks away in a place that I kept secret for years.

Because, you see, my family squatted in an abandoned diner for the first seven years of my life.

What does that mean, exactly? It means we were almost homeless. We lived in a skeleton of a business that had closed down years before. It was freezing in the winter and sweltering in the summer. The business wasn't meant for anyone to live in, but then again, my family was the true example of that saying: *Where there's a will, there's a way.*

My mom used to cook on a space heater she would turn upward so that it served as a grill. For electricity, we used an orange extension cord that was plugged in our next-door neighbor's house. Our kitchen was an empty room that had a long counter toward the back and an old GE refrigerator. I remember that fridge so well because I loved its logo. After my mom would bathe me, she would carry me to the fridge so I could touch the logo with my little, newly washed hand.

The diner we lived in had an outside bathroom. We would shower there and then have to walk to the diner. During the winter, when the weather got too cold, we would have to bathe inside the diner in order to avoid walking in the cold. My mom would occasionally bring home a ten-gallon plastic pickle tub from the Mexican restaurant where she worked. We would fill it up to mop the floors, but during winter that bucket would also become our shower. My mother would warm up water and fill up the bucket. We'd bring in the metal washtub we used to hand-wash our clothes and stand inside it, in the blistering cold, while we poured cups full of warm water over ourselves.

People love to ask me how we ended up there, expecting a fall from grace when in reality we were moving on up. My mother was a single mom who raised four kids by herself. I should mention that my mother had four children with the same man, my father. They had been married for years. Many times, when I mention that my mother had four children, people say, "Well, maybe your mother shouldn't have had four children if she couldn't afford to take care of them," because you know, that's the *only* reason we'd be poor. It *had* to be the irresponsibility of a single, Latina mother. Truth is, we ended up there because my mother had left my abusive and constantly drunk father. He had another family she hadn't known about. She was the first woman in the family to leave her husband, and since this was decades ago, she was breaking barriers. She never divorced him because she had been married in the church, and as a Catholic, that wasn't an option. She never looked at or thought about another man until the day she died. (You're probably thinking, *This is a book by a comedian?*)

Growing up in a Catholic family was great for me, but that's because my mom followed her own philosophy when it came to Catholicism. She agreed with the idea about loving and helping people, but she also taught me that being Catholic was about realizing that sometimes rules had to be broken if it was for the sake of pure happiness, like her leaving my father. I'm the only one that never got to meet him. My brothers and sister got to grow up with him for a bit, but I didn't even get a glimpse of what he looked like. My mother once told me her punishment to my father was to have him never meet me . . . and he never did.

I remember when I was a kid, I asked my mother who my dad was—and where he was. I think I caught her off guard. But without hesitation, she told me my father was El Santo, an extremely famous Mexican *luchador* who wore silver trunks and a shiny silver mask. El Santo was a wrestler known in Mexican culture for starring in movies in which he would battle vampires and werewolves using his wrestling moves. My mother told me I wasn't allowed to know what my father looked like because he wore a mask to keep his identity secret, which I obviously believed because why would the person I love the most lie to me? When I told my brothers and sister what my mom had told me, they laughed and laughed at me, and even to this day, my brother Eloy will still send me pictures of my "famous wrestler dad" on Father's Day and on El Santos's birthday. He'll tag the pictures of El Santo holding a mummy in a headlock with the words: *Hope you wished your dad a Happy Father's Day (or Birthday) today!*

There was this one time, years after my mom had left him, when I got to sit next to him—but I still didn't get to meet him. My mother needed my father to go with her to the immigration lawyer so she could become a permanent resident. He needed to sign something because they were technically still married. My mother told me I had to go with them that Saturday morning, but she had rules for me. I had to keep looking down at the floor the moment he showed up and I was to never speak to him. I was not allowed to ever look up at him and she threatened to hit me if she caught me looking at his face. That day, he picked us up in a pickup truck. It didn't have a console like trucks have now; the front was just one long bench seat. I got into the truck and sat next to my mother and father for about forty-five minutes each way, not saying a word. He tried talking to me a couple of times and my mother would tell him I was not going to utter a word. I remember seeing his right hand. It was dark and had lines all over it, as if he had done a lot of physical work. That was all I got to see. His hand.

I looked down and didn't speak for hours, feeling as if that moment would never end. The moment he dropped us off, I got off the truck and ran away. That was the only time I ever had any contact with him.

I should mention that, just like I didn't get to meet my father, I didn't know too many of my relatives either. I knew my grandmother on my father's side the best, but mostly everyone on that side of the family didn't really exist to me. I had an aunt and uncle from that side of the family that would come and occasionally visit us. I remember on one visit, they gave me a red plastic keyboard that I loved playing. It took batteries, and to this day I can still remember the demo song it would play. Then all of a sudden, that part of the family stopped visiting us completely. Every now and then, my mom would bump into a relative and they would chat for a bit as if I didn't exist. And to be honest, I don't think I *did* exist to them. They would call me "La Niña" when they referred to me —"The Girl." In a way, even though my parents were still technically married, I always felt like I was treated like a bastard child, someone that didn't really fit into the scheme of things with aunts, uncles, and cousins. I felt like a sixth finger on someone's hand. I looked like the others, but people noticed I was out of place. I didn't really get to meet a lot of relatives on my mother's side because, when I was a kid living in the diner, my mother was undocumented and most of her family was back in her Mexican village. She couldn't go back and visit her family because it was too risky, so the majority of her relatives were like characters in stories she would tell me as a child. She did have a brother named Jose that lived in the United States, in Harlingen, Texas, but he lived about an hour away from us, so we rarely saw him.

I knew I had grown up poor, but it was something I didn't talk about back then because I was ashamed of it. The shame came from years of me having kids at school point out how poor I was, like the one (and only) time a friend of mine gave me a ride home from elementary school and, while we were in the car driving into my neighborhood, her mother started narrating our car trip as if it were a National Geographic documentary. "Okay, so this is the part of town we don't normally come to. This is where the 'other side' lives. Your friend lives on the wrong side of the tracks," she said. Even now, I can hear that woman's voice in my head because it was the first time an adult pointed out that I was really poor. (The woman was a teacher at my school, which made me feel even worse.) The next day, my friend came over to talk to me and told me that for the rest of the night, her mother kept reminding her how thankful she should be for having everything she had, because "her friend" had nothing. I didn't understand why that woman would feel so comfortable talking like that about where I lived, in front of me. It was almost as if she thought growing up in poverty made me deaf to criticism.

Kids used to make fun of me for so many things. I never had the cool sneakers or clothes. There was a period in second grade when I used a purple Crown Royal bag as a lunch bag because we had gone to a *quinceañera* where they had one and I thought it was pretty, so my mom, a recycling genius, decided to use it as a lunch bag for me. Poor people are the original recyclers; we find a way to make things work. Rich people recycle now as a part of life, but they don't realize what *real* recycling is all about. Did you know that people with money use a tub of butter and then throw the tub away? Who does that? Everyone poor or resourceful knows that once you're done with the tub of butter, you wash it out, put leftovers in it, and play the world's crappiest game show called "Is It Butter?" (Guess what: It's never butter.)

The first time I admitted to someone about the poverty I had grown up in was back in 2000, the first time I was living in Los Angeles. I was having lunch with a couple of friends and the conversation shifted to one of them talking about how poor he had grown up. His family had lived in an old church. He described the way they lived: they had no plumbing, not much of anything. The more he spoke, the more familiar his struggle felt to me. I started telling him about how poor my family had been, and once I started describing it, I couldn't stop. It was like I had opened a floodgate. The more I talked, the more my friend nodded because he knew exactly what I was talking about. I felt an urgency to tell my story as quickly as I could because I had been hiding it for so long. After my welfare soliloquy, my fellow poor friend asked me to describe the house I had grown up in and I tried to but couldn't put it into words. I told him it was a big room with no walls, similar to the size of the diner we were in. I mentioned that the first place my family lived in also had a counter in it, pointed to the counter in the diner we were eating at, and said it was similar but that ours was dirtier and older. He made a joke and said, "It sounds like you lived in a diner." I looked at him and admitted I had. I had never uttered those words out loud; I had never told a soul. My friends found it fascinating and started asking me questions about my life, and for the first time ever, I felt like I could be completely honest with people about my past, and I knew why it had happened. By my friend being so honest about his difficult upbringing, he made me feel it was okay to share mine because I didn't feel alone.

Throughout my childhood, I realized that what I was shooting for was liberation. A world of freedom where my family and I were allowed to seek out more rather than settle for "just enough." When I would have a moment where I wanted to dream, I would put on the Boston vinyl and listen to "More Than a Feeling." I would sit on the floor and just listen to the words because I took them so literally.

When I was a kid, all I wanted was a Cabbage Patch Kids doll. It was the toy every girl wanted and I knew I would never get one. I rarely got new toys, in fact. My favorite one was an old Big Bird doll my mom had bought me at a garage sale for a quarter. But my sister, Julie, got a job as a server at the restaurant my mom cooked at and saved up money to get me a Cabbage Patch Kids doll. She had put one on layaway for me and gave it to me for Christmas. At times, we didn't have food to eat, but here was my sister buying me a Cabbage Patch Kids doll because she knew what it was like to not have things and she didn't want me feeling what she had felt. I still remember the happiness I felt when I got that doll . . . a white boy with light brown hair who wore a red football jersey. I cried because I couldn't believe I was holding one . . . and that it was mine.

You see, that is the kind of sacrifice my siblings and mom would make for me, and I love them for that. I don't mean to speak for everyone and generalize, but where I grew up, in my neighborhood, the family dynamics were so different because families were not just composed of parents and children. In families, sometimes relatives had other duties as well. My sister had to take care of me when I was a baby because my mother worked at a restaurant. My eldest brother, Ruben, as a teenager had to go work to help out with money, so he served as a father figure to us. My brother Eloy taught me how to play sports and tutored me like another parent. We all had to do what was needed of us in order for all of us to survive. I understood that.

Maybe it's because of this kind of family foundation that I had from day one that I always expected everything I did to not only be for me but for my family. My dream was always bigger than me, it was bigger than what I could've described. I know it sounds ridiculous but I think that's why "More Than a Feeling" was so important to me. I would use the title of that song as a line I would say throughout my life when I couldn't explain why I felt a certain way about my dream.

Coming from a world where we wondered *if* we had a future to asking ourselves what we should *do* with our future, I know my dream of leaving my little town in search of exploring what was out there paid off not only for me . . . but for my family. We won.

Every time something wonderful happens to me, I listen to "More Than a Feeling" and smile. It reminds me of a time when I realized that a dream doesn't have to make sense to anyone if it makes sense to you. It's funny that after all these decades, I still can't describe how that song makes me feel.

It really is just MORE than a feeling . . . and I'm okay with that.

Me, looking like Dora the Explorer. The little building in the back is the outside bathroom we had when we lived in the abandoned diner.

"SAY YOU, SAY ME"
LIONEL RICHIE

Sometimes I put on my OP shorts, lace up my K-Swiss sneakers, pop a cassette into my Sony Walkman, and think, *Why do people love to live in the past?*

I'm going to sound like your grandmother, but here it goes: Why haven't you called me? Not texted. Not Skyped. Not FaceTimed. *Called.* I'm a child of the eighties. Back then, we didn't have Google; we had encyclopedias (an encyclopedia is like Google in books). We couldn't binge-watch TV shows. In fact, it was the opposite. If you missed an episode of a TV show, sometimes it was gone forever. They wouldn't replay all of them, so if you were a fan of a show like *Family Ties* and missed it one week, you might not know that Tom Hanks played an alcoholic uncle at one point.

Television was very different from the television you know today. Now, if you're standing, I want you to sit down because I'm about to blow your mind. Are you sitting? I'm being serious. Okay, here goes: TV channels used to NOT run twenty-four hours a day. Can you believe that? TV channels would start and end every day. At the end of the programming day, they would play "The Star-Spangled Banner" and then go to static till the next morning. I know: the impact of my words must be blowing your mind right now. Let me blow your mind even more. Sit down again (or sit down MORE if you can figure out how that works). We didn't have as many channels as we do now. Instead of four hundred channels, we'd have about thirty of them, but ONLY if you had cable TV. I suddenly feel like a professor giving a lecture with all of this history I'm dropping.

When my family first got cable TV, we couldn't understand what we were getting into. My siblings and I were introduced to MTV, a channel that would play musical short films called *videos* that captured the essence of different songs. What? Visual radio? Get out of here! We were very poor but we always had cable TV. For my family, it made sense to spend money on it because I was a latchkey kid. My siblings and mother would go work and I'd be left alone with TV as my babysitter. They thought if I was entertained, I wouldn't think about being alone so much. It worked.

I'd come home and do my homework while I watched TV and get lost with the channels. MTV was one of my favorites because I loved music so much. I remember being so obsessed with Whitney Houston's "Greatest Love of All" that I used to watch the video over and over to try to memorize the words. I had a Hello Kitty notebook and every time the song would come on, I'd sit in front of the TV and write down a new line I'd hear. Once I had the entire song written out, I would take the notebook out and sing along with Whitney Houston. I could sing as loud as I wanted because, again, I was a latchkey kid and I was by myself. My goal was to teach myself how to be able to hold a long note like Whitney did at the end of the song. I would practice and practice every day until, one day, I held the note without having to take a breath. I was so excited.

All the same, I didn't really like being a latchkey kid. I was left by myself at a very early age and when you're a kid, everything can be frightening. A blanket folded in a weird way could create a shadow that looked like a monster. I heard noises but wouldn't investigate because I was frightened of what I would find. I would try to watch anything on TV that would make me forget about the fact that I thought something could happen to me. I was so grateful for cable TV because, in a way, television not only became my best friend, it became my security blanket.

My family loved cable TV so much that we upgraded to a super-fancy channel called Home Box Office. That's right: HBO. It was a channel that played movies. I can't even put into words how much of a game changer it was for me because I never got to go to the movies. I didn't understand that movie theaters existed until my sister took me to go see my first movie at a theater: *Sesame Street Presents: Follow That Bird*. Then she took me to see Jim Henson's *The Muppets Take Manhattan* at La Plaza Mall, but it was so expensive for us to go, it wasn't a regular outing. If I had to guess, I would say that I went to the movies less than ten times in the first eighteen years of my life. My family calculated that, back then, getting HBO was cheaper than splurging on a movie ticket, even if we had to wait months to see the big hits.

Well, actually, let me correct myself because I'm lying. We used to go to the drive-in on Mondays, but I don't count that. The drive-in we would go to played movies in Spanish. A lot of them were very similar to one another and starred the same acting duo: the Almada brothers. The movies usually featured one or both Almada brothers trying to do the same thing: use their bullets for good instead of evil. Every plot included a shoot-out between them and the bad guys (probably the cartel), and they would shoot at each other forever because both sides were terrible at aiming and never needed to reload their guns. We usually watched a double feature, but I would fall asleep pretty early, during the first movie.

When I was introduced to HBO, I couldn't understand what I was watching. I couldn't understand how it was possible that I was seeing a movie that had been in the theaters months before. Unfortunately, because this was a new concept, they didn't have the amount of programming they have available now. There were no original series like today, so back then, they tended to repeat the same movies over and over again, which I didn't mind at all because it allowed me to memorize everything I wanted about my favorite ones.

Most of the movies I used to watch focused heavily on dance. I LOVED watching people dance. I was obsessed and had no clue why. I look back at this time of my life and realize that when there is something that speaks to you, you can't control it. It's as if you see it happening but you don't know WHAT exactly is happening. I was completely unaware that my love of fine arts was being awakened during that time and it was completely by accident. My family wasn't taking me to see opera or ballet. My family was too busy working to get food on the table. There was no way for someone growing up like me to be exposed to art in my neighborhood, so cable TV brought art to me.

It was the break-dancing movies that stood out to me more than others because not only did a lot of the dancers look like me (people of color) but they were from neighborhoods that reminded me of my own; and a lot of the stories were about a group of break-dancers being the underdogs. I could absolutely relate to being the underdog. I'm not saying that it was exactly like looking in my mirror, but compared to other movies that showed a white dude dancing in the rain for fun, the break-dancing ones seemed to speak to me more.

I used to try to learn the moves and actually *did* learn some of them. I'd spend hours trying to spin on my head, but would always hurt myself. My mom got to the point where she wanted to know if someone was beating me up in school because of my bruises, but I never told her. I remember break-dancing for my PE class in first and second grade on rainy days, and no, I'm not kidding, but I do want you to notice that I didn't say anything about being great at it. The coach kept asking me to do it for everyone, so I was either so impressive that he thought my gifts had to be shared with the world, or he was a jerk that wanted the students to laugh at me.

The way that HBO worked was that they would play movies on heavy rotation for a month and once the month was over, they'd bring in a new movie to rotate nonstop. One month, I noticed HBO didn't have a break-dancing movie for me to bust out my cardboard box to practice my moves on, but they did have a dance movie I could watch called *White Nights*.

This is the point where I must explain that, in the eighties, there were a lot of movies that focused on the relationship between the Soviet Union and the United States. It was almost a genre within itself. I hate spoiling the movie for those that haven't watched it, but I figure that since the movie is over thirty years old, you've had plenty of time to see it. The plot revolves around a Russian ballet dancer (played by Mikhail Baryshnikov) whose plane has to make an emergency landing in Siberia. He is taken to the hospital, recognized as a Russian defector, and placed in custody. He meets another dancer, a tap dancer (played by Gregory Hines), and his Russian wife (played by Isabella Rossellini). The three want to defect from the Soviet Union. I guess what I'm saying is that this is a great kids' movie to show the family. I know how far-fetched this plot probably sounds to many. The notion that there would be tensions between Russia and the United States is crazy to believe because that was in the eighties and we've progressed so much since then (I hope you notice my sarcasm because there is no sarcasm font).

At first, the movie seemed too adult for me to watch and I figured it wasn't for me. But the description in *TV Guide* said it had dance in it, so I figured I'd give it a try. I couldn't understand what was happening in the movie. It all seemed to go over my head until I got to the dance scenes with Mikhail Baryshnikov and Gregory Hines. I had no idea who they were. Remember, there was no internet back then. If you wanted to learn about anything, you couldn't go online and type their names into Google. You'd have to invent Google first. My generation's version of Google was having to go to the library and find archived videos on them, read articles and books about them to really understand who they were.

I remember, days after watching *White Nights* for the first time, my brothers and I saw a music video on MTV for a song called "Say You, Say Me" by a man named Lionel Richie. I had no idea who Lionel Richie was. I had no clue he had been in a band called the Commodores. I was years away from knowing what a "Brick House" was. Remember, I was just a child when "Say You, Say Me" came out. I consider it a power ballad, meaning that it's a bit more than a typical love song. Most of them tell you how much someone loves someone else. A power ballad does the same, but they do it to an extreme level.

I liked the song instantly. As a little girl, I constantly found myself gravitating toward love songs and power ballads, as if my heart had been broken constantly since the age of four (just imagine me hitting the milk carton hard after getting dumped at a playdate). I instantly fell in love with the video because it had scenes with

Baryshnikov and Hines dancing from the movie. But then something unexpected happened that made me love it even more. There was a sudden tempo change halfway through the song that blew my mind. Without notice, it went from a slow tempo to this energetic burst. Suddenly, a compilation of my favorite scenes from the movie where Baryshnikov and Hines danced together started playing with the tempo change in the video. I watched it absolutely speechless. What was happening? Why was I so excited? I didn't remember this part of the movie. I asked what I was watching and my brothers explained to me that sometimes people would write songs for specific movies and "Say You, Say Me" was the theme song for *White Nights*.

I wish music videos were still as popular as they were back in those times because this one is a perfect example of how much power they could have when they were done well. The ways that some videos synced up with the songs were magical. "Say You, Say Me" made me love *White Nights* on another level because the tempo change in it allowed the dancing to be highlighted more. In the movie, the dance scene with Hines and Baryshnikov is brilliant and masterful, but the music they dance to in that scene is quiet and subtle. But in the "Say You, Say Me" video, there was an emphasis that made me feel like I was watching something extraordinary. It's a bit comical to think that while most kids were singing along to classic kid power ballads, like "The Wheels on the Bus" or "Itsy Bitsy Spider," I was rocking out to a song that showed clips from a drama about people trying to defect from the Soviet Union. You know, typical kid stuff.

The next time I found myself alone, living that latchkey-kind-of-life, I watched *White Nights* and found myself sitting there, waiting for the dance scenes to come on. When they did, they felt like magic. Those two men moved so beautifully and effortlessly across the floor.

I kept playing the Lionel Richie song over and over in my head, remembering how my mind had been blown by that tempo change. I thought to myself, *I have to do what they're doing. I have to learn to dance like them.* From that point on, every time the movie played, I would wait for the dance scenes to come on, and slowly, I would try to copy their moves as best I could, learning the routine in small chunks. When they moved their feet to the left, so would I. When they took three steps back, so would I. When they would kick high in the air and land on their feet, I watched them do that (I couldn't do all of the moves; I had no idea what I was doing).

I ended up getting "Say You, Say Me" on vinyl. Back then, you could get singles of songs you liked on vinyl that we would refer to as "45s" because of the speed you'd play on the record player to be able to listen to them. Every time I was at home by myself, I was either watching the movie and learning the moves or playing the record to try to re-create the dance break from the song.

I loved listening to the song over and over again. It started out so slow. The music video started with a picture of the sun. I loved that it was a love song, but it seemed like it was a love song about friends. I remember some of the lyrics resonated with me because they sounded so hopeful. They told you to believe in yourself, that you were a star. The song served as a motivational pep talk for me. Every time I heard that tempo change, I would get up and excitedly dance around the house. The song ended in the same slower tempo it started with, and I felt like that made the tempo change stand out much more because, as a kid, I thought it was like having a surprise in the middle.

My time as a latchkey kid slowly evolved into an ongoing talent show I would put on for an audience of none. I danced my heart out for myself. The more of the routine I learned, the more unstoppable I felt. I don't know if I was very good at what I did, mainly because, like I mentioned, I have never performed the dance in front of any-one. I will say, I felt like I had a good grasp on most of the moves I was capable of doing. Once I felt that I knew the choreography of the Baryshnikov/Hines duet, I wanted to tackle a bigger obstacle: I wanted to learn how to tap-dance like Gregory Hines.

Baryshnikov is great, legendary. You have to be great so that someone like me (a Mexican American girl growing up in poverty in a border town) knows who you are in a time when (once again) people had to make an effort to learn about you . . . but Gregory Hines . . . he was electric to me. He would stomp his feet on the ground, creating tapping sounds I couldn't believe were coming from one person. I had no idea what I was seeing, no clue what it was called. It wasn't like the dancing I was used to seeing anywhere else. It was beautiful and *he* was beautiful because his skin was brown like mine. It was only as an adult that I realized that, as a child, I was secretly craving for anyone that I thought looked like me to grace the screen to give me hope.

(DISCLAIMER: This is the part of the story where people start thinking, *But Gregory Hines was not Latino.* I want to explain my childhood bubble. I grew up around a heavily populated Mexican community. I personally was not exposed to a lot of diversity until I became a teenager and started visiting my sister in Dallas. Even white people in my neighborhood were rare. A lot of my exposure to different ethnicities came solely from TV and movies I would watch. My family didn't go on vacation to other places around the country. The only time we would travel anywhere was to go to Mexico to visit family. As a kid, I thought everyone that had brown skin looked like me. I unknowingly craved a connection with people that looked like me on the screen because it made me feel that if they were doing what they were doing, I could too.)

I wanted to take dance lessons. There were a couple girls at my school that I knew were taking them, so I figured I'd ask my mom if I could. I remember her answer like it was yesterday. "Oh, of course you can take dance lessons. But first, go tell your brothers and sister they're going to have to starve because you want to take dancing lessons and I'll take you." So . . . that was not only a no but also a reminder that my family was barely surviving and dreaming was a luxury we couldn't afford.

My mom used to say, "Dreams are for the rich. People like us need to focus on surviving." I felt so heartbroken when she'd say that. Why wasn't I allowed to dream like other kids? Why did *my* hopes and dreams not matter? It was because *she* had been told that. She had been told that her hopes and dreams weren't important. My mom wanted to be a singer. But how does someone become a singer if you're raised in a village that has no electricity or running water?

When my mom told me I couldn't take dance lessons, my heart broke. I would hear some of the girls at my school say how much they hated dancing, how they wanted to quit because it was "boring," and it would make me so mad because they were taking this gift for granted. They couldn't see how lucky they were. I kept thinking I was wasting my talent, and no, I don't know where I got my confidence, but I'm glad I had it back then. I told myself, "You're going to learn how to dance. You will find a way."

One way or another, I was determined to learn how to tap-dance like Gregory Hines, so I did what any kid would do. I asked my mom to buy me a blank VHS tape because I wanted to record *White Nights* on our VCR so that I could watch it whenever I was alone to learn how to dance like those men.

I should remind everyone that the reason we had a VCR (despite living below the poverty line) was because television was our way to see the world outside of our little town. We always saw television as a tool to learn about new things. It was a time before reality TV. I learned about science and reading from PBS. My family used to sometimes record the news to keep up with current events. Television taught us there was a bigger world out there that we didn't have access to, but one day hoped we would.

So, what is a VCR? I feel as if this chapter is becoming a historical account of life from decades ago because now I have to try to explain what a VHS is. Here goes. Four score and even a bunch more years ago, because I just realized I don't know how long a score actually is, there was a time in our history when we couldn't skip through the commercials when we watched TV. We were forced to watch them because we couldn't record the shows we watched and fast-forward. This is how so many of us learned commercial jingles that stayed with us forever. Even at forty, I can tell you my bologna has a first name and how to spell that name. I can tell you what makes me a Toys "R" Us kid. The good thing was that it taught many of us to make quick runs to the bathroom and kitchen between these commercial breaks so that we wouldn't miss any of the show. None of this dillydallying the kids have now where they can stop watching an episode of something and then continue it the next day. THE NEXT DAY!

That all changed with the introduction of a little machine called a VCR (videocassette recorder). My family bought one. I wasn't allowed to touch it, which meant I touched it all the time when no one was around. The best way to describe the VCR is to explain that it was a bulkier and better version of a Blu-ray player, which was a better version of a DVD player (it's like a technology set of Matryoshka dolls, where you take off a layer and a former obsolete gadget is inside another one). With this *Star Trek*–level glimpse of the future called a VCR, you could record anything you wanted to off the television.

One day, I came home from school and, as usual, found myself alone for hours. My schedule was the same. I'd watch MTV while I did my homework, listen to the vinyl records my brothers didn't let me touch (this point of the book is when they find out I did), and wait for *White Nights* to start on HBO. Once it started, I pressed record and waited. Every time the dance scenes were approaching, I'd stand up and wait to dance along with them. When the Gregory Hines tap solo came on . . . I tried to keep up, but was so unsuccessful. The tap dancing was too fast and I was dancing barefoot, so while he was tapping like a madman, my feet sounded like they had taken a vow of silence. I had to get tap shoes. But how?

My mom used to buy me one pair of shoes at a time. I would have to wear them out before getting a second pair. They were either black patent-leather Mary Jane shoes she would get from a store in downtown McAllen, or white sneakers from Walmart that used to Velcro on. I wore a pink shirt/purple shorts combo and had a bowl cut. One could say I was the original Dora the Explorer. At that time, I owned the white Velcro sneakers, which was unfortunate because I thought the Mary Janes looked more like Gregory Hines's tap shoes.

I had to work with what I had. The sneakers had a soft bottom, which at the time I thought would be problematic but turned out to be a gift. I knew it would be a challenge, but then again, so much of my life seemed to be a challenge, so this was nothing new.

I tried taping pennies to the bottom of my sneakers to make some noise when I was learning Gregory Hines's moves, but those didn't work out. I started losing pennies pretty quickly, and I couldn't afford to lose a cent. I figured I needed something I could take off and on so I wouldn't have to destroy the only pair of shoes I owned, but quickly realized I would need a more permanent solution. I just had to really think about it. I knew it would come to me, but until it did, I would have to practice my dancing silently . . . as if my tap dancing was on mute. Oh well . . .

We used to go to Mexico on Mondays to visit my grandmother. Sometimes we would drive the car over to her house. Other times, we would park the car in Hidalgo and walk across the International Bridge into Reynosa because traffic coming in from Mexico would sometimes be so heavy, it could take you almost two hours to cross back to the United States. In those days, the bridge didn't have a high fence to keep people safe from falling over. There was a rail that was low and frightened me. On one of our trips, a guy pushed me to the side and I fell against the rail, to the point where I could've fallen over. I couldn't swim and it scarred me for life. Getting to my grandmother's house was not easy either.

We would walk to the downtown part of Reynosa to pick up a *pesera*, which back in those days was an old van that had been gutted to remove the seats in order to pack in more people. The van would have plastic milk crates in it that you could grab and sit on, if you were lucky. If you couldn't find one, you'd sit on the floor. We had to pick what route to take because we had to take the "five route" and there were two choices: Pemex or Charco. Pemex was considered the "express" route that would cut stops and drive us through the Pemex refinery. Most of the times, the side door to the van was left open to make getting in and out easier and, as a kid, it could be pretty terrifying. Sometimes I felt like I could fall out of the van when the driver would make hard turns, but, hey, that was the only choice we had. I would guess that the trip would take a little under an hour each way.

Once we got to my grandmother's *colonia* (a dirt road she lived on), we would get off the van and walk blocks to her house. The worst days were when it rained because the dirt roads would flood easily and become very muddy. If you weren't careful, you could fall into puddles that were deceptively deeper than they looked.

One of the best things about visiting my grandmother was that her neighbors next door had a little makeshift store that sold lots of Mexican candy. I loved going over there and getting *tamarindos* (tamarind candies, usually spicy). On this specific visit, I went over to see them and one of the owners' daughters was sweeping the store's dirt floor. It was covered in bottle caps to help make it feel more like an actual floor. Sometimes they'd wet it to add more bottle caps or to make adjustments because it was always shifting shape. This was one of those times. I grabbed the bottle caps and tried to help her by pushing them down on the ground to make them stick. I used to try to help because sometimes I would get free candy. After that was done, I found myself making a clicking sound every time I took a step. I picked up my foot to see what was making the noise and saw that I had unknowingly stepped on one of the caps. I tried taking it off but it was stuck on my white sneaker because I had stepped on it with the bottom of the cap facing up. That's when it hit me! The noise I was getting from my sneaker sounded like the sound I would hear Gregory Hines make when he danced in the movie. Could I have found the way to get my tap shoes? I HAD! I asked my friend if I could have some bottle caps to take home with me and she said yes. I got eight of them; four for each shoe. I remember going home as if I had won the lottery.

The next day was business as usual for me. I went to school but couldn't stop thinking about the day being over so I could go home and work on my shoes. Once the bell rang, I got home and my Mac-Gyver skills went into play. I grabbed my Mexican Coke, Jarritos, and Joya bottle caps and got to work. I placed them the way I wanted them on my shoe and tried to step into them with my sneakers the same way I had accidentally stepped on one of them in Mexico, with the flat part on the floor. It wasn't easy, but eventually I got them on.

I stood up with the bottle caps on the bottom of my Dora the Explorer sneakers and tried tapping. IT WORKED! The caps at the front of my sneakers would fall off every now and then, but I could deal with that. I was ready to do my version of tapping! I started the movie and fast-forwarded to Gregory Hines's tap solo. The moment he started tapping, I started doing my version of it. I wasn't even close to doing anything he was doing, but I can tell you what I felt because I remember that moment of my life so well. I felt *pride*. I felt like I could accomplish anything I wanted. I learned that being told no was not going to ever stop me from doing what I wanted to do. I had found a way to work on my dancing even if my family didn't have the means. I felt so powerful and so proud. Nothing was going to stop me.

Every day, I would come home and work on my dancing. I'd work on the duet Baryshnikov and Hines did. I would work on Baryshnikov's ballet and Hines's tap solos like I was getting paid for them. I did the ballet stuff barefoot. I would wear my bottle cap white Walmart sneakers for the tap portion. I was doing my own kid version of *Fame*, sweating my butt off trying to teach myself how to dance. I started checking out books from the library about dance to learn what I could and see if I was even close to doing it right. I learned the names of certain moves but really had no idea what I was doing. All I knew was that I was mimicking what I was seeing on the screen and I felt unstoppable.

After months of learning the dance moves, I would perform the scenes with Baryshnikov and Hines as best as I could, and each time it came more easily. Learning the choreography made me feel like I had won. It gave me confidence that eventually left me wanting to learn more. I didn't want to only learn about other dance styles. It made me want to immerse myself in this different and beautiful world of fine arts. I discovered operas as a kid (the first one I saw was *Carmen* by Bizet on video at the public library). I did all of this when I was alone. I hid my love of this stuff from everyone like it was my secret porn stash. I never told my family what I did when I was by myself. I was a little embarrassed by it because I couldn't explain what my love of this was to anyone. I was already made fun of by kids at school, and my family was the typical family that would make fun of one another for the most ridiculous things, and I wanted to be spared the humiliation of being this nerdy kid that liked "fancy things." That's how I saw it. I thought dancing and operas were fancy things that only the wealthy had access to and I didn't want anyone making fun of me.

Well over a decade later, I ended up taking a dance class. I remember being so excited for it. I felt as if the little girl in me was finally getting to take the dance class she had longed for so much as a kid. I was terrified that I would be terrible at it. A couple classes into it, my teacher told me he thought I was good and asked me what I had studied. Instead of naming different types of dance, I named movies. He was the first person I told and he said I was good. I wanted to cry. I felt like I had gotten the validation I wished I had gotten as a kid when I didn't know what I was doing.

While writing this chapter, I was having dinner with a friend. We were discussing what I wrote in regard to Gregory Hines. Halfway through our conversation, he said, "Isn't it crazy to think how far you've come from those days? This all started when you were a little kid. Can you imagine how different your life might've been if Gregory Hines hadn't been in that movie?"

More than thirty years after that time in my life, I sat there, speechless. I had never thought about that. It felt like his words hit me straight in the heart because he made such an important point. If Gregory Hines hadn't been in *White Nights*, would I have gotten into dance with the intensity that I did? I'm not sure I would have. Seeing Gregory Hines in that movie made me feel like I could do what he was doing. I made a connection with him because I thought he looked like me. His dancing opened a door for me into a world that I never knew existed.

This is why I think representation is not just important, but absolutely vital. Kids like me—the ones that are growing up poor, squatting with their family, wondering how they'll survive—need to see their own Gregory Hines. They need to see that greatness is attainable and that they can surpass any economic challenge they may have.

The biggest takeaway I got from this part of my life was that it taught me that I am a lot stronger and more persistent than I give myself credit for. As a little kid, I refused to let a *no* get in the way of what I wanted to accomplish. I learned that poverty and the lack of basic needs were not excuses to not do something. Poverty and need made it a lot harder, but it didn't make it impossible. That is how I've approached most of my life. When I get to a point when I think something seems impossible, I look at it and think, *Cristela. You just have to make your own tap shoes. You did it before and you can do it again. You can do this.*

To everyone that has been told "no" to their dreams, all I have to say is that while it might be difficult . . . it IS possible. I'm proof of that. It may take longer than it takes for people around you, but I always say, "If you have a lifelong dream, sometimes it can take a lifetime to attain it, but it will be worth it." All you have to do is dance to your own beat—sometimes literally.

"THANK YOU FOR BEING A FRIEND"
THE GOLDEN GIRLS

This picture shows two of my biggest loves: Legos and *The Golden Girls*.
It's also the closest I would get to doing a crossover episode.

Picture it: San Juan, Texas, 1987. An eight-year-old girl lives with her family in a border town, when suddenly, out of nowhere, she meets four older women. They live in Miami, yet somehow, the five of them become best friends.

"Thank You for Being a Friend" was a song released by Andrew Gold in 1978 but really became a staple of American pop culture when Cynthia Fee sang a version of it that would serve as the theme song for the hit NBC sitcom *The Golden Girls*. This show first aired in 1985 and, decades later, is still shown daily on TV and has taken on a life of its own. The song starts with piano and then breaks into a verse that talks about the strength of friendship and how grateful one is to have such an incredible friend in their lives. Basically, the Golden Girls were *begging* me to become their friend because they knew how great I was. I had to oblige. Before we get to the story of this lifelong friendship between the ladies and me, we must first learn how it happened. I guess I should modify the beginning of this chapter to paint an even clearer picture.

Picture it: San Juan, Texas, 1986. [*Whispers*] And also a year prior . . .

I have already mentioned that I was a latchkey kid, but I want to write about how my love of television started from a very early age.

I am a first-generation American raised by my mother, an immigrant from Mexico. She didn't speak English, which meant that, as a kid, I obviously didn't speak it either. Spanish was my first language by default. My mother had a rule that in our house we were to speak only Spanish because she wanted to be able to understand everything that was being said unless my brothers and sister were translating things for her, whether it be the local news (which she'd watch in English because there was no other option) or important documents from the government.

I am the youngest of my family, the age gap being ten years between me and my sister (the closest sibling I have in age). I spent so much one-on-one time with my mom that my English was very limited during my early years. I could speak it enough to talk to my siblings, but when I went to Head Start, kindergarten, and first grade, I spoke more Spanish than English. It didn't help that most of the television we watched were Spanish channels, but then again, if my mother couldn't speak English, why would we watch things she couldn't understand? The tricky thing about watching so many television shows in Spanish as a kid was that there were many American shows I first saw dubbed in Spanish that made me think they were Mexican shows. I had no idea what dubbing was, so I used to think *Knight Rider* was Mexican. I used to watch the old *Batman* episodes and loved that Batman was Mexican (I guess I could've referred to him as Señor Batman). Even the kid shows I watched were in Spanish, which made it hard for me to learn English because I was being taught things that didn't exist in the English language, like the extra letters in the Spanish alphabet (letters and combos like *ch, ll, ñ,* and *rr* don't exist in the English one).

The Price Is Right was one of the shows I learned to speak English from. Yes, I learned how to speak English from television (I told you TV was my teacher). When I started watching it regularly, I was convinced I would name my firstborn kid "Plinko" because I loved the word so much (thank God I didn't because I don't think my hypothetical child "Plinko Alonzo" would've liked that very much).

I remember the summer before I went to first grade. I started watching a lot of American television with my brothers and sister because they were out of school for summer vacation. I would plop down on the floor and watch whatever they had on. I started mimicking people from the shows we saw, trying to speak like them, and was able to pick it up pretty quickly. I started watching more American shows during the day when my mother was at work, and I would pick up new words here and there.

My English was getting better. What I hadn't noticed was that because I was learning English from watching TV, I was also learning how to speak the language with the accents of the actors I was mimicking, therefore creating my own inflection. Even to this day, I speak with a different accent than my siblings because they spent about a decade living in Mexico before moving to Texas. You can hear a Latino accent that comes out of them. Meanwhile, I speak with an accent that at times sounds like I'm Bob Barker trying to make you guess the price of a box of Rice-A-Roni to win a Vespa.

When summer ended that year and I started first grade, everything was business as usual for me in school, except a certain number of us in the class would have to break off from everyone and go into a different class. We would read books in Spanish, and the teacher would teach us how to say commonly used words in English; I didn't know what it was, but I liked it. It would take me a couple of months to realize I had been placed in something called an ESL class: English as a Second Language. I couldn't understand why I had been placed there because I thought I had learned to speak English in the summer from TV. I asked my teacher (in English) if I didn't speak English (because I thought I did) and she told me I could speak it but I needed a little bit more help. It was so confusing. If I couldn't speak English, how could she understand what I was saying? I felt I needed to watch more TV to improve my English.

The shows that gave me the best representation of what "being American" meant were those half-hour comedies that used to heavily revolve around the lives of families that would solve problems in twenty-two minutes (without commercials). They would have a mix of pop culture references and jokes about current events set in a world where a super-witty family lived. They were called *sitcoms*.

Sitcoms can be wonderful and, at the same time, so ridiculous. Watching sitcoms occasionally did really feel like I was doing anthropological research. I took everything I saw to heart and assumed that life in sitcoms was a true representation of what life in this country was really like. I would think to myself, *I don't think my family knows how to be a family because we don't do any of this.*

A lot of the shows kept the same formula. The theme song would play and a scene would start. The family would make jokes at one another that for some reason no one else in the scene would ever laugh at. I thought that was weird because, in my family, if someone said something funny, everyone laughed. Suddenly, a problem would come up. This is where the ridiculous part comes in because many times I couldn't relate to the problems the families would have because they seemed so small compared to the ones my family had. I'd see an episode about a crazy mix-up regarding a birthday cake and the first thought to pop into my head was *Wow. Birthday cakes are real?* (No one in my family ever had a birthday party.) In my house, a similar episode would've been about having a crazy mix-up about who was supposed to have gotten the money order to pay the electric bill.

Sometimes when I'd see these sitcoms, I'd feel that, while two of my siblings and I were born in Texas and my family was living in the United States, my family wasn't really an "American" family. At least, not in the way TV showed a family to be. Their experiences and the way they interacted with one another seemed foreign to me.

Television was an early example of how hard it would be for me to find my identity as a first-generation Mexican American because, again, while I was born and raised in Texas, I was living a pretty Mexican lifestyle—that's obviously all my mom knew. My mother couldn't teach her kids about American culture because she wasn't familiar with it, so we had to figure it out on our own. Not only that, once her children learned something new, we would have to teach it to our mother so she knew it too. In my family, the kids were responsible for teaching the parent about life in this country.

Then one Saturday night in 1986, I changed channels to NBC.

They had *Gimme a Break!*, *The Facts of Life*, and at the eight o'clock hour they had a sitcom called *The Golden Girls*. I loved the theme song right from the get-go because of the piano and it was easy to sing along with. I didn't know the words, but they repeated the line "Thank you for being a friend," so I caught myself singing it.

The moment I realized I was probably going to love this show was when a character named Sophia Petrillo made her entrance. She was a little lady that came in with a big presence. She was abrasive, made fun of everyone, and didn't care if she hurt your feelings. The moment she said her first insult without a care in the world, I thought, *Oh my God. She is exactly like my mother!* My mother was about five feet tall but would insult you as if she were a giant. That was how she showed you that she loved you. I had never seen a woman like that on TV. Sophia had suffered a stroke and the part of her brain that censors what she'd say had been destroyed, which allowed her to say whatever she wanted whenever she wanted. It made me wonder if the same thing had happened to my mother.

I started really looking forward to Saturday nights. I looked forward to hearing Sophia throw her barbs at everyone. I would look at her and imagine that my mom would sound just like her if she spoke English. After about a month, I had learned the words to the theme song. Every time I heard the piano start playing, I got excited. If I was in another room, I would run into the living room to catch it from the beginning.

Theme songs are not as prominent now as they used to be back then. I wish they were because they are such a vital part of television history. Some of the most iconic theme songs felt like they were their own character in the show because they served as a reminder of the world you were about to enter. Take, for example, *The Golden Girls* theme song. It did a great job of setting up that this world was about a different kind of family. It was a family made up of strong bonds of friendship. Every time I heard the song, I was reminded that in this specific world, we were going to follow the lives of Dorothy, Blanche, Rose, and Sophia as they showed us what true friendship was all about, and that is exactly what they did in every episode. The more I saw the show, the more I felt a connection to it. I liked how the women interacted with one another. There were constant insults thrown, similar to the kind my family would use. I loved when they would do that because the characters would acknowledge when a person said something insulting, either by having Dorothy do a clever retort to Blanche implying she wasn't attractive or at times Rose just giving a look that said, "I know you think I'm not smart." Amid the insults, there were also moments where they were so supportive of one another, just like my family. They would constantly tell one another how much they meant to one another. I thought of *The Golden Girls* as a feel-good show that offered a reality that aligned more with my reality. The women didn't always get along. In fact, they had their fair share of arguments. I loved that because it felt real.

The more I watched the show, the more connected I felt to the characters. Part of it was due to the theme song. I used to find myself singing it at school a lot. I would be in class and, out of nowhere, I found myself going from quietly humming it to belting it out like I was Patti LuPone. I couldn't help it; the song made me happy. One of the powers of a great TV show having a great theme song is that when the song gets stuck in your head, it makes you smile because it's a reminder of how the world of the show makes you feel. That's what that song did for me.

Courtesy of Ruben Alonzo

Me in my English as a Second Language (ESL) class trying to learn the language. Sometimes I would come to school early to have extra time to learn.

After making such a concerted effort to improve my English, I quickly started noticing that I was making a lot of progress with my ESL class in school and thought it was largely due to the amount of American TV shows I was watching. Obviously, the teachers were an integral part as well, but considering the amount of time I had with them, even they were surprised at the pace in which I was becoming fluent. Who knew TV would help me with school?

I was eventually able to leave ESL months later. When the teacher told me, I looked at her, pointed at her, and said, "Thank you for being a friend!" She laughed—a sound I still remember.

It was then that I realized I was getting a new responsibility that came with being a bilingual first-generation American. I had to join the ranks of my siblings and serve as a translator for everything my mother needed. It was as if I were having a linguistic *quinceañera* thrown for me, except that instead of a party, I was handed government paperwork I had to fill out for my mom. IT SUCKED.

There was a lot of pressure that came with having to translate for my mom as a kid. It made me grow up quicker than my friends. I was dealing with adult responsibilities that some kids couldn't imagine. While friends were collecting rubber bands to make their own Chinese jump ropes, I was walking with my mom to the post office so that I could buy money orders for her that I would fill out and send off to pay bills. One of the things I hated doing the most was having to translate the news for her because I didn't know what they were talking about. Imagine an eight-year-old girl trying to explain the Russian nuclear reactor exploding at Chernobyl and releasing radioactive materials throughout Europe! I had JUST gotten out of class where English was my second language and now I was trying to explain to my mother nuclear war? Who was I? Rose Nylund from *The Golden Girls* episode where she wrote to Gorbachev and Reagan asking them to get rid of nuclear bombs?

It became part of my life. Every night, I would have to sit on the floor next to my mother and translate the news. The news anchor would say a headline and I would have a couple of seconds to translate it into Spanish. That was usually the easiest part of the job. Then I'd have to listen to the actual story and translate the big bullet points to my mom. This part was a guessing game because I had to find a quiet spot in the news story that would give me enough time to translate for my mother without lagging too much, and do it with enough time left over for me not to miss the next story. Every night felt like I was doing a book report on what was happening in the United States (the news broadcast) for the Mexican government (my mom).

I slowly started getting the hang of it and found myself learning who the politicians were. So many times, the news was just continuations of headlines I had already learned about, so it became easier for me to reference people to my mother because I would just remind her of what I had already told her previously.

I found myself feeling older than my classmates. I know how ridiculous that sounds considering I was eight, but I had too much on my mind. Being a translator for my mom meant that I had to know everything that was going on with her. I was there to explain the pills she would have to take (because, you know, I'm the star of that hit TV show called *Kid Pharmacist*). If one of our utilities was disconnected, I would have to go down to the office with her, pay the bill, and set up a reconnection date (it was the eighties, so it wasn't as convenient as it is now). I basically became the kid sitting around the lunch table with my classmates, slamming milk cartons like they were pints of beer. I'd hear a kid talk about a broken toy and I'd stare at her and say, "You call those problems? I can't remember if I told my mom to take one or two pills this morning. I could kill her if I make a mistake. Tell me about your doll again, Maria . . ."

My mother wouldn't let me see friends outside of school because she hadn't been allowed to do so as a child. Therefore, she was unable to understand why people did that. Having to spend so much time by myself made me crave human interactions I was not able to have, meaning I had to create my own friendships the best I could, which is what led me to gravitate toward *The Golden Girls* because the theme song was literally about friends. They were good friends, I needed good friends. It was a match made in heaven.

I looked forward to the show every Saturday night because the women seemed so familiar to me. The stories Sophia Petrillo would tell about her village reminded me of stories my mom used to tell me about her growing up. As time passed, TV shows would come and go, but *The Golden Girls* seemed to stay. The longer a show is on the air, the more the characters develop, and the more we become familiar with each one as their own personality. I saw the evolution of the mother-daughter relationship between Sophia Petrillo and Dorothy Zbornak as very similar to the kind I had with my mother. We would make fun of one another at times, but we did it out of love. One time, my mother and I were in bed and my mom started telling me a story. She said, "*El año era como 1955, yo no sé, y era una niña buscando comida . . .*" (The year was around 1955, I don't know, and I was a little girl looking for food . . .) I laughed because I realized that it sounded like a Sophia story. I couldn't explain that to my mother because she didn't know what *The Golden Girls* was. She was at work when the show would air and had never seen an episode.

The more I saw the evolution of Sophia, the more I thought of her as a wonderful homage to immigrant mothers because she reminded me so much of my mother, my relatives, and friends of my mother. Sophia constantly talked about her village, like so many women I grew up with. No one could ever beat Sophia at how hard she had it, just like my mom. Sophia would talk about her kids in such a way that you always knew where you were ranked in order of favorite to least favorite, again just like my mother. I find the similarities I discovered between this fictional Italian mother and my own Mexican mother interesting because it taught me that two people who seem to have nothing in common can have similar histories, regardless of skin color or background. Sophia came to the United States from

Sicily so her family could have a better chance at life, just like my mom. Dorothy Zbornak was a first-generation American, just like me. I also liked that the other characters in the show would reference their cultures as well. Blanche Devereaux was a Southern belle who spoke fondly of the South in a way that by today's standards would've made me want to ask her some serious questions about her lineage. She would tell stories of her upbringing that included a debutante ball (which is like a *quinceañera* for white people, I guess) and how she was raised on a plantation. Rose Nylund was from a small town in Minnesota and often told tales that were as outlandish as Sophia's but always seemed to have a touch of ridiculousness in them that made me want to visit St. Olaf in real life.

What I liked about the show was that it allowed me to grab a little bit of every character that I could relate to. The show didn't have moments where one character would tell Rose, "Oh, Rose, that's soooo Scandinavian of you!" There weren't instances where cultural moments were explained and others would question their validity. I thought this show would be a good barometer of what life would be like in regards to how people related to one another. I thought *The Golden Girls* was one of the most relatable shows I had seen up to that point in my long (but actually short) span of life.

I used to reference *The Golden Girls* episodes a lot in school. If someone said something that would remind me of one in particular, I'd ask other kids if they had watched it. They usually hadn't. I'd get offended. After a time, I started getting on students' nerves because of how much I loved that show, and ended up annoying my classmates for not one but many school years to come. I was rarely in trouble, but did end up going to the principal's office twice when I was in the fifth grade because of *The Golden Girls* theme song.

It was the first day of school. While other students showed up with their basic school boxes filled with pencils and crayons, fifth-grade Cristela showed up for the new school year carrying a big, aqua-colored plastic briefcase. I loved school so much that I used to show up like I was going to an office job in corporate America.

My fifth-grade teacher let us pick where we wanted to sit and I picked a seat toward the middle of the classroom. I was in the gifted and talented class and usually sat in the front of the room because the students there would get called on the most. I had always been one of the first to raise my hand, to the point where my fourth-grade teacher told me to stop answering so many questions and give others a chance. I figured I'd try something different and move toward the back. Now, in hindsight, I realize that was a dumb decision on my part. I was minimizing my love of learning, and one thing I've learned as an adult is that trying to minimize what you're good at doesn't serve anyone at all.

Once I picked my seat, I sat down, opened up my plastic briefcase, and took out all my school supplies to set them up on my desk. I took out my pencils, *then* took out my pencil cup, which I had made out of Legos that summer (I was a super-cool kid). A girl sat in front of me. She was dressed really cute and had long hair up in a ponytail. She was new at the school. I didn't recognize her. She seemed nice.

The first day of school went as usual. We did introductions, did some "getting to know you" activities, went to lunch. The afternoon is when things went downhill. We were in the classroom, writing something. The class was quiet. I started singing the piano portion of *The Golden Girls* theme song. "Dun, dun, dun . . . Thank you for being . . . ," I quietly sang. After a couple more times of me singing, "Dun, dun, dun . . . Thank you for being . . . ," out of the blue (though as an adult I know I absolutely deserved it), the new girl turned around and told me to shut up. I got mad because of her tone. She turned to face forward and I just stared at the back of her head, thinking, *I'm sorry, did this really just happen?* It was on. I honestly didn't expect what followed, and neither will you.

This is the part where this book becomes a Choose Your Own Adventure! If you think I stopped singing, go to page . . . just kidding. You're a smart person who realizes I was joking about this being a Choose Your Own Adventure book and we can be friends, because of course I kept on singing. NOBODY PUTS BABY "SINGING *THE GOLDEN GIRLS* THEME SONG" IN THE CORNER!

I sang the song a couple more times. She started getting angrier. I started getting happier. After a few more times, she did the unthinkable. She turned around, grabbed the Lego pencil cup holder I had made, and put it on her desk. Oh no, I KNOW this little girl had not taken my Legos away! I got so upset that I started singing more. It was easy to not get too much attention because, again, I was toward the middle of the classroom. There were more than thirty kids in class, so it was easy to blend in. Then she turned around and started taking away more of my stuff, and finally said the words that would burn in my soul: "Stop singing. I hate that song!" To look me in the eye and say you *hate The Golden Girls* theme song? Not on my watch. She went on to say that she didn't like the show and basically suggested that I wasn't cool for liking it.

That's when I did the unthinkable.

Picture it: *San Juan, Texas, 1989. A ten-year-old Cristela sits in her classroom with a broken heart after being told blasphemous news. She gets her plastic briefcase and grabs her scissors. Cristela then grabs the girl's ponytail and cuts off a small part of her hair, intentionally making it crooked. I tell the girl, "I DO NOT thank you for being a friend." The girl feels it and stands up to tell the teacher what has happened. The teacher calls Cristela to her desk and asks for more details. Cristela tells the teacher what happened and gets sent to the office.*

When I got to the principal's office, she asked me to explain why I was there. I told her everything. She listened, asked me if I was aware of what I had done, and I said yes. I told her I felt really bad (because I did). She asked me what the name of the student was, and when I told her, she looked at me and told me a fun fact: I had just cut the hair off of the principal's daughter. Well, I had not seen that coming. She punished me. I can't even remember what it was, but I assume it was nothing extreme or else it would come back to me. I do recall I had to apologize to the girl and was moved away from her because obviously if I cut her hair once, I could do it again. Who knows? All I knew was that I was happy to not sit near someone who couldn't see the magic of *The Golden Girls.*

Now we get to the part where I have to unfortunately admit I am well aware that I was an annoying kid when it came to my love of TV. I used to quote episodes and movies all the time. I picked it up from my family. We still do that. When we're all together, we'll quote movies like *Airplane!*, *The Naked Gun*, and *Back to School*, mixed in with TV shows like *Family Ties* (it's Proper Penguin!—writing that solely for my brothers) and *El Chavo del Ocho*. It's weird how as a kid you are at times unaware that you are being annoying. It took me years to realize the extent of frustration I occasionally unleashed on people, and for that, I apologize.

I was different from other kids and that was okay in my book because I didn't know how to be anything but myself. Some kids thought I was weird because I didn't really interact with them directly. I would usually be the student who finished all her work first and had to find a way to kill time to avoid boredom. I was known for saying jokes out loud in class to make everyone laugh. I didn't have my own jokes, so I would just repeat jokes from TV shows I watched. It usually worked. I would quote TV shows so much that, one time, my teacher wrote a note on my progress report that read "Cristela is a bright student but quotes TV shows a bit too much."

In hindsight, it is only as an adult that I realize how those moments would be indicative of the kind of life I would have. It is a recurring theme for me. I'm better at being alone than I am at being surrounded by people because I was never taught how to interact with them. Again, remember that I wasn't allowed to spend time with friends outside of school, so I missed out on a lot of important moments in my formative years that would have taught me how to deal with people. I never had a sleepover. I never went to a birthday party. Nothing. When I wasn't at school, I was at home, usually by myself. The only friendships I had were the ones I had created in my mind with characters from my favorite TV shows because those friendships were easier to maintain than ones in real life. It was all I knew how to do.

Fast-forwarding to the present day, I find myself at the age of forty and still watching reruns of *The Golden Girls*. It's comforting. I know the episodes so well that I notice when jokes are edited out for running time or content. When I watch and see Sophia break into a story, I can remember how it felt to touch my mother's hand because it was something I used to do a lot. I remember her hands, her left one having a big vein that protruded from it. The wrinkles, the hardness of them. I hear the stories about Sophia Petrillo's childhood in Sicily and imagine what my life would be like if my mother was still around now to tell her stories.

I see *The Golden Girls* reruns and feel like I'm watching a glimpse into a relationship that I thought I would have with my mother in the future. I thought we would end up like Dorothy and Sophia. I didn't know who the Blanche and Rose would be, but it didn't matter, because all I was sure of was that I had my own Sophia.

I still sing a lot, and what I think is hilarious is that even as an adult, I still bust into *The Golden Girls* theme song without notice. Some things never change. You can take the girl out of the hood but don't you dare take her homemade Lego pencil cup holder away because she will cut you (or rather your hair). Oh, and that girl whose hair I cut? We ended up becoming friends all the way through high school.

TV shows can be magical. They were for me. I take them very seriously because I know the effect they can have on someone. They can be so special to people like me, the little, lonely girl that had no friends growing up, because they made me feel like I wasn't alone. That is what I believe TV could and should do. After my sitcom was canceled, people kept asking me when I was going to come out with a new idea, and I always said the same thing: "I don't know." I'm not trying to force the next thing to happen. I'm not trying to come up with something merely for fame or money. This journey I'm on has never been about any of those things. It has always been so much bigger than me. This journey is about creating a world that speaks to people on a personal level. It's about finding a story and creating a world that makes people feel the same emotions I felt when I saw my favorite TV shows. It's about trying to reach out to the kids growing up like I did, and create something that will stay with them for the rest of their lives. It's about creating something that could be what *The Golden Girls* was for me, for someone else.

Sometimes when the stars align, you end up with the perfect combination of actors, writers, tech crew, hair/makeup, audience coordinators, network executives, craft service, and whomever else, syncing up to create magic. I list several people you might not think about because it's important to realize there's a world of people involved in putting together a great TV show, and everyone is important to make it succeed. It takes a village, a village like the kind Sophia Petrillo used to talk about.

In *The Golden Girls*, that perfect combination is Dorothy's sarcastic retorts while she listens to Blanche's stories about her never-ending trysts as Rose talks about people in her hometown with names you can't pronounce. Sophia then enters wearing pajamas, *still* carrying her wicker purse in the middle of the night, and they share not only a cheesecake but their friendship. They were an unlikely group of friends to this little Latina. They helped teach me English and how important friendships can be. To this day, they are still the longest friendship I've had.

So, to the ladies, to the writers of the show (one ended up writing on my sitcom—I love him), to the people who worked in front of and behind the screen of *The Golden Girls* . . .

Thank you for being a friend.

"ONLY THE GOOD DIE YOUNG"
BILLY JOEL

My mom and me dressed up for church. When we went, we attended Spanish Mass because my mother never learned to speak English.

While I was born and raised in a small town, one thing that wasn't small was the presence of God. My hometown is the home of a huge Catholic church called the Basilica of Our Lady of San Juan del Valle–National Shrine, or as I like to call it, "the Big Church." I come from a very Catholic family. We used to light candles for the candles we had just lit, just in case. And even though there were five of us living under one roof, we had to also make room for the Father, Son, and Holy Ghost.

We were the kind of family that would go to church for fun. We used to go to church on Mondays to get out of the heat because it was my mom's only day off. I grew up in a very Catholic family, after all. My mom was so Catholic she made nuns question their commitment to God. To be honest, I think she just felt like she was more Catholic than the nuns because so many of our relatives were named Jesús.

On my mother's day off from work, we would walk there and spend hours sitting and praying, walking around and seeing the statues. When I was in high school, the church added the Stations of the Cross—an outside path you could walk and see a set of sculptures depicting the crucifixion of Jesus Christ. Every time we walked that path and got to the last station, where Jesus was laid to rest in his tomb, my mom would make us do the walk in reverse so that at the end of our walk, Jesus was still alive. THAT is how Catholic we were.

My mom wasn't like the ones you see in TV commercials, in which the kid spills orange juice on the floor and they have a talk about how "mistakes happen and it's no big deal." She was the kind of woman that would get upset about my spilling orange juice because it was so expensive. She was also a Catholic woman, which meant that would also limit the life lessons I would get from her.

My mother never talked to me about the birds and the bees unless she was literally talking to me about the birds and the bees. It was more than just sex too. When I was in seventh grade, I started my period and thought something was wrong with me. My mother had never taught me that menstruating was something that happened to women. For months, I would hand-wash my clothes if I stained them to hide them from my mother because I didn't want her mad at me. She finally found out what I had been doing and it was then that I had a rare moment with my mother that I had always searched for. I remember when I finally had to tell her what was happening to me, I was bawling my eyes out, hoping she wouldn't hit me. She looked at me, cried, and hugged me. It was then that she explained a little bit of what was happening. That moment was the closest I ever got to having my mother be open about anything like that with me, which is disappointing because I wonder how many embarrassing and trying times I could've saved myself from if I had just been allowed to ask her things.

When I think about my Catholicism, I can't help but think of "Only the Good Die Young" by Billy Joel. Billy Joel was my first concert and I have seen him more times than I want to admit. What can I say? I'm a sucker for any guy who can play piano. I don't care if you're Billy Joel or the guy at a Nordstrom during Christmas season, if you're tickling the ivories, you're tickling my fancy. The first Billy Joel song I fell in love with was "Allentown" from *The Nylon Curtain*. I was about six years old and it was my "kid song." A kid song is what I call the random song a child connects with and will sing along or dance to when it comes on. It's become a thing for parents to post videos of their toddlers singing along to Katy Perry, Bruno Mars, or whatever other artist has performed in a Super Bowl. Well, mine was Billy Joel. Now thinking about it, the fact that I used to "rock out" to a song about the decline of American factory work and the diminishing of the manufacturing industry seems pretty prescient for a little kid.

"Only the Good Die Young" was one of my anthems because it focused on the religious part of me that most songs didn't really ever focus on. After all, Catholicism was ingrained in me as if it were as important to my identity as my family's being from Mexico. I used to love watching religious cartoons and did so until I was a teenager, learning lessons about being good and bad. The moral of the stories was always the same: help people that are in need, faith is what keeps us going, beer before liquor, never been sicker . . . You know, the usual.

I am grateful for having had the Catholic upbringing my mother gave me because it was based on the idea that it was important to have faith. Faith meant the impossible could happen. It also meant that we didn't have the right to judge anyone for what they were; rather, we *loved* them for what they were. My mom would always tell me that she didn't believe in judging people (even though she did it like it was her part-time job) because she knew what it was like for people to do that to her and she never wanted anyone to feel the way others had made her feel.

Having said all the obligatory stuff about Catholicism, I will admit the religion did stifle me a lot and still does now into my adulthood because it held me back in a really important part of life: relationships, dating, "doing it." I mean, look at how I refer to sex. I say "doing it," for God's sake! (BRB, going to light a candle for writing "for God's sake" because I think I just took the Lord's name in vain.) Aside from the "Don't judge, love everyone" narrative, I was also taught the "Wait until you're married to do anything" narrative.

My sister ran off with her boyfriend when she was eighteen. No one in my family knew she was even seeing someone. He lived in Mexico, near my grandmother's house. She would go and visit my grandmother on the weekends, and then one weekend, she didn't come back. I was about eight when it happened and I remember how furious my mom was. She hit me because she thought I had lied about not knowing my sister's boyfriend (I had had no clue). I understand why my sister did what she did. She just wanted to flee our house to have a chance at being like girls her age. She wanted to taste some kind of freedom. So she took the first opportunity she had to leave home and didn't look back. Seeing her leave home felt like the part in *The Shawshank Redemption* when we find out Andy Dufresne escaped from jail in the middle of the night. She had done it!

Unfortunately, I had been left behind to deal with my mother. After my sister left home, my mother was convinced that she had not been strict enough. What had happened with my sister was NOT going to happen with me. My mother decided to become stricter. She decided she would fix the mistakes she thought she had made and would keep me by her side at all times. If I thought she had been strict before, then I had no idea what was coming to me.

I was not allowed to date. I was not allowed to even have a crush on a guy. My mom's thinking was "You can date when you get married." I don't think she got how dating worked. Back in my mom's village, you didn't really date. At least, my mother hadn't been allowed to date. She had basically been kidnapped by my dad, who had taken her from her house and pretty much made her his property. "That's how they did things back then," my mother said. I still don't know why the Hallmark Channel hasn't done a rom-com about this.

My mother was hardwired into believing that dating was an express lane to getting pregnant. She couldn't understand the concept of having a boyfriend, one that would take you to school dances or a movie. My mother wanted me to know that doing anything with a boy before marriage was a sin. ANY KIND OF ROMANTIC CONTACT WITH A BOY WAS A SIN! I think it was easier to use Catholicism as a way to shield me from boys rather than try to explain that teen pregnancy was high in my hometown; the next best option was to instill the fear of God in me so that I would never want to ever go out with anyone. I had it in my mind that God was like Santa Claus, in that he saw everything I did, and I didn't want him to see me doing anything that would go against what I was taught.

It worked until the eighth grade . . .

Courtesy of Ruben Alonzo

I was in eighth grade and was always expected to dress up like I was selling insurance to classmates.

I had been a straight-A student my entire school career leading up to junior high because I had to be. You know the term "Tiger Mom"? My mother was a "Los Tigres del Norte Mom." On the very rare occasion that I would get a B, it was always with notes from my teachers telling my mom that I talked too much in class and distracted students by trying to make them laugh (I know, go figure). She would "fix" the problem by hitting me. She believed that by doing so, it would scare me into getting A's—and this usually worked. But in eighth grade, I found myself bored in class, being disruptive, and talking more because I would finish my assignments before everyone else.

There was also this guy in one of my classes that I could not stop thinking about. He was cute, a jock, AND A HARD-CORE CATHOLIC! Come to think of it, he was so religious, I'll call him Jude because St. Jude was both of our families' saint (yes, we both had a family saint). I loved that he was religious because it made me feel like that meant I was safe from having any physical contact with him. What could go wrong? (Insert the biggest eye roll here.)

Months into the school year, Jude asked me for my phone number. No boy had ever asked me for my number and I knew that I couldn't give it to him, so I told him I didn't have one and ran away. All I kept thinking was *What if I give him my number, he calls my house, and my mother answers the phone?* I was NOT going to get hit over this stupid, good-looking jock that liked me. Or was I?

I ended up realizing I liked Jude a lot and made up a story a week later about how my family had just suddenly gotten a phone and NOW I could talk to him. Needless to say, I have never been a suave person. I remember I gave him my phone number on a Monday, which at the time I didn't realize was a Monday until I got home. The reason that Monday is important to this story is because it was my mother's day off from work. When I got home and saw her sitting on the couch, I freaked out. What if he called me that day? A boy had NEVER called me at the house before. What the hell had I been thinking?

I sat at the kitchen table and started doing my homework. The only phone we had was in the living room. I calculated that if the phone rang, I had about ten seconds to run and pick it up.

That wasn't going to be so hard. My mom didn't like answering the phone, so what was the big deal? A couple hours passed. At around 5:30 p.m., my mom told me she wanted me to take a shower. OH GOD, NO! That meant I would have to be away from the phone while I was showering. NO! I told her I had barely touched anything and was probably pretty clean from yesterday's shower. She told me to go shower anyway. I could be in and out of the bathroom in about five minutes. She finally snapped at me and said, "GO SHOWER, CRISTELA!" and I ran. It was the quickest shower I had ever taken. A cat licking itself probably did a better job than me that day, but I didn't care. As long as I hadn't heard the phone ring, I was okay. I got out, got dressed, and walked into the living room. I sat down near my mother as she watched TV. We sat in silence for a couple of minutes until she finally said, "You got a call while you were in the shower." NO! I pretended it was no big deal. I asked her who it was. She replied, "It was a boy. He asked for you. I told him to never call here again and hung up on him. Who is that boy?" I lied and told her that he was a boy from school that I had been paired up with to do a project, but I had told him he couldn't call me at home and I was going to have a talk with him at school tomorrow to tell him as much. In my mind, though, I was so embarrassed at the thought of having to see Jude at school the next day. Even worse, I was terrified at being so close to my mom. Was she going to hit me again? I sat there, waiting for her to decide my fate. She kept watching TV. I had gotten away with it . . . or so I thought.

She started hitting me, yelling between smacks: *SMACK!* "I can't believe you're ruining your life for a stupid boy!" *SMACK!* "You're a child. What are you doing with that guy?" *SMACK!* "I'm doing this to teach you to be a good person!" *SMACK!* "Boys only want one thing. Wait until you're married!"

I didn't know what she meant by that. I was only fourteen. But as an adult, I've come to understand that my mother was the way she was as a by-product of the way she was raised. She came from a family where her parents weren't the only ones allowed to hit her, but her brothers could as well because they were men. After hearing stories my mom used to tell me about her childhood, I knew that when she hit me, I was still doing better than what she had lived through. It didn't make it hurt less, though. I had been "bad." In my mom's mind, the mere fact that a boy had called the house looking for me meant I had sinned, even though I hadn't.

I knew what would happen next. I had to stay out of my mother's way until she cooled down. Sometimes it would be quick; other times she would hold a grudge—and boy, could she hold a grudge. If the Olympics had "holding a grudge" as a category, she would've been its Michael Phelps.

After she stopped hitting me, I sat by our record player and waited to see if she was done with her punishment. Once I saw she was, I took out Billy Joel's *Greatest Hits Volume I and II* records and played them. When "Only the Good Die Young" started playing, I thought Billy Joel was singing about me. The song described this girl named Virginia and how Catholic she had been raised. There was a lyric in the song that specifically talked about how her parents had built this girl a temple and imprisoned her in it. When I was at home, I felt like Rapunzel. I felt like I was imprisoned in a tower, kept under lock and key. My every move was supervised. I had to ask permission to even get any food from the kitchen to eat. I had to follow rules, and there was always a constant reminder that you had to be a good person because God was always watching.

The next day I went to school and saw my crush. He told me what my mother had said and, to my surprise, said he understood and respected it. He thought it was "cool" that my mother was so protective. WHAT? Was this the nicest guy ever? We kept talking and getting to know each other. We'd talk about church, sports, church, music, church music . . . Notice a theme? Jude eventually asked me to have lunch with him and I thought, *AM I HAVING MY FIRST DATE?* and said yes.

I didn't know what to do. My best friend at the time was a girl that was raised in a strict Jehovah's Witness household and she was also not allowed to talk to boys. Put us together and we were pretty useless when it came to dating. So I figured I'd wing it. I met Jude for lunch, not knowing what to expect. We sat next to each other and then he took it out. No, not what you think. He took out a folder with a bunch of papers in it. He spread them on the table. Lying in front of me were all these photocopied pics of squiggly figures, maybe a baby? I couldn't make it out. He started telling me about the pictures. They were of aborted fetuses. He started going into a lecture about abortion and being pro-life. What the hell was going on? I kept thinking, *Oh my God. Is THIS what a date is?* I liked him a lot, but this was weird. Yet there I sat, nodding and trying to eat my sloppy joe as he showed me graphic pictures and taught me about the word of God. That lunch, that lecture would be the first time ANYONE, including my mother, would talk to me about sex. He didn't even go into detail, he just told me that babies were made from sex. From that point on, I thought that this was what dating was. Going out with guys and having them lecture you about the Bible.

I didn't know why my friends were so into dating, and more important, I didn't know why my mother didn't want me to do this more.
Even after our weird lunch sermon, we kept talking. We never did
anything. He hugged me once. We never even kissed or anything.

I remember being really sad when the school year ended because
eighth grade was over. The next school year, we'd be freshmen, and
many of our friends would be going to different high schools. I was
devastated at the thought that I might not see Jude again. How were
we going to say goodbye?

On the last day of school, our principal let the eighth graders
request songs to be played over the intercom as a way to say goodbye
to friends. I remember walking from my locker, looking around the
school, and dreading the end of the day. Then, over the intercom, I
heard my name. My crush had dedicated Boyz II Men's "End of the
Road" to me. As I'm writing this sentence, I'm laughing at remembering how excited I was. I actually saw him while this song was playing and we hugged goodbye because I knew that there was no chance
I was going to see him over the summer break. My mom would never
allow that. As I left school that day, I kept hoping I would see him at
the start of high school in the fall.

And I did.

We had English class together. I remember being nervous when
I saw him again. What if things were different? What if he didn't like
me anymore? We sat across from each other and caught up with the
basic questions:

JUDE: How was your summer?
ME: Good. Did a lot of reading.
JUDE: Oh. I didn't do that.

ME: How was your summer?
JUDE: It was cool.
ME: Cool.

I felt different about him and he felt different about me too. I couldn't put my finger on it. We were both trying to pick up where we had left off, but it wasn't happening. We would talk, but things were different. I chalked it up to our being busy. He was playing football, I was doing volleyball, theater, and academic decathlon (not to brag).

A month after school had started, he told me he wanted to talk to me about something. Oh, boy, it was coming. He was seeing someone—of course he was. I wasn't allowed to even talk on the phone with him and here I expected him to wait for me? Wait for what? Again, I was like Rapunzel, living in my tower where no one had access to me outside of school.

He sat me down and I immediately expected the worst. And that was pretty much what I got—the worst. He told me there was this girl. (I slowly nodded. *Okay.*) They had known each other for a while and had been talking to each other. (I slowly nodded again. *Got it.*) They had hung out in the summer. (I nodded so much I probably looked like a Pez dispenser. *Yes, I'm listening . . .*)

And she was pregnant.

Um, I'm sorry. What? He was going to be a father? We were both fourteen years old. I couldn't process what he was saying. *How* was he going to be a dad? I mean, I guessed *how* it had happened. I had started seeing the R-rated movies on Cinemax months prior; I could figure it out. I just kept thinking about how different our summers must have been. He's having sex with this girl while I'm at home trying to beat Sonic the Hedgehog? He went into this long monologue about how confused he was. He was having a baby with this other girl but he "liked me so much" too. He kept telling me he was in love with both of us and didn't know what he was going to do. I sat there and listened to everything he had to say. Then I asked him if he was done talking and carefully thought about what I was going to say next. Then, very adult-like, I told him that he shouldn't be confused about anything. It was obvious whom he had picked. I reminded him about that lunch we had had and how, looking back, he talked about being pro-life, but not once did he mention anything about waiting till marriage to have sex. So I told him to go on and be a dad. That's what he had chosen. I was just glad I wasn't the one to whom it had happened.

I went home and again put on my main man, Billy Joel. "Only the Good Die Young" started playing and I realized that it was the first time I'd really had my heart broken, or what I thought was having my heart broken. In part, I blamed my upbringing. Why couldn't I have been "normal"? I was so aware that I wasn't having the typical teenage experience my friends were having, and I hated it. I couldn't talk to boys, I couldn't go out on a date. I was expected to keep to myself, get good grades, and completely ignore the fact that I was slowly becoming an adult with all these new thoughts and feelings I didn't understand. I couldn't talk to my mom about this. I couldn't talk to anyone about it. I just had to suppress everything I was thinking and hope it went away.

The way I heard that song changed that year. It made me feel good by making me feel bad. It was like that moment when you go through a breakup with someone and play love songs that make you remember the good times and make you even more miserable—

which is somehow therapeutic. Every time I played the song and listened to the lyrics describing how the Catholic girls were depicted, it reminded me that I was different from everyone. It was almost in a mocking way—but I still loved listening to it.

My freshman year in high school put me on an expressway to boys. I was not only forced to confront my awkwardness; I had to find a way to deal with it. I was a big tomboy. I didn't really wear makeup or dress up very girly. I remember my favorite shirt was this old-school Mötley Crüe one I bought at a Goodwill for three dollars. I liked watching *Star Trek: The Next Generation* and played a lot of video games. I remember playing Super Mario Bros. and thinking, *I don't get why this plumber keeps trying to save the Princess. You've saved her so many times, you've even gotten your brother involved and she STILL won't go out with you.* I hung out with my brothers a lot as well, so I guess for the most part, I always saw guys as buddies. Girls that were the opposite of me seemed to get all the guys. They were the ones that wore makeup every day, dressed up to go to school. They were so not me.

That was also the year when I got really into theater and entered every competition there was. In one of the tournaments during my freshman year, my school had shared a bus with our neighboring high school and I ended up hanging out with a group of freshman guys. I knew some of them from competing in theater in eighth grade, so I was excited to see them because I didn't get along with my fellow high school drama thespians. (I had no idea that what was happening at that moment was the start of some heavy-duty bullying. But just you wait: we'll get to that in a later chapter.) When

I wasn't competing in events that day, I was hanging out with these guys. We talked about heavy metal, sports, and video games while at the same time quoting *Wayne's World* nonstop. I had no interest in any of those guys, I was just having fun hanging out with them. We were talking like I did with my brothers and I felt completely at ease. That night, after the awards ceremony, we got on the bus to go back to school. I picked a seat by the window and placed my trophies next to me. One of the guys from the group I had been hanging out with asked me if he could sit next to me and I said yes. We sat and chatted a bit. He told me he liked my trophies and I remember telling him, "Duh. Show me someone that doesn't like winning." Then he leaned in and kissed me. Like, KISSED me where he opened his mouth and I felt his tongue. I freaked out and pulled away because I felt his tongue. I had no idea what had just happened or *how* it had happened. I hadn't been doing anything with this guy and here he was pretending I was drowning and he had to give me CPR! What was going on? I remember I could feel his lips even after I pulled away from him. I was fifteen and had just had my first kiss with this guy that a while ago was singing Hendrix's "Foxy Lady" with me as Garth from *Wayne's World*. The first thing I thought was, *Oh my God! Am I pregnant now?*

What I wrote is not a joke. I'm embarrassed to have to write it, but I have to be honest. I thought that this guy had gotten me pregnant because he had kissed me. I KNOW! How on earth does someone get the idea that a kiss is what sex is? Well, my Catholic upbringing and the suppression of anything involving sex helped, but Mexican telenovelas were partly to blame as well. I was in high school, yes, but no one had taught me about sex, so I had used context clues from TV/film to guess what sex was and how it worked. I used to see telenovelas with my mom all the time. The difference between the telenovelas and the soaps in the United States was that the tele-novelas would have a beginning and an end; they were limited series. Meanwhile, the US soap operas lasted decades. In the same four months that a telenovela would start and finish, you'd have love, lust, crime, heartbreak, and death, while American soaps would take the same four months to cover two days of the characters' lives.

The stories in the telenovelas I grew up with in the eighties and nineties were very similar to one another. A pretty, young (usually poor) girl would fall for the handsome, older (usually wealthy) man. Sometimes the roles were reversed, but let it be known: someone was poor and someone was rich. There was always a villain because you can't have a love triangle without one or else it'd be a "two-way street" kind of love, and who wanted that? The villain's goal would be to destroy this budding relationship by any means possible. Usu-ally the villain's worst actions were done on a Friday to make peo-ple have to watch on Monday. The thing that really confused me was that in the telenovelas I watched, they'd have a moment in the story when the couple would realize they loved each other and would kiss. Sometimes the camera would slowly pan to a side and cut to commercial. A couple episodes later, the girl would find out she was pregnant. The stories were always presented in a very conservative manner. They would never show anything sexual, but would rather subtly insinuate it, which was very confusing for me since I took things pretty literally. Oh, I forgot to mention that at some point in the telenovela, if our heroine was confused, she'd go to church and pray for guidance. (This happened a lot in one of my favorite tele-novelas of all time, *Rosa salvaje*.) These soap operas were the closest and most frequent examples I would see from my childhood about what relationships were all about. After all, my mother raised me by herself; my parents had separated; so it wasn't like I had any real-life relationships to learn from.

I was in shock for about a week after being kissed for the first time. I felt like I wasn't a good Catholic girl anymore. I was tarnished and I had to tell my mom what had happened. I was stressed out. I really thought I could be pregnant. I wanted to take a pregnancy test. I finally mustered the courage to tell my friend what had happened and she started bawling. She could not stop crying from all the laughter. She thought I was joking. "Wait, how can you be so smart and so dumb at the same time? How is that even possible, because you're SO dumb right now." She told me how it all worked. I finally ended up getting a version of the sex talk . . . from someone my age. I felt stupid and embarrassed because it was, again, one of those moments when I felt like I wasn't normal. To this day, I still remember how much she laughed because I felt like the laughter was proof that I was weird. I was not like anyone else I knew.

I figured the best plan for me to survive high school was to be a jerk to guys so there was no chance they could ever like me. I started doing it all the time; it became my go-to. I was awful; I know that. If I knew a guy even remotely liked me, I was terrible to him and I did it intentionally so he could hate me and not want anything to do with me. I knew I could never have anything with any of them, no matter how much I liked them. It really used to make me feel awful to do this because, in so many cases, I really liked the guys but felt like I had no other option.

My plan ended up working. Guys didn't want to date me or want anything romantic to do with me—which was the goal. Then came the moment I was introduced to irony. This was at the same time my mother started getting concerned, wondering *why* I wasn't so girly and not interested in boys. She wanted to know why I wasn't like my older sister. She had liked guys. She was girly. Again, she had also left home at an early age because she didn't like how strict everything was. My mother wondered what was wrong with me. Little did she know, she was a big part of the problem.

She started wondering if I was gay since I hadn't shown any interest in guys. I found it incredible that she was completely unaware that she had scared me into suppressing that part of myself. I had become this teenage girl that constantly talked about how guys didn't matter to me and how I believed love was a stupid concept. I thought that was the only way to get her off my back. I had created this faux illusion that I was this asexual person that wasn't interested in anyone. It was my way of trying to get my mom to lay off of me, but now she was determined to get me to come out of the closet.

My mom used to watch this salacious Latin American TV talk show that would constantly have episodes featuring gay teenagers that would come out to their parents. Most of the time, the parents would get so upset, they'd pick up chairs and try to hit the kids with them. My mom used to watch those episodes and feel terrible for the kids. She couldn't understand how parents could just stop loving their children for something they were. She was very progressive when it came to matters like the LGBTQ community. She was the person that would say that it didn't matter who you loved as long as you were happy. I couldn't understand how loving she could be in that regard because if a boy called our house asking for me, she'd hit me.

We used to watch the show together a lot and I started noticing my senior year that every time there was an episode about a teenager coming out to their parents, she would look at me and ask me different questions to feel me out. We'd get to the part of the show when the teenager would reveal he's gay and a parent would get mad, then she'd casually throw out, "You know, if *any* of my kids were gay, I wouldn't love them any less," as she slowly moved her head to look at me. Okay. If there was a commercial with a pretty girl in it, she'd ask me if I thought the girl was pretty. Um, I guess. She asked and asked around it and then finally, one day, asked me, "Do you like girls? Are you gay? I won't be mad if you are. I just want to know. I will love you the same." I told her I didn't think I was. It was such a weird thing for her to ask me, not because she was asking me if I was gay but rather because I didn't know if there was a right answer. I lived on pins and needles with her. I told her I didn't have any kind of feelings for anyone, which was a total lie because I had a crush throughout high school on this guy that was a year older than me. He liked me too. We used to talk on the phone when my mom was at work. I was head over heels for him, but couldn't do anything but talk to him on the phone. That was how I dealt with my strict mother; I lied a lot to her about my feelings and who I was.

I didn't go to my high school graduation; that was my choice. Once I knew I had enough credits to graduate, I stopped going to school because I figured there was no point. I had always felt like I didn't fit in, so why keep going if I didn't have to? I had been taught to treat school like it was work, and I didn't have that *big* group of friends that I was going to miss. I really only had two friends throughout high school and they were a year younger than me. I had decided to go to college in St. Louis, and in my mind, I was already living on my own. My mom hated that I was moving away. I think my mom was hurt by the fact that both of her daughters left her the moment we could, but could you blame us?

The first day I got to college (and I mean within hours), I met a guy. He was living in my dorm and just started talking to me. We hung out for a bit. He was from Dallas; my sister lived there, so we had that in common. He seemed nice. Cut to a couple hours later, we were making out. Scratch that—let me correct myself. He was making out with me and I was trying to figure out what "making out" was. All we did was kiss, and I remember that I couldn't enjoy it because I kept wondering if I was doing a good job. I felt like I had lied on my résumé and gotten the job and now I had to do the thing I absolutely did not know how to do. All I'm saying is that I am grateful that Yelp reviews for making out didn't exist back then. I was completely unaware of what was happening to me, but now, looking back, it was so obvious. It was the first time I was on my own with no parental supervision. I could do anything I wanted and it was overwhelming. I was going crazy, or rather I was going my version of crazy. With this newfound independence, I was making up for lost time. I just wanted to make out with every guy I saw!

Did you think I was going to say I slept with every guy I met? Ha. Have you not been reading this chapter? Pages ago, I thought I had gotten pregnant by a kiss and you think I'm going to give it up that easy? Come on!

Looking back, I realize I didn't have too much of a problem telling people I had never had sex; I had a problem with certain people's reaction to it. Sometimes, if it would come up in conversation, there would be people that acted like there was something really wrong with me. They suddenly wanted to make plans for me to lose my virginity like I was some teenage guy in a high school movie desperately trying to get laid before graduation. People kept asking me why I hadn't slept with anyone yet, and the truth was simple: I didn't date and I had never had a boyfriend. The opportunity had never come up. It wasn't this religious thing I was holding on to. I just hadn't gotten around to it, in a way.

Years later, on my twenty-first birthday, I was working as a server at a restaurant where everyone knew I was a virgin and they decided to pitch in to get me a gift and surprise me with it. As they brought it out, they told me that I was required to take it home with me the way they had given it to me and they would make sure that I left with it intact. They also told me that they would give me the money from the tip jar the next day if I did what was told of me.

I didn't see what the big deal was because, honestly, I'm the person that had no shame. I'd walk around in a onesie that made me look like a horse, and I was pretty well-known for singing in the kitchen during my shifts when the patrons would clap and tip me after songs. What on earth could they ever do to try to embarrass me?

They brought out a huge cookie that read "Happy Birthday!" and then another server said she was going to get my "gift." When she came around the corner and I caught a glimpse of it, I wanted to cry. It was a male inflatable sex doll that had a penis sticking out of it. He was a brunette with chest hair drawn on him. He kind of looked like Burt Reynolds.

And yes, it was inflated.

They started laughing and couldn't stop. I was terrified. The server handed it over to me and said, "Have fun going home with it." Did I mention that I didn't own a car at the time and took the bus home? After my shift that day, they watched me leave the restaurant and walk to my bus stop, carrying this inflatable dude under my arm. The moment I was out of their sight, I started deflating the guy, but it was taking him too long to deflate and my bus got there. I walked on and took a seat while people stared at me, and I just kept telling people it was a joke birthday gift. I was so embarrassed. Slowly, within a couple of blocks, the doll was nothing more than a blob . . . a blob with an erect penis.

Look, I was twenty-one when I lost my virginity. It was obviously to the inflatable Burt Reynolds look-alike doll the servers got me. (Just kidding.) I would rather not talk about who the guy was, just know that I really liked him and thought he was great. The truth is, no one knows who it is. The guy who thinks he was my first was actually my second. I wanted to keep the first one a secret because of this story I'm about to tell.

I met the guy at work. Not at the restaurant, but at another job I had. I usually had more than one job at all times back then. He was good-looking and super sarcastic. We weren't allowed to go out with coworkers, so we would go out of our way to hang out outside of work. After months of hanging out, we slept together. It just happened. I had not been waiting for marriage because, honestly, I wasn't sure if I ever wanted to get married. We went back to his place and drank some beers, eventually making fun of each other, and then one thing led to another. We ended up in his bedroom. I remember exactly what I was thinking when it was happening: *Am I doing it right and what am I supposed to do here?* Again, the closest I got to an idea of what to do was from watching the late-night Cinemax movies, but the only thing I learned is that sleeping with random guys was the only way to keep a bikini car wash open.

The next day, when I woke up, it took me a second to realize that I hadn't dreamed what had happened. When I realized I wasn't in my apartment, I looked over and saw the guy's face. My eyes widened as if I had just realized I was being haunted by a ghost. I turned away from him and kept mouthing, "WHAT DID I DO?" over and over again.

The guy woke up soon after I did and wanted to hug me. He asked me if I wanted breakfast. I didn't know if I should have breakfast. Was breakfast a part of the whole process? I quickly jumped out of bed and told him I was running late. I had nowhere to go, but I had to get there quickly. I don't know what came over me, but I went from groggy to freak-out immediately. He offered to give me a ride home (remember, I was taking the bus everywhere), but I told him that I was okay. I gathered my stuff and sprinted out his door.

I didn't know why I was leaving so quickly. I technically had not done anything wrong. *Technically.* Notice that word? I had "technically" not done anything wrong, but I realized in that moment that I felt as if I had. Here I was, thinking that I was okay sleeping with someone because I wasn't waiting for marriage, but in reality that thick layer of Catholic guilt washed over my body like the moment the Red Sea came together after Moses parted it. It was at that moment that I realized what I was feeling was this guilt that I had been taught to have. It felt horrible. I didn't know what to do to make me feel better, but more important, I didn't know how the hell to get home. Where the hell was the bus stop? I finally ended up catching a bus, and once I got near my neighborhood, I got off at a stop I was very familiar with. I ran from the bus stop to a Catholic church I used to go to. I ran in there like I needed an exorcism and went into the first available confessional booth I could find. I went in there and confessed to the priest that I had slept with a man, though the more I confessed, the more I felt that even the priest thought I was weird. He had a tone in his voice like he was expecting there would be more to the story. I kept trying to say the same thing in a more dramatic tone to see if I could get more of a shocked reaction from him. "I SLEPT with a man. I slept . . . WITH A MAN!" He told me a couple things to say and, boom, I was done.

I left the church that day feeling so stifled. I had done a completely normal thing that a lot of adults do, and here I was, completely incapable of handling it. It was then and there that I realized how stifled I was when it comes to so much because of the "proper" way my mother raised me, which really meant pretending most of what was normal didn't exist. The way I had been raised was a mix of being a devout Catholic and also supposedly trying to be prim and proper.

I always found it weird that the base of what was taught to me as a Catholic was to always try to be honest, when in my case, Catholicism was more about hindrance than anything else. I'm not knocking the religion at all. I am still Catholic. It's a part of me that I can't shake off. If I have free time and I'm near a Catholic church, I go to it. I have a St. Jude altar in my apartment. I think one thing I've realized as I've gotten older is that there can be a balance between one's faith and one's growth. One can work hand in hand with the other without stifling and canceling it out. It's taken me years to understand this, and I'm still learning.

I'd like to think that I'm still religious because having come from nothing, you realize faith is all you've got. That is until you can find yourself. In the words of Billy Joel: "Only the good die young."

I don't want to die young. I want to die old, which means I think I have to be a little bad for that. God willing.

Selena Quintanilla is someone I connected to despite having never physically met her. She is a prime example of what one is capable of when being oneself.

"DREAMING OF YOU"
SELENA

It was 1995 and I was in my high school French class wondering why, in every foreign language, it's so important to learn how to ask directions to the library. I used to imagine that maybe that was a required thing when you went to foreign countries; you had to go to the library for some reason that I would find out about as an adult.

I had to take a foreign language course for credit and wanted to challenge myself with French because I already knew Spanish. Of course, I was a big nerd that liked to challenge myself with schoolwork, and I did take French for years, though I can't speak or write it anymore. It wasn't that hard because French has the same verb conjugations as Spanish.

On March 31, 1995, my principal abruptly interrupted class to make an announcement. "Sorry for the interruption, but we have an important announcement to make. We have just learned Selena Quintanilla has died."

The class was quiet for a little bit, and then everyone started crying. I was having trouble processing what had been said. A girl that sat diagonal from me looked at me and said, "Why are you crying? Did you even like her?" I replied, "Yes, I liked her. We were both in the same PE class." That's when she told me I had killed the wrong Selena in my mind. The Selena that died was the Tejano singer. I was so embarrassed. I had confused the Selenas. There *had* been a Selena in my PE class, but come to think of it, I didn't know what her last name was. I just assumed that because so many people in my class were crying about it, it had to be a student, right? Once I realized which Selena it was, I was even more devastated, and that confused me. I actually knew the girl from my PE class personally, but the singer? I had never met her. How could I be feeling so devastated by the loss of a stranger? I knew her music but not her.

Before I continue, I should give a crash course for those unfamiliar with Selena Quintanilla. Selena was a Mexican American singer born and raised in Corpus Christi, Texas (which is a two-hour drive from my little hometown of San Juan). She was the singer in a band called Selena y Los Dinos, which was managed by her father, Abraham Quintanilla. In a way, it was kind of like a Mexican American Partridge Family. She became famous singing a genre of music referred to as Tejano music, which I guess you can say is a kind of Latino Texan music. It can typically have elements of polka and rock, with songs being sung in Spanish. She is lovingly known as "The Queen of Tejano" and achieved this status by becoming the most successful Latino artist in the nineties.

My family used to catch Selena y Los Dinos a lot on a show we watched on Sunday mornings called *The Johnny Canales Show*, a weekly variety program that showcased prominent names in Tejano music. In our family, watching Johnny Canales was a part of life. We'd sit on the floor of our house and eat breakfast as we watched him. Every week, we'd see him throwing out his catchphrases that became classics. "Take it away!" and "You got it!"

French was my last class of the day. My brother picked me up and, as I got into the car, I remember hearing a Selena song playing on the radio. When it ended, the radio DJ was sobbing as he repeated the news, "Selena Quintanilla has died," and then continued playing more of her music. My brother asked me if I had heard the news. I had, but hearing her music made me sadder. I had trouble accepting what I was hearing. I didn't instantly mourn her; it was a slow build within me. When we got home, my mom was crying about Selena. It was the first time I had experienced this phenomenon firsthand: a famous person dying and having everyone around me react to it on this level, like we had all lost a member of the family.

One of the ways I could tell Selena's death was different from others was that the announcement of it had made it to my mom's mattress. My mom used to keep the most important documents under our mattress in that gap between the mattress and box spring; it was like the family safe. Anytime we needed to get an important document, one person would raise the mattress so the other person could find the paper that was needed. It was kind of like a poverty game show because we had to try to find the thing we were looking for before the person holding up the mattress started getting tired and dropped it. It was interesting to see the random things my mom kept under there; it almost served as a time capsule for what my family represented. It had the check register for my mom's bank account that never had more than three hundred dollars in it (the only time we had that much money in the bank is when my mom would get her income tax refund). There were also school pictures that we never framed. They weren't even ones we bought. Most of them were pictures of us that had the word *sample* watermarked on them. There was a picture of Jesus Christ that was so old but that my family refused to throw away because we thought it was sacrilegious to do so. There were envelopes of my mom's taxes from H&R Block and my mom's newspaper clippings. The newspaper articles she would keep said a lot about her. They showed what mattered to her. She had clippings from random things like a cutout of the US flag, articles about the big Catholic church in our town, an article profiling John F. Kennedy . . . but the big, dominant one was the front page of our local newspaper, *The Monitor*, announcing the death of Selena. My mom kept it because she deemed it important to the history she wanted to remember.

I'll admit, I didn't understand why my mother had kept that clipping and put it under the mattress, but I was young. It wasn't until I saw the movie starring Jennifer Lopez that I understood.

The movie had me from the beginning, showing a little Selena looking up at the sky and making a wish. I used to do that every day when I was a little kid. The more I got into the movie, the more I started realizing what I loved about her. I personally didn't have dreams of being a Tejano music star, but I caught glimpses of familiar things like the dynamic she had within her family. Their energy seemed like mine in that the siblings liked being around one another and the parents were overprotective but loving. I loved seeing that she lived in Corpus Christi because I had never been to a "big" city like that, so different from my little town of San Juan. I compared it to one of those big metropolitan areas like San Antonio, which I thought of as being like New York City.

A moment that really stuck with me was a scene in which Selena and her friend are looking at a dress in an expensive store. Her friend wants to try it on and the sales associate at the store assumes they can't afford it and doesn't want to waste her time helping people who are not serious shoppers, because obviously you can tell that about someone when they walk through a door. In that part of the movie, someone recognizes Selena and they run out and tell someone else; the domino effect begins. In the next scene of the movie, there are groups of Latinos crowded around the store. It eventually leads to the sales associates in the store figuring out that Selena is some notable singer (that they obviously hadn't heard of). The thing that stuck with me from that scene was that her fans were blue-collar, working-class Latinos that had jobs as delivery persons and janitors. That scene spoke so much to me because it was then that I realized that I came from a family whose matriarch had that kind of job. It made me realize how important it was for people like my mom to see someone that seemed familiar to her. It also made me realize that regardless of how big Selena was for the Latino community, she wasn't as famous as I imagined she was outside of the community.

There was a bigger lesson I learned from that scene, one that I wouldn't completely understand until I was older. It was that, despite being as rich or famous as you can be, there will always be people that assume you can't do things because of the way you look. They will think that you can't afford something or that you don't belong where you are. I've had my share of this. A couple of years ago, I was shopping for a new car. My TV show was on the air and I wanted to buy a car because now I could afford a new one. I had my friend Steve go with me to the dealerships because I don't understand the automobile industry at all and Steve not only used to sell cars, but one of his childhood best friends was a manager for a car dealership in Texas.

We were in the Beverly Hills area and drove past a nice dealership. Steve suggested we stop by and look at the cars. I had already looked at that specific brand of car but didn't imagine I would buy one because they were pricey. But I figured, why not? Let's go check them out. Steve had helped me whittle down some choices and I wanted to specifically test-drive two of their models. I was wearing an old, tattered yellow *Golden Girls* shirt that I still wear to this day, and a pair of denim shorts with sandals. I will never forget that outfit. Steve and I looked around the car dealership for a bit and noticed no one had come to help us. We both figured that it was the kind of dealership where maybe people didn't want to seem so aggressive, so we ended up walking to the information desk to ask for a salesperson. The woman paged the sales department and up walked this man who immediately looked at me and made a face. I thought I was imagining things. I'd told Steve I wanted him to do the talking because moments like that intimidated me, especially since I didn't know much about cars. Steve told the salesperson that I wanted to test-drive these two specific cars. The salesperson looked at me and said he didn't have any cars for me to test-drive. Steve thought this was weird. How could a car dealership not have any cars to test-drive? Steve asked him what cars he *did* have available and the salesperson said, "Well, which one do you want to buy?"

I said, "I'm not sure. That's why I want to test-drive a couple."

The salesperson said yet again that he didn't have any cars for me to try out. Steve repeated that there were two models I was looking at, and the salesperson said he couldn't help us in such a condescending way that I told Steve we should leave, which we did. We walked out and Steve could not understand what was happening, while I, on the other hand, knew exactly what was going down.

As we walked back to my car, Steve said he was so upset; he wanted to do something about it. He called his friend in Texas and told him what happened, and immediately his friend said that this was absolutely not normal. He told him it was obvious that the sales-person didn't want to help me. Steve's friend told him that coincidentally another one of their old friends from Texas was the regional manager of that car brand for southern California. He told Steve he was going to call him and tell him what happened.

While Steve was on the phone, I sat there in the driver's seat of my car, stunned at how I had been treated. Whenever those moments happen (and, yes, they still do), it feels like the first time. I feel anger, but I feel hurt as well. It's a different kind of hurt. In a way, it's a combination of feeling like I will never do enough to make some people think I matter and a bit of "Why must I have to accomplish incredible things for you to acknowledge me as a human?" When Steve got off the phone, he said his old friend, the regional manager over at that specific dealership, had called the general manager of the dealership and told him what had happened. The general manager was in his office at the dealership and wanted to talk to Steve and me. I told Steve I didn't feel comfortable walking back in there again. Yes, I know some people would've taken a more aggressive route and charged in there to show them what was up, but I didn't feel like that at all. I started crying and told Steve I couldn't understand how (back then) I had a show on network TV, was cohosting *The View*, and was still treated like there was no way I was good enough to buy a car.

Steve went back into the dealership. He wanted the general manager to know how that salesperson had treated me. I stayed in the car. Steve called me a while later from the dealership and told me the general manager wanted to talk to me. I didn't want to go. At that point, I was now so angry that I didn't want to be near that building.

When he returned, he told me the general manager apologized and had sent that salesperson home. He wanted to make things right and give me a deal on the car. He said he felt bad because his wife was Latina and he couldn't believe that something like that had happened. He even told Steve that if I didn't want to go to the dealership, he understood and would bring the car to me, wherever I wanted, to test-drive it. Days later, I told Steve I wanted a car brought to the studio where I was shooting the show to get a test-drive and asked for a salesperson of color to bring the car because I wanted them to get the commission. When the salesperson showed up, we drove around the neighborhood and I asked Steve to help me negotiate the deal. Once it was done, the car was delivered to me, again at the studio . . . by a Latina. She told me she had heard what had happened and she felt terrible. She gave me the keys and thanked me for giving the dealership another chance.

When I told a friend of mine about what had happened, she told me I had had a "Selena moment," and we talked about the scene with the dress. We talked about how, at times, it didn't matter to some people who you were because look at Selena. She was an icon to many and she had been judged by *what* she was. I still think about that from time to time.

I couldn't help but root for Selena. She had this likability that oozed out of her; she didn't have to say a word to make you feel it. She had an incredible smile that demanded you know how special she was . . . and you did. My favorite part about her was that she looked like me. She was a Mexican American girl with brown skin and dark hair. She reminded me of so many girls I knew, and I loved that. The music she was known for was sung in Spanish but was made here, not only in the United States but near my little blip of a town that wasn't big enough to be listed on maps. She was so different to me because I had grown up listening to predominantly Mexican songs sung in Spanish by Mexican singers. The idea that this girl (and when I discovered her, she was a teenager) was a Mexican American like me and straddled both cultures made me root for her. She sang in Spanish but spoke in English. So did I.

The thing I loved the most about her was that she was a Latina I could look up to. She was "the girl next door" that came off as approachable—and more important, she was a local hometown girl. She lived two hours away from where I lived, and growing up in a big state like Texas, where at times there could be so much open land between towns, you quickly discovered that two hours was nothing. There was also a vibe she gave off that is hard to explain, but I think the best way to describe it is that it felt very "south Texan" to me— meaning *extremely familiar*.

I've always struggled to describe where I grew up because it's different from other places. What I learned about spending time in my life living in Texas, New York, and Los Angeles (among other places; I'm a nomad) is that the Latino community is very similar yet different at the same time. (FYI: There is no country called Latinolandia.) There are differences within Latin American countries that set us apart from one another, like the language. While a lot of us speak Spanish, we sometimes speak different kinds of Spanish; words have different, subtle meanings in different countries.

The biggest lesson I learned (and am still learning) is that even from within my own Mexican community, our worlds can be very different from one another. The Mexican culture that I grew up with in Texas at times differs from the Mexican culture I've come across traveling the country.

I think it's important to focus on what makes the people within the Latino community different from one another. For far too long we have been forced to try to fit into the box we have been put in. I've noticed that quite a bit working in the entertainment industry.

There is also a struggle that exists where I feel like I have to inform people about things they're unfamiliar with while trying to explain why certain stories are important to tell. In those instances, I often wonder how I expect them to understand my plight if I have to educate them along the way. I remember when my show was about to premiere and I had to do press to promote it. The powers that be found out I spoke Spanish and, lo and behold, I ended up doing more interviews in Spanish than I did in English because people thought that me speaking in Spanish would appeal to more Latinos. Why? I tried to explain to them that my show was in English and, therefore, the interviews should have been too, but they didn't listen. What they thought was that I spoke Spanish and all Latinos spoke Spanish, so let's pander to them.

To be fair, I think Latinos like to put one another in boxes too. I dealt with this issue when my TV show was on the air. I would get people telling me, "Latinos don't do that!" or "Latinos aren't like that!" I would always agree with them and say, "I know." The name of my TV show was *Cristela*, not *Every Latino in the World*. It's impossible to meet everyone's expectations and we shouldn't have to. I grew up watching shows like *Roseanne* (the original, not the reboot) and not once did I assume all white mothers were like that. I just figured that was the specific story they were telling. I figured I would get the same respect that I gave to shows, but nah . . .

As part of the Miami trip I was doing to tell people about my show, the powers that be thought it would be good to screen the pilot for different Latino groups. I was vehemently against it because I felt as if targeting specific Latino groups and screening the pilot for them implied that I was asking for their permission to tell me that my life was worthy of their attention. I wanted to premiere it and have everyone react to it simultaneously. After the first pilot screening in Miami, a woman said she didn't like the show because it was "too stereotypical," which I took offense to because the show was based on my family and was very accurate to what our dynamic was. Was she implying that my family was a stereotype? She gave the usual "Latinos aren't like that." I asked her what she meant by that and she continued with "Latinos aren't like that. The mother in the show is too stereotypical. We're not like that." The moment she said that, I smiled at her and asked, "What mother are you talking about, because there are two mothers in the show: my mother and my sister. I just want to make sure I reference the correct one." She said she was talking about my mother and I began to explain the intent of the show. I wanted to take people on a journey to show how certain situations can reflect the changing of the guard, so to speak, about how we handle specific situations depending on the context. It was important for me to show a stark difference between the mothers in the show and also between them and me. You could say you don't like the show, that's fair, but I couldn't understand such a blanket statement like "Latinos don't do that." Breaking news, lady, that thing you didn't agree with? I *did* that and my family did that. My only goal with the show was to show my reality in hopes that it would speak to others, not to try to be the perfect example of what we're all like. I could never do that. I didn't live your life.

The overall story I was trying to show in my sitcom was how ideas and thoughts evolve through generations, because that's what happened in my family. My mother was an old-fashioned, old-school mother who was strict and always told stories about how she had had it worse than all of us combined. My sister had three children and I noticed a change in the way she was with her kids compared to how our mother had been with us. Because my sister had grown up in the United States, in a culture that was different from what she had been used to in Mexico (my sister lived there for the first ten years of her life despite having been born in Texas), she was able to understand that some of the thinking my mother had was out-of-date. Subsequently, she became a more "modern" mother, though she still had a tinge of that old-fashioned thinking at certain times because children learn what their parents teach them. While my sister was more of a modern thinker than my mother, she also married and had children at a very young age. I didn't marry or have children at an early age because I wanted to go out and work on my dream and build a career instead. This put me on a different trajectory from my sister's, and, therefore, I evolved into a person that still was connected to my family roots but was also different than the rest of my family.

At the same time, I understand why people can be very critical about the depictions of their community on-screen. They crave to be represented and want to feel a connection. They want to give their input, which I absolutely welcome, but I believe that we can change our intent and our meaning by merely rephrasing how we say things and have better conversations with each other. Instead of saying that "Latinos don't do that" or "You forgot when we . . . ," you can say, "When I was a child, [insert nostalgic thing here]," or just plainly, "My family didn't do that," but you can't negate MY life or experience because it didn't happen to you. How can we evolve as a community if we don't open up and allow ourselves to be exposed to stories that don't fit the narrative we know? How can we make any progress and get more representation if people are ready to disregard someone else's story at a moment's notice and call foul but not offer a solution? Can you imagine if we did that all the time and disregarded stories that were different from ours? As a Latina that grew up in a border town in south Texas in the eighties and nineties, what kind of stories would I have to relate to as a child? What shows did I have available back then? There weren't stories that fit my mold. That was the reason I wanted to tell my story on TV. I hadn't seen a story like mine on television before and wanted others that maybe lived like I did to know they weren't alone. I wanted to tell my story, the story of an average girl that got to do extraordinary things. That is the reason that Selena Quintanilla is an icon not only to me but to so many others. She was the "average" girl that was anything but. Her girl-next-door appeal made me feel as if I was capable of achieving greatness because she had done it, and she didn't feel as if she was special, but that was what made her special.

Selena accomplished what I am currently trying to do: live my dream on my own terms. She was a musician that didn't live in Los Angeles or New York City. She got to live her dream from the town she grew up in. That is big for me. I grew up in a tiny town and I wanted to go out and explore the world, but the fact that I had to leave my tiny town to try to chase after my dream was terrifying. I realized that if I wanted to have a chance, I was going to have to leave everything and everyone I loved behind and accept that I could live in loneliness, surrounded only by my hopes and dreams. I had saved up money and hoped it was enough to get by. I lived in my car when I moved to Los Angeles. I've slept outside in parks. I didn't have a bed from the age of nineteen to twenty-five; I slept on the floor. All of that was necessary and part of my plan to get to do what I wanted to do. Selena did it, though. She accomplished her dream, and not only from Corpus Christi, she did it with her family by her side. They were part of it and I loved that.

I grew up being really close to my family. I love them and would do anything for them. At eighteen, when I told my mother I was leaving home to study theater, she told me not to go. She forbade me and told me she wasn't going to allow it. I had never, ever gone against my mother's wishes, but decided it was necessary. I told her I was still leaving. She didn't think I was being serious because, again, I was the kid that always listened to her mother, but the day she realized I was serious, she lost it. She got down on her knees and begged me not to go. She had tears streaming down her face. You never forget the moment you break your mother's heart. I remember looking at her and saying, "You think I want to leave you? This thing . . . it's bigger than me and it's bigger than you. I have to go try. If this works out, it's going to be good for all of us. I promise." That moment stayed with me forever because having to pick between staying with the life you know or risking it all in hopes of winning a long-shot dream is difficult. If I could have done it, I would have loved to have brought my family along for the ride but, unfortunately, what I wanted to do wasn't something a family could do together. So I left.

My mother wanted me to stay close to her because she wanted to protect me, both from the heartbreak of disappointment and big-city life. I found it pretty comical when we talked about that because it was really the pot calling the kettle black. She wanted to shield me from the same exact thing she had done. She had begun her life in a tiny village in Mexico and moved to a foreign country with a second-grade education, not knowing the language, in search of a fighting chance at life. She said, "Yes, but I did it because I had to. We didn't have any food. We were very poor." I looked at her and said, "I know.

You gave us a better life than what we would've had in Mexico, but we still grew up in poverty here. I want to leave to chase my dream because our family STILL doesn't have food and we are STILL very poor. I want to do what you did for the same reason. Don't you see that?" She didn't. I know it seems crazy, but having followed Selena's ascension into success, I felt like it was possible for me too. I felt like I had a chance . . . and that's all I wanted . . . just a chance.

After Selena Quintanilla had dominated the Tejano music market, she recorded songs in English and planned a crossover but died at the hands of the president of her fan club before it would come to fruition. I'm going to be honest. The death of Selena was brutal to accept because I felt like I had lost my blueprint. She was showing me the way to chase after my dream; it was a map for me. She was leading by example. What was I going to do now? Figure it out on my own? Her death crushed me because it meant the death of a hope of what could've been.

I had a hope that Selena would cross over and let the rest of the country in on a secret: Latinos are just like everyone else. I thought everyone would fall in love with her and she would make others realize that people like me were worthy of respect. Selena was someone that could show the country we weren't all these tired stereotypes depicted in TV and film. We are not all housekeepers, we are not all gang members, we are not all problems. I never understood why there were so many more stories that categorize Latinos merely by their occupation rather than by their history, as if we're merely human vacuum cleaners that don't have people we love (and who love us) in our lives.

I think about how my mother was a cook at a Mexican restaurant for years. She worked double shifts. One might've caught a glimpse of her and thought that's all she was, but she had a heart, a soul, and a rich history that entailed struggles with the patriarchy that existed in her old-fashioned family and how she forged through years of pain and suffering to end up working in a restaurant in a tiny town in south Texas. I want to hear that kind of background more often in stories about characters we tend to overlook because, in that example, that woman is not "just a cook," she is a mother to her children and a daughter to her parents. How on earth can people find the humanity in those characters if there is no humanity written in them to be found? Aside from speaking about delving into making characters "real," I also think it's important to tell the stories of people that maybe didn't have the "hard" struggles typically associated with the community. There are Latinos living in this country that have had numerous generations of their ancestors living here and might not have the same kind of connection to their ancestors' country as someone like me that is a first-generation Mexican American (or someone who was born there) does, but that doesn't mean they're less Latino than others. There are some Latinos that can't speak Spanish—so what? That does not make them less Latino. Not being able to speak Spanish does not diminish their history. They are still part of the community and need to have their stories told.

A couple of criticisms I used to get about my own show was that they didn't know why the family in my show had to be poor. I would get asked, "Why can't they be successful and have money?" I'd always reply with the same thing: "The family in the show is poor because the show is based on my life and my family was poor." I didn't understand why people couldn't understand that. If I had written a show about a fictional family, then yes, I would love to depict a family with success, but in this particular show, I wanted to paint a picture of what my life was like, and trust me, I had already thought the way my family was depicted in the show was too rich. The fact that they lived in a huge two-story house made no sense to me, but I felt like having us live under the same roof was a compromise where the studio/network could have their standard "big, attractive" house and I could keep my truth that we all lived under one roof. What I had intended to depict in the show was the ascension from my family's low economic status to a better one as I continued to chase after my dream because that was honest to me. That was what my real life was about: leaving my house to chase after the dream, which, once I attained it, would allow me to take my family to a new level of life.

I kept getting notes from the network/studio that "families love aspirational shows," which I took to mean they meant they wanted the family to start off successful. I only guess that because they kept mentioning it and mentioning it and we'd fight about little things like when I asked, "Should the kitchen have such an expensive stove in it if my family couldn't afford it?" The answer: No, it shouldn't. I remember I had specifically asked that the kitchen in my family's house have an old refrigerator and stove. They didn't want it. I tried explaining to them that my goal was to have old appliances because I wanted to do an episode where my brother-in-law would surprise the family with new ones and we had to explore what that meant to us as a whole. That came from my life. I was in high school when we finally got a stove with an oven that worked, and for weeks, my mom and I kept making stuff to put in it. We would put food in the oven and turn on the light to see it, thinking technology was amazing because we couldn't understand how the food cooked and we could turn on the light to see it but the lightbulb was okay. And yes, we thought that was technology. A storyline like that was real to me. A big purchase like that meant that the family was either doing well or they had finally gotten their income tax refund. Whatever the reason, it was a positive sign.

I knew they didn't understand how that could be "big" enough to do a whole episode about it, but that was because the concept was foreign to them. They struggled to see the bigger picture of what something like that represented for a family like mine. Imagine the speech my mother would've given in the show as she chronicled her life from where she started to where she ended up at that moment. She went from milking cows to owning a stove with a working oven *and* a refrigerator that dispensed ice . . . without having to use an ice tray! My brother-in-law could have a moment where he talked about how he felt like a good provider, a hunter and gatherer like his ancestors, to which I would've joked, "Because the cavemen loved Frigidaire?" My sister would have taken selfies with the appliances to let her friends know she had gotten them and I would've had a hard moment where I had to thank my brother-in-law for surprising everyone. I thought exploring themes like that would make the show stand out because of its authenticity to my life, but I never got to tell that story. Therefore, my TV house never got a new fridge, yet it had a really nice, fancy stove because the idea of showing a struggling family on network TV can be a challenge.

My idea of what an aspirational show is was different from what others thought it was. I thought that an aspirational show should have characters that you root for. I didn't think you could root for a family that is introduced as being successful in the same manner that you would if you witnessed a family with nothing, ending up with so much more, because it gives hope to families that find themselves struggling. I thought it would make families feel like they had a chance to change their situation because they had a family that was doing the same and succeeding.

Look at Selena Quintanilla. She was the girl next door who happened to have brown skin. She was the girl who gave a nod to the culture her family roots were from while still appreciating the hometown she was living in in south Texas. Selena is someone that reached a legendary level rarely seen by a Mexican American (much less a woman) by being herself, which makes me wonder why there aren't more stories like that being told. How do we not have more stories that show different sides of the culture when we have proof of how successful they can be with a real-life example like Selena?

For years, we have talked about how important representation is and how important it is to see more of our stories in film and on television, but the truth is, it's bigger than that. We need to see each other in music, sports, news, and politics. We need to have a more accurate representation of what the numbers really show, not just for Latinos but for every ethnicity out there. We need to show what life is really like because only with accurate representation can we begin to have a lasting domino effect of change. A change that includes everyone, regardless of what they look like, being treated like they matter. In order to do that, every group should be represented. If we can get a change to happen, then maybe one day some of us can enter a business without having to worry about people thinking we don't deserve to be there.

I loved how the *Selena* movie chronicled her life. We see her marry her boyfriend, Chris. We see her recording her songs in English. We see her become a fashion designer. Then we see the iconic image of a moment that has become synonymous with Selena: the Houston rodeo with the infamous purple jumpsuit. The year was 1995, about a month before her death. She played for Tejano Day at the Houston Rodeo. Over *sixty thousand* people were in attendance.

She came out and gave a concert that would be considered a high-light of her career. It's hard to explain how monumental that moment was for people. So many remember where they were the day of that concert. They remember the bigness of it and that despite the enormity of that event, where tens of thousands of people were flashing their cameras to take pictures, Selena's smile shined brighter than all of them. With all the hope and joy I felt when I saw that, I would soon be crushed because that beam of light would dim and fade to black. I had approached the crushing ending of the movie. That moment (even after decades) makes me cry every time, as if it's the first time I've ever seen it. A white rose falls on the ground. Music starts playing. It's one of her songs in English, "Dreaming of You."

The song starts off slow as we hear Selena's voice. In the third line of the first verse, she talks about wishing on a star, hoping that person she's singing about is thinking of her too. That precise moment the line was sung, I remembered the beginning of the movie where a little Selena looks up at the sky and makes a wish. The image of this sweet little girl popped into my mind, as I knew what was coming and absolutely dreaded it. As the song progresses, there is a montage that shows quick cuts of real news footage about her encounter with the woman that killed her. When the news story came out in the montage, I was instantly taken back to the day she died and felt the sadness all over again. Then there is the part in the montage when doctors tell her family (the movie version, not the real one) that she died, and in those faces, you see such pain from losing their beam of light, as her song "Dreaming of You" keeps playing over the sequence of events. It's weird to think how fitting that song was for a moment like that because it was a love song and one would assume that a love song is usually about lovers, not about a future folk hero. But then you realize, a love song is about whatever kind of love you want it to be about.

   She didn't have to try so hard to make us love her. She was just herself. Thinking back to how my show was promoted, heavily in Spanish and with so many things that were against my wishes, it proves that networks and studios don't have to try so hard to "get" us. I always think about some of my favorite things and *why* I like them. I love shows like *Doctor Who* and *Star Trek*. I don't watch those shows because they have pictures of Vicente Fernández hanging on the walls in every episode or because there's a Juan Gabriel song playing in the background (though if that was something people wanted to explore on a real basis, I'm open to it). Those are just good shows to me. I don't watch some of my favorite movies like *Die Hard* or *Hot Fuzz* because they have mariachis in them. I watch what I watch because I think it's good. There shouldn't be such an extra effort happening in trying to appeal to a specific community because, a lot of times, it ends up feeling inauthentic. I should know. I struggled with a lot of those same issues in my show and I won a number of them because I realized I had nothing to lose. That was one of the most powerful lessons I learned growing up as poor as I did. My poverty made me fearless to make choices without worrying about the outcome, because what was the worst that could happen? I go back to being poor? I grew up in that lifestyle; I'm used to it. I've always liked fighting for things and don't mind if I lose in the end because I know I am fighting for what I think is right. Were there people within the show that were critical about me behind my back? Yes, there were, and I know who they are. I figured as much; I didn't care. I am proud of what I tried to make my show be and was happy with the stories we got to tell. Did it have a lot of stereotypical things in it? Some people might say yes, and maybe for them it *did* seem like too much, but it was pretty accurate to my life.

Authenticity is what I have to offer and I learned that from Selena. She wasn't trying to inspire people, but she did it by just living her life. That inspired me. I learned to speak English from watching TV shows and then decided I wanted to make TV shows. My whole life has been a long shot; I'm used to this journey.

Even if you don't understand her cultural importance to someone like me, you can understand her impact from a business point of view. Because, let's face it, the universal color everyone recognizes is green. It's amazing to think that even after having died over twenty years ago, her legacy is just as strong as it was when she was alive. Anytime a product bearing her name is released, it sells out. The Selena Quintanilla collaboration with MAC Makeup was such a successful launch that it sold out instantly online and had people waiting in line for hours to try and score any of the items packaged in the iconic Selena purple (also a shout-out to my Latina groundbreaking friend Patty Rodriguez, who was responsible for starting the whole thing and making it a reality). A Texas chain grocery store, H-E-B, released a line of reusable grocery bags with her face, and people bought them like they were made out of gold. But why? How is she still such a commodity? It's a pretty simple answer.

Personally, I know I like to keep her memory alive because I don't want her legacy to be erased from history. It is absolutely necessary that people remember that a strong, Mexican American woman once graced us with a legacy that has surpassed her death by decades. To people like my mother, Selena made her feel good about where we were headed as a community because she had a similar hope to my own. She hoped that people would see how great our culture was by having someone like Selena not only be allowed to shine, but to thrive.

I've had so many conversations with people about how Selena was our beacon of hope. She was one of the only beacons I had and that's okay because some people never get to find their beacons. I think the manner in which she died is what made it so devastating. She didn't have an illness that took her life slowly, she didn't get to live a long life that spanned decades. My beacon died when she was shot by her fan club president when the family discovered money missing. It's a tragic way to end the hope that so many had. Even years after her death, her light keeps guiding me and reminding me that everything I do must be done from an honest place of who I am.

I'll admit something that I haven't told anyone before. Every time I hear "Dreaming of You" on the radio or from a shuffle playlist on my phone, I always stop what I'm doing and just listen to it and remember her. If it's nighttime when I hear it, I look up at the sky, pick a star, and make a wish, like I did when I was a kid, the same way little Selena did in the movie. In those fleeting moments, I believe anything is possible for me. I think about where my life started and where I currently am and wonder how on earth I got here. I think about what Selena represents to me, and that is a combination of hope, ambition, and faith.

Selena Quintanilla is an important part of our history. She is an example of what we're capable of with a mix of what could've been. But besides her million-dollar smile and her voice, Selena was also just a little girl from south Texas who chased after her dreams and caught them. She made me believe I could as well because I am also just a little girl from south Texas chasing after her dreams.

That is what true representation is all about.

One of my last high school plays. During my high school career, I won about two hundred trophies in drama competitions.

"LOVED BY THE SUN"
TANGERINE DREAM

I hate high school reunions. I don't understand the point of them. Every ten years, you get an invite that basically says, "COME AND SEE THE BULLY THAT MADE YOUR LIFE A LIVING HELL! HE CAN DRINK LEGALLY NOW!" One of the reasons why I don't understand them is probably because I absolutely hated high school. Why would you want to go back and reminisce about the bad old days? Can you imagine making anyone go back and rehash terrible things they want to put behind them? "Hey, Great-Grandma, remember when you were on the *Titanic* but your friend died? Let's go back and relive that!" I'd rather have reunions about the times I drank too much in my twenties. I'd love to have a "Blackout Reunion" where people show up and tell me what I did on nights I can't remember. Come to think of it, isn't that what Facebook has become? A high school reunion that never ends? Sometimes I'll get friend requests from people that were terrible to me back then and the first thing I think is, *Do you have amnesia?*

"Loved by the Sun" is the best theme song I could've chosen for my time in high school because it was an important song for my drama class. It's by Tangerine Dream, an electronic band from

Germany, and it was featured in an eighties movie named *Legend* that starred Tom Cruise because he's been around that long (think *Mission: Impossible* but with unicorns). My high school had made it a tradition to play this as the last song before each school play began, as the audience filed in, because we obviously wanted to show everyone how cool we were. The moment we heard "Loved by the Sun," we would get more excited because we knew the play was about to start.

It really is a lovely song. It has an ethereal sound to it, the kind of music that creates a heavenly vibe that would make any sentence sound majestic. You could have a line like "I hate ketchup on my hot dog," but add the style of music for which Tangerine Dream was known and it would turn that line into a battle cry you could sing before slaying a dragon. It made sense having it in a dark fantasy movie like *Legend*. I feel like fantastical movies used to be more prominent in the eighties. Movies like *The NeverEnding Story*, *Willow*, and *Labyrinth* told stories with dragons, mystical creatures, and monsters. As a Latina, I think it's interesting to wonder how these stories about magical worlds had more of a chance to be made than a story about Latinos just living their lives, but I guess demons battling for control of a world seemed more realistic than a woman of color trying to become an engineer as she put herself through college.

Every time I listened to that song, as we ran to get into our places before the curtain went up, I felt so hopeful. The last words of the song, "To believe in the good in man . . . ," repeated several times as it slowly faded away, and I remember believing that line was true. It was something I really believed in: the good in man. I believed (and still do) that we are capable of greatness and of good. I believed that if you tried to be a good person, people couldn't find a reason to dislike you.

I was wrong.

Part of the tradition tied to the song was that the cast of the show would gather around in a circle and hug one another and give one another words of encouragement behind the curtain. But those words of encouragement rang hollow to me. The song I had once looked forward to hearing because of the hope it had given me slowly evolved into a song that scarred me for life. The truth was that every time I heard it, I didn't hear hope. I heard my pain. Every line that offered love and understanding changed into a constant reminder of the hell I was experiencing, because during my time there, whenever we got to the part where the cast would gather, there were three guys in that circle who didn't want me there. They were guys who loved to make me feel terrible about myself. They were my bullies, led by their friend, a guy who was a year older than me. This guy would spend years terrorizing me for fun. When I heard that line "To believe in the good in man . . . ," I would hope there was a chance he would listen to those words and stop being cruel, but he never did. He loved my misery too much.

I was a nerd in high school. I was on the academic decathlon team. I was a member of the Masterminds team, a local quiz game show where high schools competed against one another. I was also the photo editor of the high school yearbook. Despite all these things, I was better known in high school as *the* drama nerd. I was president of the Drama Club and won more trophies at competitions than anyone else. I used to average a minimum of about five trophies per tournament, which led to my winning around two hundred trophies while I was in high school. Impressive, huh? I would dedicate my entire summer to preparing for the next school year to try and dominate those theater competitions. You might think I was a well-adjusted teenager who must've been popular and really happy in school, right? Wrong. I was miserable.

There was a reason I worked so hard to win so many trophies: revenge. I worked so hard on winning trophies because of my high school bully. He didn't bully me simply because I was a theater geek. In fact, he was a theater geek too. I actually never fully knew why my high school bully made my life a living hell. I think that's the worst part of getting bullied: you always wonder what you did that made someone decide to make it their job to make you feel terrible.

How can a nerd bully a nerd? The idea makes no sense. I was so grateful for having found theater because I felt like, in so many other parts of my life, I didn't fit in—but in theater, being different was not only accepted, it was celebrated. When I started performing, I thought it would be my salvation, but in reality, it would become yet another world where I didn't fit in because of that bully.

I fell in love with theater after seeing the Tony Awards in 1991. I was twelve years old and had turned the channel one random Sunday night to CBS to watch an episode of *Murder, She Wrote*. The show was not on that week. Instead of seeing Jessica Fletcher fly to yet another location where she'd have to catch a murderer because the cops were so inept, they were airing an award show for Broadway. I had no clue what Broadway was, but back then, I would watch CBS on Sunday nights no matter what, so I watched it. I saw Jonathan Pryce perform a song called "The American Dream" from a musical called *Miss Saigon*. He was playing an Asian character, but I knew he wasn't Asian. He came out and started singing and dancing onstage. The chorus of the show came out and danced in the background. The stage had bright colors that popped as he sang about what his version of the American Dream was. I was instantly hooked. Whatever this was, sign me up! What would my version of the American Dream be? I remember watching the entire Tony Awards with so much awe, not capable of understanding that what these people were doing were real jobs you could get paid to do. How can a job be fun? How does one break into it? I was always taught that jobs were something you hated but dealt with because food and rent cost money. I was completely unaware that most of these performers had studied and worked on perfecting their art by taking acting, dancing, and singing classes. I was completely unaware that drama class was even a thing in school until I was in eighth grade. I had been in choir up until then, but that class had been removed from our curriculum due to lack of funding—because, you know, the arts aren't important (they are). I decided to sign up for a drama class because I had been in plays in elementary school. The first play I was in was *Hansel and Gretel* in the first grade. I played the evil stepmother. In third grade I played Snow White's evil stepmother, the Queen. In fourth grade I played Clara in *The Nutcracker* and in fifth grade I was the CPU in a play that described how a computer worked. The CPU is short for the central processing unit. The way my teacher had explained it to me, I was the "heart" of the computer. Without the CPU, there would be no play, so basically if this play was the *Titanic*, I would be the boat. As you can tell, I was a child with a lot of range.

The idea of drama class intrigued me. I figured we would put on plays a couple of times a year, but there was also a part of me that thought I was signing up to be in the cast of *Fame*. (For some reason, I thought I might have to buy leg warmers for the class.) The first day, I showed up and we did the obligatory introductions of ourselves. I didn't really know anyone else in the room, yet our junior high drama teacher made us do trust exercises with one another. I had no idea what the hell was going on. What was a trust exercise, and would it burn calories? We had to do a trust fall—you know the one I'm talking about. The kind where you fall backward and "trust" the people behind you will catch you. If you knew my neighborhood, you knew that wouldn't go well. The sense of humor we grew up with in my hood meant we would tell people we'd catch them and then let them fall and laugh as the person writhed in pain.

In another exercise, our teacher asked us to pick an appliance we would pretend to be. What the hell had I gotten myself into? He said, "GO!" and all the students started to shake their bodies like they were vibrating, jumping around like they had been bitten by fire ants. This reminds me of the part in the song "Nothing" from *A Chorus Line* in which the Morales character is incredulous at the acting exercises that everyone is doing because she doesn't understand it. I was similarly confused. I'm surprised I didn't die from rolling my eyes too much. I just stood there, not moving, while my classmates were all simultaneously acting like they had been possessed. The drama teacher walked over to me because he wanted to know why I wasn't doing the exercise. I told him I was. He asked me what appliance I was and I said, "I'm a vacuum and I'm broken." He let it go.

The next day I was in history class when I suddenly got called into the principal's office. When I walked in, I was told that my schedule had been changed without my consent. I had no idea what was happening. I liked my schedule. My best friend and I had the same lunch. This new schedule meant I was going to have a different lunch period from that of my best friend, and that couldn't happen. I was told the drama teacher had moved me to the competitive theater class. Competitive theater class? What the hell was that about? The principal told me there was nothing I could do about it.

I confronted the drama teacher in his classroom and demanded answers. He told me he thought I needed to be in the advanced theater class. I remember asking him if he was punishing me for the vacuum remark I had said the day before. He explained to me that he liked my answer and thought theater was something that could be really good for me. I fought it and got upset, but in the end, he told me what the principal had told me: I had no choice. I was stuck in this new, stupid class and I had to report there in a couple of hours. He explained that part of the curriculum of this class was to compete in theater tournaments and that we would be graded on how hard we worked on our competition pieces. The teacher explained the tournaments were mandatory.

This was unacceptable. I couldn't compete in tournaments. My mom didn't let me do anything after school hours. If school ended at 3:00 p.m., I was expected home by no later than 3:15 p.m. My mother oversaw every move I made practically down to the minute. When I explained this to my teacher, however, I think he thought I was lying. He told me I had to figure it out.

I went home and tried to explain to my mother what had happened. She instantly thought I was making up the whole thing to hang out with my friends after school. I kept telling her it was the truth. I then explained to my oldest brother what had happened. Since he had started teaching and understood how things worked, he explained to my mother that what I was saying was true. After I begged my mom for weeks, she finally allowed me to go to *one* tournament, but only because she saw that, in my progress report, I wasn't doing well in theater. I reminded her that the reason for this was that competing in tournaments was part of my grade.

I remember telling my drama teacher about the first time my

mother gave me permission to go to a tournament. He gave me a look like "Really?" There was actually a tournament coming up that very week that I could attend. One of the students had signed up but couldn't go anymore and he offered me the spot in an event called "prose." Prose was basically narrating a story in about seven minutes with some inflection to text but still having a natural flow. In junior high theater, though, prose meant to overact words as if they were all written in capital letters and underlined.

My teacher told me all I had to do was go up and read the story as if I were living it myself. This sounded easy enough. Then he asked me if I wanted to do another event involving a thing called improvisation. He told me all I had to do was pull a piece of paper about a topic and talk about it for about five minutes. I remember thinking, *This event should be called life. Isn't that what we all do? Get a topic and just talk off the top of your head?* I agreed to do that one, too, because I thought it would help my grade.

The day of the tournament came and I had to get my brother to drop me off super early on a Saturday morning to get on a school bus taking us there. I didn't know what I was doing or what to expect. I did as I was told. My teacher told me where to go and basically told me that all I needed to do was read the story and go to the other event and talk. I could handle that. After I was done, I told my teacher that I had done my part of the deal for the grade. I thought I was done for the day.

I wasn't. Soon after, my teacher told me I had advanced to the semifinals in both events and that I had to do it all over again. Then I advanced to the finals in both events and ended up getting first place in both. My teacher was obviously really happy and the only thing that crossed my mind was *Does this mean I get an A?*

After I won those first two trophies, my teacher obviously wanted me to keep competing, and to tell you the truth, I did too. It was the first time I felt part of something. Winning made me feel good, and I *never* felt good about myself. I have always suffered from extremely low self-esteem. I always say that I have low self-esteem because it has half the calories of regular self-esteem. So finding something that made me feel like I was not only able to do it but do it well was new to me. My mom started slowly letting me go to more tournaments— not all of them, but a couple more.

I ended up falling in love with theater. The more I immersed myself in that world, the harder I fell for it. The more tournaments I competed in and won, the more I began to wonder if it could be that I was actually good at something. Could that even happen to someone like me?

By the end of eighth grade, theater had started giving me a confidence that was helping me with the fear I had of going off to high school the next year.

Freshman year can be tricky to navigate. Most of the classes you have are with students in your own grade, but sometimes you're clumped together with people in the same class that are older than you, sometimes way older than you, and you are supposedly seen as equals. That was drama class. All the students who competed in contests and were in all the school plays had the same class. I hated the idea of being grouped with everyone because I was always very awkward in social situations. I know that sounds weird, considering that I'm a stand-up comic, but being in rooms with strangers has always made me very nervous. I fake that I'm okay, but really, if I don't have a friend in the room, I always want to blend in and leave as soon as possible. Those feelings came from my mom having taught me never to stand out—which made my interest in theater even more bizarre to her. (Little did I know that, decades later, I would find out I suffer from severe social anxiety.)

Things started out okay for me in theater. Then one day, I noticed this guy making comments about me . . . in front of me . . . to other people.

I guess I should mention (because it's an important part of this story) that I have struggled with my looks my entire life. When I was a little kid in elementary school, I was ridiculed for having a "dark complexion." Kids used to make fun of my skin and call me names. Mind you, many of these kids had brown skin themselves; I was just a tad darker than them. I used to spend recess running around with the guys playing freeze tag and I would get a tan from the sun, but I was also just naturally darker than the kids that would ridicule me. I always thought it strange that within my own Latino community back home, I could be ridiculed for my skin color, considering most of us had brown skin; I just didn't seem to have the "right hue" of brown. In the summer months, my mom wouldn't let me go outside, so I would stay indoors and I would lose some of my tan; I noticed as I got older that I would get complimented by students when I'd come back from summer break because I was "lighter." As a kid, you don't want to be made fun of, because it hurts, so when I noticed kids weren't making fun of me because I wasn't as dark, I started avoiding going outside because I didn't want to hear kids telling me how ugly I was. (God, I hate writing those words.) It took me years to understand how wrong that thinking was; that my skin was part of my beauty and, more important, it was part of my history.

Another thing that was "wrong" with me (from what other kids told me) was that I had an "ugly" crooked front tooth. It had grown in crooked, but I had also been punched by a girl in sixth grade who had made it even more crooked. My family struggled to get by; there was no chance of going to the dentist. (I only got it fixed in my late thirties because I couldn't afford to do it until then.) When I was a freshman, I usually didn't think about my crooked tooth on a daily basis. But that day my bully mentioned it in the most brutal way.

I will never forget that moment. My bully and his friends were sitting on some risers we had set up in front of the stage in our theater classroom. I was sitting on the other side from them, reading a script. He was there, with three of his friends, including one that was in my grade. I heard my bully talking, but I didn't pay attention to him. Then he slowly started getting louder and I started hearing him talk about me. It sounded really harmless at first, and for a second I thought he couldn't have been talking about me because I never really interacted with him. Then I heard him talk about my crooked tooth. I stopped what I was doing and looked up at him. He continued to have this conversation with his friends, acting like I wasn't supposed to hear but speaking very pointedly at me. He talked about how weird I looked when I smiled. He started opening his mouth really wide and letting his lip curl up so he showed his gums. His friends started joining in and agreed that I had an ugly smile. I said nothing. I didn't even understand what was happening. I hadn't done anything, but he kept talking about how ugly I looked when I smiled. I started getting emotional and tears were building up. And he *loved* this.

I went and told the teacher what he was doing, but since this guy was one year older than me and I was a freshman, the teacher was more familiar with him and told me that was just what this guy did. He was being "funny," so the teacher did nothing about it. I figured he was right because he knew this guy better than I did. Maybe I was overthinking it.

I wasn't.

As time passed, this guy got worse. One of the drama teachers showed us the movie *The Breakfast Club*. I can't remember why, but there was a valid reason. We all watched it as a class and, afterward, the teacher made us go around in a circle and say what character we thought we were. Everyone said their answer with no pushback or criticism, except for me. I said that I considered myself more of the Ally Sheedy character, the "weird" one. I chose her because the Molly Ringwald character was far too girly for me. The moment I said this, though, that guy started making fun of me. He made remarks about how I was nothing like her and how I was making myself seem cooler than I was. Again, his friends chimed in. I was a loser, I wasn't anything like her. It went on and on. The teacher eventually told him to stop it.

I really struggled with theater my freshman year. I loved it so much because it had given me hope that maybe, just maybe, I had found a world in which I was accepted, but at that point, I really didn't feel like I was being accepted by the people *in* that world. The guy became bolder with me and just flat-out cruel. I'd mention it to the two drama teachers (male and female) to no avail. He wasn't physical with me, they said. At one point in my freshman year, the male teacher suggested I maybe try another club like JROTC. I couldn't believe what I was hearing. I refused to quit because even if drama class sucked, theater was the only thing that truly made me happy.

I had started doing the humorous event, but it was a hard event, especially because not a lot of women advanced in it; the final round was usually all guys. At this specific tournament, I had actually made it to the finals and a lot of people (including me) were *really* shocked that I had because I was young and the only girl. I was really excited about it until I learned that the terrible guy from my drama class had made it too. When he and his friends realized this, they started saying crappy things to me. It got to the point where our female drama teacher stepped in and asked him why he was being such a jerk. He had no answer. And she had had enough. She stood up for me, and at that precise moment I realized that I hadn't been crazy. I hadn't been imagining things. This guy was being terrible to me, and not only had she noticed it but she felt compelled to bring it up to him. It was weird because I felt happy that I had been right all along—but also felt terrible that I had been right all along. I ended up getting last place in that round. I want to say he won third, I'm not sure. All I remember is that on the bus ride back to the school, he made snide remarks about me getting last place because I obviously had to be reminded that I was a loser. I looked at him the entire way and said nothing. Once I got home, I started bawling.

I was really happy once school let out for the summer because I couldn't mentally handle this guy anymore. I had to decide if I was going to let him force me out of doing the thing I loved doing or if I would hang in there and know that my life would be hell for the next three years. What was more important, my mental health or my love of theater? Theater won. That summer, I wondered what the best way for me to protect myself from him would be, but I realized that there was nothing I could do. This guy was only going to get worse because he was getting to know more about me, which meant he had more to say about me. I started wondering if I could possibly do the same thing to him and in some way bully him back, but how? Then it hit me. In the last tournament we had gone to my freshman year, I had made it into the finals of this humorous round, an event that a lot of people held dear . . . especially the guy who was becoming my night-mare. A student would perform a condensed version of a comedic play. It was one of the more popular events, the kind where everyone would go see the final round because the performances were usually very funny. I knew that guy thought he was funny. I knew he wanted to win. I knew he wanted to be known as the star of our team. I knew what I had to do: I decided to work hard and beat him at everything he tried to do. If he was going to hate me, make fun of me, and make me cry, then I would give him a reason to do it. I didn't want to make him think he was a loser, I wanted him to know that I had made him *become* a loser to me.

That summer leading into my sophomore year, I decided to work on my stuff for next year's theater competitions. I had my brother Ruben drop me off at the McAllen Public Library daily. I would stay until closing time so that I could spend the day reading every script I could get my hands on. I decided to sign up for every event that jerk wanted to compete in and every other event I had time to do. I wanted to win every damn tournament. I wanted to hold those trophies in my hands and look at him while I received them. When school started back up again, I found myself in drama class with that guy and his friends making their snide comments about me. He'd plan a get-together for people and would intentionally invite everyone that was sitting around me, except me. One time, someone asked him if he was going to invite me since I was sitting next to them and he bluntly said, "No. Why the fuck would I invite that?"

Then it was time for our first tournament of the year. I was curious to see if I had prepared for it as much as I thought I had. To prepare for tournaments, we were expected to set up practice sessions with the drama teachers. I didn't want to do that because I didn't want anyone to know what pieces I was doing—at that point, we had gotten a new female drama teacher, and to tell you the truth, it had become difficult for me to trust people because even people that I thought were my friends would hang out with my bully. There was no loyalty.

The day of our first tournament came and we went off to compete. I had signed up for seven events, which was considered an insane number, but I assured the teachers I was ready for all of them. That day, I went and competed in the seven events and found myself advancing to the finals in *all* of them, including humorous. I found myself going up against my bully in that category. No one at my school knew what I was doing because, again, I had intentionally withheld everything from them. I remember getting to that humorous finals round late because I was running around doing the finals in the other categories. When I got there, I was the last to perform. I went up and did it. I had picked a play where I had to perform eight different characters, which was super fun. Since I had learned English from TV shows by mimicking the way actors spoke, I had accidentally learned how to do different voices, so each character I did had their own accent, their own *everything*, which not everyone could do. I did really well in that round, but since I had arrived late, I hadn't seen my bully perform. I just hoped for the best.

At the awards assembly for the tournament, we all sat down by schools and they started announcing the winners of the events. I had won first place in a couple of them right out of the gate. I kept winning more; they kept announcing my name over and over again. Then came the humorous category. Now, what this specific tournament was doing was naming third place and up, so anyone who got fourth through sixth place wouldn't get mentioned. They used to do this to save time. I was hoping to place but wasn't expecting it because, again, I hadn't seen anyone else's performance and not too many women ended up in the finals. As they started naming the winners, I stared at my bully's face to see if he would win. Third and second place were called; it was neither one of us. People thought he was going to win because who else was left, right? When they named the first-place winner, the name they called was mine. I HAD WON THE EVENT! My eyes opened up wide and I smiled my (according to him) ugly smile with my crooked tooth. I remember staring at him for a second too long as I made my way up to collect my *seventh* trophy. I had won a trophy in every single event I had competed in. Everyone on my team was shocked. What I thought was even better than winning the trophies was that I noticed my bully was a lot quieter on the bus ride home. That started a pattern for me. I started winning an average of five trophies at every competition I went to. I was becoming the stand-out of the team and I loved every minute of it. The more I won, the more terrible he got. It sucked. I hated this, but there was a comfort in knowing that, again, if he was going to hate me, I was going to give him a reason to do so.

I started getting cast in the school plays, which was good and bad at the same time. It was good in that I was getting roles, but it was bad in that when I was doing the plays, I was reminded I wasn't anything. He still dominated our drama group. He was the more popular one. In fact, I think that now I was actually more of a target because I was the one who always won at tournaments. During rehearsals for the play, he would just say terrible things about me to everyone around me and to my face. They were *jokes*, though, so nothing could be done because it was all in "jest." It got even worse when my mom got me a used car. It was an old Camaro she bought me because she wanted me to be able to drive her everywhere. When my bully and his friends discovered I had a car, it was game over. After rehearsals, they would gather around it, bend down to grab it from the bottom, and just start shaking it for fun. I would tell them to stop, which only made them do it more.

One of my favorite (and I mean that sarcastically) memories of him was a time when we were doing a play and I couldn't find my car keys after we were done. I spent so much time looking for them to no avail. I eventually ended up calling my brother to come and pick me up. We had no spare keys, so we had no choice but to leave the car in the parking lot overnight and have me keep looking for them the next day. I couldn't understand what had happened to my keys. I always kept them in the same spot. I just hoped that I could find them. When I showed up the next day, I discovered my car had been vandalized. The tires had been slashed, the windows had been smashed. It was ruined. My family was upset because it was going to cost money we didn't have to fix it and, miraculously, I found my car keys in the drama classroom, where I had looked for them the previous night with no luck. They had just popped up out of nowhere.

I never had any proof that any of those guys had anything to do with the damage done to my car, and honestly, there was a part of me that hoped they weren't responsible because that would've meant they were just evil. Whether or not they were involved, what happened that night pissed me off. We were doing our play the next night and everyone was running around, getting ready. I was really miserable because I was preoccupied thinking about what had happened to my car and was moving slower than usual. Right when the show was about to start, the song "Loved by the Sun" began to play. We all gathered around in a circle, and as part of the tradition, people started trying to give their pep talks. That's when the guys, including my bully, started giving *their* version of pep talks, all of which had to do with my car. They mocked me, they made fun of what had happened, and I just had to stand there and take it.

When my bully's senior year approached, it felt like it was my senior year too. I couldn't wait for him to be out of my life. I never wanted to see him again. At this point, I was winning all the time. I had become the anchor of my drama class. I had the lead in the shows, I won a bunch of trophies, and the guy I despised would soon be gone. The last week of school that year, he showed up in class carrying some invites to his graduation party. He handed them out to everyone (except me, obviously). His big last middle finger to me was making sure everyone, including my best friends, were invited. He gave them an invite right in front of me, and if I'm not mistaken, I think they might've ended up going to it too. At that point, I didn't care. I was just grateful that I would never have to see him again. Ding, dong, the witch was dead (to me, or so I thought).

Senior year high school ID. One of the few pictures from school that I have left.

But I would have to see him again. We ended up going to the same college. Isn't that hilarious? And by "hilarious," I mean I wanted to grab a fork and stick it in my eyes so I wouldn't have to see him again. Once more, he had the upper hand because he was a year older than me and people knew him and I was new. Now, I had hope that maybe a year in college might've made him mature, but I was wrong. The terrorizing started pretty quickly.

It didn't matter. The summer after my freshman year in college, my mother told me I had to drop out of school because my sister needed help with her kids. I didn't want to drop out. I had always planned on graduating college, but as I constantly say, "Sometimes life gets in the way," and this was one of those times. I dropped out and moved back to Texas. While my heart was broken about leaving when I didn't want to, I was happy that I wouldn't have to deal with my bully again. It felt like a heaviness had been lifted from me. I remember my brother Eloy went to pick me up on campus to drive me back home. As we pulled away, Green Day's "Good Riddance (Time of Your Life)" started playing and it felt like a scene from a movie. I was leaving this place that in theory I didn't want to leave, but I was so happy to never have to see my bully's face again.

I hated that I would never get closure with him. I hated that I was leaving without getting some kind of payback. I wanted karma to show me that it existed. I wanted that stupid Tangerine Dream song to ring true . . . I wanted to believe in the good in man. I wanted the good guy (me) to win! But that doesn't happen in an everyday, normal life, does it? A normal person that has been subjected to bullying just has to live with it and move on. A regular person rarely gets their moment of Armageddon. Thank God I wasn't a regular person.

At twenty-six, I found myself living in Los Angeles, touring the country, serving as an opening act for a well-known comedian at the time.

In October 2005 I had to fly to New York City on a red-eye flight because the comedian I was opening for was doing a weekend at Carolines, a comedy club in Times Square. I didn't have a chance to sleep when I landed because I had to meet up with him and his crew to do press. His crew consisted of his assistant, his wife, a photographer, the other opener, and his tour manager. My boyfriend at the time was still living in Dallas but had planned to fly up to New York to meet up with me and would catch up with us later.

We were all exhausted and started our day at Sirius XM radio. None of us had gotten any sleep and we were just trying to trudge through it all. While we were waiting, the comic's assistant tried to liven things up. She took out her phone and said she was going to read us the "Chi of the Day." It was a daily motivational quote that she was sent from something she had signed up for. She read the chi and it talked about being thankful for both your friends *and* enemies because they both make you who you are. When she read that, I was the first one to say that I believed in that and started telling them about my bully. Because we were waiting for a bit, I told them all kinds of stories and how my wanting to beat him in high school made me work harder than him. In the end, I was grateful that things were going so well for me and I just hoped that if I ever saw him again, I would have the upper hand.

Hours later, my boyfriend met up with me. I was so exhausted. I just wanted to do the radio show and get to bed, but I had to go to Carolines for the first show of the week. It was sold out, and although exhausted, I was really looking forward to doing it because it was my first time doing stand-up in New York. After the show, the group was hungry. We were looking for a place to eat that was close to the club because no one wanted to waste time. The manager told us that the restaurant next door, Ruby Foo's, was open late, so out of convenience we all walked over there.

We got there and sat at this big, round table; none of us had any energy left. We looked like a table full of zombies that just wanted to eat some quick brains and leave. I kept yawning. Everyone had reached peak exhaustion. I tried to liven things up and asked the assistant to give us the "Chi of the Day." She laughed when I asked and reminded me that it would be the same quote she had read that morning. We laughed at how I had forgotten we were still living the same day, but she took it out and read it again to kill time as we waited for the server to come and get our drink orders. She repeated the thing about being grateful for both friends and enemies, and I leaned over to tell my boyfriend that I had mentioned my bully to them. He was familiar with stories about this guy by now. Then our server showed up; he was standing behind me. He welcomed us and asked for drink orders. The moment I heard his voice, I froze. *Wait. I recognize that voice.* It couldn't be. Could it? My boyfriend saw my face change; the entire table did. Everyone knew something was wrong with me, but they didn't know what. I slowly turned around, hoping I was wrong in guessing, but as I slowly moved to look behind me, I saw that I was right.

The guy who had made my life a living hell, the one who had made me hate myself, was standing behind me. My high school bully was our server!

He looked at me, completely surprised, and said, "Cristela?" I awkwardly said hello and asked for a beer. Everyone else gave their drink order and the moment he walked away, I had a bunch of questions that I couldn't answer. I was absolutely paralyzed. The comedian I was opening for asked me what was wrong and I finally mustered up the words "That guy? The one I told you who made my life a living hell? The one I had never told you about until this morning? That's him. Our server!" No one could believe it. Why would they? What were the chances of that even happening? The comedian asked me if I was joking. I said no. I told the table that if they had doubts, they could ask him questions about how we knew each other. When he got back with the drinks, that's exactly what they did.

As my bully set our drinks down, the comedian asked him, and the bully told him we had gone to high school together. Then other people at the table wanted to ask questions, so they found out we had both done theater together, we had gone to the same college for a bit; everything I had said was being verified. My boyfriend kept asking me how I was doing throughout the whole meal and I honestly didn't know what to say. I felt as if I had instantly been taken back in time and I was the teenage girl he had terrorized. That feeling quickly subsided when the comedian asked my bully what he was up to. He told the table that he was living in New York with one of his high school best friends (one of the jerks that used to hate me too) and they were trying to break into acting. I wanted to tell him that I was doing really well, but I didn't know how to do so without coming off like I was desperate for him to know that. That's when the comedian stepped in and said, "Oh, that's cool. Cristela told us you guys went to school together. You know, she's doing great . . ." He started talking about everything I'd done, and I got so happy inside because I loved that my bully was hearing all this but that I wasn't the one who had to tell him. It became a game for them. Every time my bully would come to our table, someone had to mention something great I had done and kept making remarks about how "crazy" it was that he was my server. I loved it.

Since the table now knew he was indeed my old bully, they found themselves trying to make him work harder too. They would ask for refills, ask him to bring extra things we didn't need. We did anything to make him run around and serve us more. In the middle of the meal, the bully mentioned that he had tried to get tickets to see the comedian I was opening up for but the tickets were sold out. Now, I KNOW this guy was not trying to fish for tickets, right? YES, HE WAS. The moment he said that, I blurted out, "All the shows are sold out. Sorry." The comedian corroborated this.

At the end of the meal, the comedian paid for the dinner and I didn't know what to do. Did I leave without saying goodbye? I despised him, so it made sense, but was this dinner enough of a payback for me to forgive him and move on? Our group walked out of the restaurant and the comedian asked me what I was thinking. He knew I had something on my mind because I tend not to hide emotions very well. I told him I wasn't sure what I should do. He stopped me and told me I had two choices. I could either be the bigger person and go back in there and give him tickets to the show so he would have to go and watch him perform, which also meant having to see *me* perform, or I could walk away knowing I would probably never see him again and leave with the satisfaction that I ultimately had the upper hand because I was doing so much better than him. Then he asked me what I wanted to do. I looked inside the restaurant and thought for a minute. I looked at my bully and said I never wanted to see that guy ever again. I wanted his last interaction with me to be that he served me. I wanted him to always know that every time he brought me a new beer, I smiled my "ugly smile" with my crooked tooth and knew that I had beaten him. I walked away and didn't look back.

I had never expected to see that guy again, but I'm glad I did. It gave me a chance to give that part of my life an ending. Not many people get to do that. The last I heard about him, he was doing theater in Alaska. I wish him the best, and by that I mean I don't at all.

The movie *Legend*, in which "Loved by the Sun" was featured, told the story of a person who ultimately has to battle against Darkness, personified by a creature that in the end is defeated by good. Before he disappears, Darkness reminds people that evil lives inside everyone and we're all capable of it, so in theory, Darkness can never truly die. That's kind of fitting for me in this episode of my life. While I defeated my own Darkness, I understand that he still lingers within me. He forced himself into my mind, and whether I like it or not, he is part of my history. The thing is, I now have the power to always defeat him.

That night, I got back to the hotel, put my earbuds in, and listened to the Tangerine Dream song, and for the first time, it felt different. For the first time in decades, I felt the same hope I'd felt when I first heard the song. It was the first time, as an adult, that I could listen to that song without crying. When I got to the part of the song that speaks about believing in "the good in man," I couldn't help but laugh because, in the end, my life had resembled the movie *Legend*, because after all that time and hurt, Darkness had finally lost.

"SHAPE OF MY HEART"
BACKSTREET BOYS

Courtesy of Ruben Alonzo

My mother and me at the little house we lived in after the diner. I never imagined that, years later, this picture would be used for a *New York Times* profile on me.

This is the chapter where my mother dies.

I didn't write that to sound melodramatic but rather to serve as a warning. I have spoken about my mother and her death a lot in the past and I cannot begin to tell you how many times I have had people break down and cry when they meet me because they say my mother reminds them of their mother. I have had conversations with people about the death of a parent and how you never really recover, especially when you were their primary caregiver. I was that for my mother and I wanted to be sympathetic and make sure that people reading this book are mentally okay to get into this chapter and also to let you know that it's okay if you can't. I struggle with bouts of severe depression, anxiety, and social anxiety and I know how hard something like this can be for people. First and foremost, I want to make sure that you (the reader) are prepared. I will be honest: This is the chapter I was scared of writing the most and that took me the longest to pen, and I most certainly cried a lot while doing so. With that caveat, here it goes.

I grew up loving boy bands: Menudo, New Kids on the Block, New Edition, Backstreet Boys, Boyz II Men, 'N Sync, etc. Basically, if there was any chance of a music video featuring four or five men singing their undisputed love to a woman in the rain, it's safe to say I was a fan. Which, by the way, always confused me . . . When the boy bands confess their love to someone, are they doing it to the same person?

"Shape of My Heart" is a love song by the Backstreet Boys that came out in 2000 as part of their *Black & Blue* album and I loved it. It was a love song, though if you asked me what it was really about, I couldn't tell you. The music video showed them all taking an acting class and that left me very confused. I bought *Black & Blue* at our local Walmart in McAllen, Texas, in the middle of the night and, no, I wasn't a hard-core fan that camped out and waited for the CD to come out. I was doing one of my middle-of-the-night Walmart visits with my mother because she couldn't sleep . . . again. I think the reason I became so connected to the CD is because when I bought it, it was one of the only earthly possessions I had.

I am the youngest child out of four and was always at my

mother's side; it was just understood that I would be. One thing I didn't realize is that having the responsibility of being by my mother's side meant having to be part of her good and bad times. When I was around eight years old, I was lying on the twin bed my mom and I shared till I was eighteen. We would sometimes lie on it and just talk and laugh like we were best friends—because we were. She told me she wanted me to be the one who would take care of her when she got older. She said she knew I would do it and I told her I would, not knowing what I was agreeing to. Frankly, her comment had come out of left field and really took me by surprise because it was at that moment I realized that my mother wasn't immortal. As a child, you think your parents will always be around. She also told me about wanting to own a house; that was her American Dream. She didn't want anything fancy, just a house that had plumbing that worked.

I remember her dream house. It was a brown manufactured home from a company in New Braunfels, Texas. We'd pass that company and some of their model homes when we'd drive up to visit my sister in Dallas. We once stopped to see the outside of the particular house that she liked. It was one of the few times I remember my mom's face full of awe and me thinking, *I'm going to get her that house.*

I was in junior high when we first found out about my mom's high blood pressure. I had to miss school that day to take her to the doctor because she hadn't been feeling well. I always had to miss school to do things for my mom and family. We walked to the doctor's office because I wasn't old enough to drive. We literally lived on the other side of the tracks—seriously, we had to walk over actual tracks past our usual Greyhound bus stop to get to see Dr. Boneta. Now when I look back, I can't help but think how ridiculous it is that my mother felt sick and had to walk herself to the doctor (that she couldn't afford) to find out what was wrong with her. Having high blood pressure wasn't that devastating because a lot of people have it and a combination of a lifestyle change and medication can control it. The medication part was the problem for us. After the doctor gave my mom a prescription for the pills he wanted her to take, we crossed the street to Medico, our local pharmacy, to get it filled. It cost fifty dollars for a month. My mom was shocked because the pills cost a third of what she received in her weekly paycheck. We couldn't afford to pay that amount for a medication every month. That was when my mom told me we'd have to go and price the medication the next time we went to Mexico. That was one of the best things about growing up in a border town. You could go to Mexico and buy medications a lot cheaper than in the United States. When we crossed the border into Reynosa, Tamaulipas, we went to the closest pharmacy, where a month's supply cost under five dollars. Mexico actually saved my mom's life (that time).

Occasionally, when I mention the lack of money for doctors or medications my family struggled with, I'll have people say, "Why didn't you check into [insert name of government program here]?" or "Why didn't you go to [blah, blah]?" I always answer, "We didn't know about any programs or any help that was available to us." You see, it's hard to know what's available when you're neglected by most of society. My family was the poorest of the poor. My dream was to be able to live in the projects because it would be a step up for us. You must also remember that during this time, we had no internet available to us. We couldn't google key words and get answers that could help us when we were sick. Going to the doctor was our last resort because it meant that by going, we would have to do without trivial things we needed like food. For my family, going to the doctor was our last Hail Mary.

Throughout my life, I have seen my family get very sick and we just pray and hope for the best. I remember one time when my mother got sick for days. I wasn't sure what was going to happen to her. She was so ill, she didn't go to work. I knew it was a big deal because if my mother did *not* go to work, the situation had to be serious. She was weak. She stayed in bed for days. It was as if she were a different person. I kept asking her if she should go to the doctor, but because she had not gone to work for days, she refused to go because her job didn't give her sick days, so they would dock her pay. I remember staying home from school during that time to take care of her because, again, that was the responsibility she had asked me to take on.

That would happen at different moments throughout my life. The moments when I would be asked to stop my life and give up my dreams in order to come and take care of my mother. I dropped out of college to help my sister with her kids the first time, then tried to go back to school but had to quit again the second time to take care of my mother, who was starting to have more health problems.

My life completely changed in 2002. I was living in Los Angeles and my brother called, days after my birthday, which is on January 6. Things hadn't been going well for me in my time in LA, especially that specific week that I got the call. I had recently been fired from working at a boutique travel agency that catered to celebrities. It was a bit of a concierge job, in a way. Imagine the movie *The Devil Wears Prada* but with a Latina assistant that never got the "makeover" to fit in. Basically, any whim a celebrity had, I had to find a way to fulfill it, whether it was finding a pair of boots that were in cargo at an airport from a client's European tour and rushing them to Los Angeles for a music video shoot in about a day (months post-9/11), to finding a DVD player in Amsterdam in the middle of the night that was compatible to play DVDs from the United States. I was fired because my boss found out I was looking for another job. I didn't blame her. She had found a résumé on my desk while I was out working on an assignment.

I couldn't mentally handle the life I was living at that point. My job was 24-7. I was sharing a studio apartment with two roommates. I was sleeping on an inflatable mattress that I would sometimes have to move into the "kitchen" portion of the studio so I could make calls to Europe in the middle of the night. It would annoy me at times that I would have to buy expensive candles for a client, whose grand total would be more than what I paid for rent. (What I'm trying to say is: That job was not for me.) My car had been towed because an old roommate had driven it and had received parking tickets without telling me. I had finally saved up money to pay the tickets and get my car out of the tow yard. If I remember correctly, I had to pay around $1,200. Once I got my car back, I went home, parked it, and went to bed. When I woke up the next day, my car had a boot on it. I called to find out why and it turned out that the money I had paid for outstanding tickets hadn't covered *all* of the tickets. There were more from LA County and I had to pay *more* money I didn't have.

I remember crying. I sat on the curb, staring at the boot on my car, and just bawled. I didn't understand why these things were happening to me. I was trying so hard to get by. Was this a sign that I wasn't supposed to be here? It's at these times that people start telling you clichés. "What doesn't kill you makes you stronger." Yeah, how about instead of telling me your greeting card phrases, you tell me your ATM pin number? I couldn't call home and ask for money. My family didn't have any to spare; I had to figure things out on my own. I sat there, crying nonstop, realizing that I was going to lose my car. There was no way I was going to raise the money necessary to pay the tickets and pay for the towing again. It was a catch-22. It had taken me so long to gather the money the first time that my towing fees kept going up for each day it stayed in the yard. I was broke, out of a job, and soon to be carless, and in a month or two, homeless (again). I kept thinking that things couldn't get worse.

Then they did.

My brother called to tell me our mother was on her deathbed. She had gotten pneumonia a month before. I knew that because she and I would talk on the phone practically every day. She was the kind of person that couldn't understand how far I was from her. If it started raining in my hometown, she would call me in Los Angeles to tell me to be careful because it was raining. My mother had asked me if I could come visit her when she had pneumonia, and I wanted to go but my boss wouldn't let me because it was Christmas, a really bad time because our clients were super busy traveling. So I told my sick mother I couldn't go. And I regretted that because I never said no to my mom. Luckily, once she recovered from it, I felt less guilty because if anything had happened to her, I wouldn't have been able to live with myself.

But there I was on the phone with my brother, and I had trouble understanding what he was trying to tell me. It must have been one of the hardest calls he had ever had to make.

My mom had had a relapse. She had gotten pneumonia again and was not expected to make it. One of her last wishes was to see me before she died.

Okay. So now, officially, things had gotten worse and impossible. I remember the first thing I thought was *How the hell am I going to get home?* I couldn't drive. My car had a boot. I looked up buses from Los Angeles to Texas but realized it would take days to get there and I didn't have that kind of time to waste. I didn't have money to fly, especially last minute, and honestly, I didn't want to. I didn't know what to expect. Saying goodbye to my mother was something I felt I obviously needed to do, but I was also terrified of doing it.

I told my roommates about everything that was happening and one of them called his father and asked him to help me. Within hours, his father had used miles to get me a one-way plane ticket to go home. I had wanted a one-way because if my mother was dying, I wasn't sure how long I'd be gone. I packed a small bag of clothes, and as I left my apartment I told my roommates I would keep them updated.

When I landed in McAllen, my brother picked me up at our little airport and took me straight to the hospital. As we drove, we were awkward with each other, a bit too silent. Our family had never had any kind of discussion of what we would do if anything happened to one of us, and now that we found ourselves in this situation, neither one of us had any idea what came next.

We arrived at the hospital and took the elevator to my mom's floor. My brother Ruben warned me she looked different. He wanted to prepare me because he didn't want me to be scared. I walked slowly into the room and there she was, lying on the bed. I remember how excited she got when I walked in. God, I remember her face in that moment. She was so happy to see me, her baby. I was technically an adult, but to her, I would always be her baby. She was ecstatic, yet Ruben was right. She *was* different. Her face was swollen from surgery. Yes, surgery. What we weren't prepared for were all these tests the hospital had run on her that she had never done before. It was then that we realized how sick my mom was. She had numerous health problems that would've been easily treatable *if* she had been able to take care of herself. The biggest problem the tests revealed was that my mother had unknowingly suffered strokes throughout her life and each one had weakened her heart more. Let that sink in: my mother had strokes she just forced herself to live through.

When you're with someone on their deathbed, you find yourself hanging by a thread, knowing the heartbreak is coming but with no idea when. I slept in the room with her that night. I was ready to say goodbye to her at any moment. Actually, I'm lying. I wasn't ready to say goodbye to her, but the moment was coming whether I liked it or not. I remember thinking that this was my chance to tell her everything I wanted to tell her. Sure, we hugged and kissed all the time, but we never had those "I'm glad you're my mother" kind of moments and I figured this was my chance. So I did. I told her how much she meant to me, how I knew that no one would ever love me as much as she did, how a piece of me would die along with her . . . I told her everything I wanted to say to her before she died.

And then she didn't die.

The next day, she got better. Within a couple of days, she was walking. There were footprints etched on the hospital floor that helped measure the distance you walked, so she had daily goals to accomplish. We held hands as I grabbed her arm and helped her walk. It was a miracle of sorts. I wasn't expecting her to live. They had told us she wouldn't. Days later, the doctors told us she had gotten better and could go home. We were surprised. Having grown up in a religious household, I couldn't help but think this was what faith was, the idea of putting your heart and mind into a concept you couldn't tangibly see. Part of me thought I was being ridiculous until my brother told me something. He told me not to let my mother know that he was telling me this. When my mother was dying and asked to see me, she had him get her a picture of me and a St. Jude prayer card. She had taken my picture, tied it to the St. Jude card, and prayed for me to come home to see her before she left us. I realized that all my mother wanted in what she thought was the last moment of her life was to have me by her side.

After she left the hospital, we went back to our little broken-down home. Since she was feeling better, I was beginning to wonder when I could go back to Los Angeles. That is when my mother told me, "Cristela, I got better because you were here with me. Please, don't go back. Stay here with me. I need you here with me."

I wanted to go back and try to chase after my dreams, but looking at my mother's face, what other choice did I have but to stay? She had stared down the face of death and defied the odds to beat it. This was a recurring theme in her life. She had come to this country not knowing the language, having little education, married to an awful man, and still she hadn't given up. I knew that I had no choice. I had to be there for the woman who had always been there for me. I called up my roommates in Los Angeles and told them what was happening. I asked that they gather my belongings and give them away to a thrift store. I didn't have to worry about my car. After being towed, it now belonged to the city of Los Angeles. I had to try to accept the fact that Los Angeles wasn't going to be an option for me. I had tried and it hadn't worked out. There was a moment where I thought maybe my mother was right in telling me that dreams were for the rich. Us poor people had to resign to the fact that our dreams were meant to remain just that: dreams. I stayed home and took care of my mother, not knowing when I would have a chance to live my life, if ever.

Once my mother was home, we started doing the math and

realized that her hospital stay was going to bankrupt us even more. If there was a way to be triple-poor, we found it. The doctors had put her on medications that without health insurance would cost $500 a month. Going to Mexico wasn't even an option at this point because now you needed to have a passport to cross the border, unlike when I was a kid. I had one, but it had expired and I couldn't afford to renew it, nor did I have the time.

My mother was never the same after she came home. I had to sleep next to her—that is, when she *could* sleep—but more often than not, the nights consisted of her moaning in pain. Sometimes she would get hit by strong anxiety attacks that would wake her up and keep her from sleeping. I stayed up with her every time she couldn't sleep. I had to, since I slept next to her. I had really just entered my twenties and had no idea what I was doing. I wanted to help her but had no idea how. I started thinking of ideas to distract her from the anxiety she was feeling (again, I was clueless) and decided to take her to a wonderland filled with thingamabobs as far as the eye could see. You guessed it. I was taking her to the Walmart that was open twenty-four hours a day.

The first time I drove her to Walmart, she couldn't understand why we were going when it was so late at night, but she also realized that she needed to do something. We rarely slept anymore. Her anxiety would make her cry a lot, and watching my mother cry was something I didn't want to do.

We'd go to Walmart anywhere from midnight to four in the morning, walking around the store, trying to steer clear of the pallets of new merchandise the workers were setting up for the next day. I would get my mom a shopping cart to serve only as her walker, as we weren't planning on buying anything.

During one of these trips I saw that Backstreet Boys CD, *Black & Blue*. I bought the CD on one of our late-night "Walmart Walks" and popped it into my Discman on the way home.

I listened to it a lot. I think at times it served as a way to keep me connected to a version of me in another dimension that I imagined was still living in Los Angeles, trying to make something happen. I remember listening to "Shape of My Heart" and thinking it was a pretty song. I imagined all the girls my age getting to experience lives where they dated guys, went to college, and got to graduate, got to live their lives. Meanwhile, I was sitting at home, listening to this pretty song, and a lot of times, the background vocals were the painful moans of my mom piercing through my headphones.

Every now and then, my mother was able to sleep through the night. I wasn't that lucky. I had been used to being on high alert and any sound she made woke me up and kept me up. Sometimes I would just stare at her sleeping, thanking God that she was able to doze off that night. I'd put on the Backstreet Boys CD and I used to be really happy when I could hear it all the way through because it meant that for that short while, she wasn't in pain. And neither was I.

Shortly after moving back home, my family realized that things were not working. My siblings were trying to pay for the medication, which really set everyone back. I couldn't get a job because my job was to take care of my mother 24-7. My sister offered to move my mother and me in with her so that we could save money to pay for her medications. Her house had heat and air conditioning and for us it was a no-brainer. We had to move in with her because it was best for our mother. Ruben drove us up to Dallas with only what my mother and I were able to fit in the car. My part was easy since I had left everything I owned in Los Angeles. My mother, on the other hand, had to condense everything she owned into what could fit into my brother's car. It was painful for me to see that my mother's entire life had to be reduced to what could fit into the trunk of a car. And within a couple of days, we were living with my sister in a Dallas suburb. We had moved from our little town of San Juan to the big city of Carrollton.

This is an interesting side note that I think I should mention here. The sitcom *Cristela* I had on network TV for a year was based on this time in my life when I had to move in with my sister and help take care of her kids and my mother. I originally wanted to share this part of my life to show that so many of us had to live this kind of life whether against our wishes or not. It was just something you had to do as a member of the family. I didn't really go to law school. In real life, I wanted to perform, but I picked lawyer as the career I would pursue in the show because I thought law was easier to explain than wanting to act. I wanted to show how my family stayed strong together during this time, while we were all scraping by; it was a time when I felt the closest to everyone because we all had a common goal: to save our mother.

My sister had set my mom and me in my niece's room. She was a little kid and was going to sleep with my sister and brother-in-law in their bed. My niece's room was tiny and had no bed, so my mother and I had to sleep on the carpeted floor on top of blankets. Neither of us cared, since, like I mentioned previously, the house had heat and air conditioning, so we were living on our version of easy street. It felt weird to me to be back living in my sister's house. I had lived with her before when I first helped take care of her kids and I never thought I would be back again, and now adding my mom to the mix.

We were in Dallas for a while. To be honest, I don't know how long. During that period of my life, I really lost any concept of time.

I didn't want to keep track of it, especially because with my mother's moaning and constant struggle with pain and anxiety, this part of my life felt like one single day that never ended. The schedules were the same. We'd wake up, my sister and her husband would go to work, and I would stay home watching over my mom. We would clean and do chores around the house to pass the time, and also because it's the kind of people we were. I would drop off and pick up the kids at school, help them with their homework, and do anything that was needed of me. Again, since I couldn't get a job to help out, I tried to do what I could to not feel like such a nuisance to people, but in all honesty, I always felt like I was in the way and really felt bad about myself during this time. I was trying to take care of my mother's needs and tried to make everyone feel happy, but really, I was miserable. I felt like a loser.

I remember one night when we had all gone to sleep. The house was quiet and all I could hear were my mother's moans. She slept inches away from me and it just seemed like the volume of every moan was magnified by a thousand. I was sick and tired of it. I put the pillow over my head and just thought to myself, *Please stop. Just stop. I can't take hearing you anymore. Please stop. I can't stand it anymore.* I still think about that night and can't help but think what a terrible daughter I was. What kind of person was I to think that? Sure, my life had changed in a second, but so had hers, so had all of ours. My mother couldn't help her moans. I knew that, but I also wasn't a superhero. I was a girl in her twenties wondering if this was what my life was going to be like forever . . . But it wasn't going to be like that forever. In fact, soon after that night, I got my wish and even now I still can't help but look back and feel guilty about what I thought. I still carry that guilt with me today.

My family had been invited to a party for one of our cousins on our father's side. If I remember correctly, one of my cousins was throwing a *quinceañera* for one of her daughters. We were rarely invited to anything like that, so once we got the invite, my mother was determined to go, which meant I had to go and I didn't want to.

We needed to find my mother a dress for the party, so my sister drove us to some stores to find something to wear. My mother had been complaining about how bad she felt that day and I kept asking her if she wanted to go to the doctor. She kept telling me she was going to be okay. We had hit every low-budget store we usually hit. I call them the "Low-Budget Trinity." In Catholicism, when we talk about the Trinity, we mean the Father, Son, and Holy Ghost. The three entities are the same divine being. My Low-Budget Trinity included "the Marshalls, Ross, and T.J.Maxx," meaning three stores that are the same example of big, big savings. The last store we went to was in fact a Marshalls. The three of us scoured through racks trying to find a dress. Finally, after looking for what seemed an eternity, we found a navy dress my mother liked for around forty dollars. My sister paid for it and we went home.

My mom kept complaining about pain for the rest of the day. I kept telling her we had to go to the doctor, but she kept insisting she was going to be fine. After hours of telling her we had to go to the hospital, she finally agreed. I will absolutely never forget my mom's face when she agreed to this. It was full of defeat. I think she felt that if she went to the hospital, she would not come back alive. I think that's why she held off as much as she could, but there was that moment when she realized going to the hospital was her only alternative . . . and she was terrified.

We called for an ambulance that quickly arrived at my sister's house. They came in and started asking a storm of questions. "How many medications is she taking? How long has she had her symptoms? Does she have a nurse?" I answered every one of the questions since I was her primary caregiver. They put her on a gurney and asked us which one of us was going to ride in the ambulance with her because they needed someone to translate. Everyone in that room stood silent and I remembered what my mother told me when she had come home from the hospital: "Stay here with me. I need you here with me." I said I would ride with her. They loaded her onto the ambulance, I sat next to her, and we rode off. I held her hand because she kept telling me she was scared. She kept asking me to stay with her. I kept assuring her I was going to be right next to her for the whole thing. I wasn't going anywhere. On our way to the hospital, we rode with no siren, no flashing lights, and for a moment it made me feel better, as if they didn't consider my mom's case so urgent.

Once we arrived at the hospital with my family driving right behind us, we were told they were sending our mother to the emergency room and I was the only one allowed to go in with her. I hadn't expected that. Hospitals, doctors, needles, they all made me nervous and scared the hell out of me, and here I found myself in the middle of my own nightmare, still holding my mom's hand. It was the only thing I could think of doing that would make her feel better. It felt like we were there a long time. It's weird how sometimes good times seem to pass in an instant while painful times seem to linger longer than normal.

Nurses came in, asking me all kinds of questions about my mother. There were rumblings about her possibly needing heart surgery. There was a point where a nurse came in to tell me they had to insert a tube in her to help her urinate. I helped the nurse do that. I never thought I'd ever have to do anything like that, but there I was, helping this nurse stick this tube inside my mother, who was freaking out and wondering what was happening. I feel as if at that exact moment, I became an adult. I was no longer allowed to be young anymore. In that moment, I had aged decades. The nurse left and soon the doctor came in and informed me that my mother was indeed going to need surgery and that there was a good chance she was not going to make it. However, the surgery was the only chance she had to live. I had to translate what the doctor told me to her. Can you imagine having to tell the most important person in your life such a thing? I didn't want to scare her. I tried to hold back my tears as I told my mother that she was going to have surgery. I didn't tell her that she might not make it because I wanted her to fight for her life. I didn't want to give her a chance to think she didn't have to fight anymore because I wanted her here with me. The hardest thing at that moment was me having to take my mom's ring off. It was a gold band she wore on her wedding finger. In my entire life, I never saw her take it off, but I had to; the nurses had told me to. As they were sedating her to prep her for surgery, I whispered to her and said, "I'm taking this ring off because I just want to make sure no one is going to steal it." I was trying to make her smile before they took her away. And within a short while, she was on her way to the operating table.

I was twenty-three years old at this point. While friends of mine were graduating college, I was at a hospital, wondering what was coming next. I went out into the lobby to meet up with my family and tell them everything that had happened and everything I knew, which wasn't much. My family had already contacted my brother Ruben back in our hometown and told him what was happening. He had gotten into his car and was making the nine-hour drive to Dallas to try to see my mom before she possibly died.

My family just silently stood by one another, trying to crack jokes because that was our go-to defense mechanism, but really, we were broken. Then, in that moment, we found a family of four African American women who were in the lobby. Their father was sick, but they were hopeful. They had been told that things were looking good for him. They asked us why we were there and we told them. They asked us if it would be okay for them to gather in prayer with us; they wanted to say a prayer for our mother, and we said yes. We needed all the prayer we could get. We stood in a circle, holding hands with these beautiful women who said a prayer to God about our mother, and for a second, I felt the beauty of humanity in a way I hadn't before. These women were strangers to us, yet in that moment, they rallied around us to pray for someone they had never met but by just looking at us could feel how important she was to us. After that prayer, we said goodbye and, for the first time in what seemed like an eternity, my family felt a little better.

A while later, the doctor came to tell us that our mother had made it through the surgery and that we were about to go into the most critical time where we had to sit and wait to see if she was going to survive. He told my family they could go see her in a bit, but he told me that I could go in and see her immediately, warning me (just like my brother had previously) that my mother didn't look the same. Her face was swollen and she didn't look at all like herself. As I walked into the room, I realized they were right. I didn't recognize her. Her face was so swollen that besides recognizing her hair, I would've had trouble believing it was her. I had to go out and tell my family what she looked like to prepare them. As they entered the room, Eloy and Julie slowly walked in to see her. We were trying to talk to her as if everything was normal, to try to make her feel comfortable. We kept getting updates saying that she was actually doing well, which made us feel better. We were eventually told that visiting hours were ending soon and the doctor suggested we go home to rest. I wanted to stay with her but was told that I especially needed to go home and rest because I had been right there with her since the start of it all, so we took his advice.

Once we got home, I went into my niece's bedroom and put on my Discman. The Backstreet Boys CD was in it and I played "Shape of My Heart." I listened to the song on repeat and, unbeknownst to me, was sobbing the entire time. It took me a couple times listening to it to realize that for the first time since I had moved into my sister's house, I was listening to the CD without interruption. My mother wasn't moaning. The only sound beyond my Discman was silence. I remembered the night that I had put the pillow over my head, wishing for silence, and now that I had it, I hated it with all my heart.

For the next couple of days, we would go to the hospital to see how our mother was doing. Ruben had gotten into town and showed me that he had brought with him a little box of cassettes my mother had, all of Mexican bands and singers. He told me he had listened to nothing but those tapes as he was driving, hoping he'd get to see our mother, and he did. Things weren't looking better for her, though. We started preparing for the worst because it seemed that *this* was exactly where we were heading. On the third day of our mother being in the hospital, the doctor informed us that she was not improving. She was on life support and we had to consider taking her off of it, especially because, without insurance, every day was costing my family thousands of dollars.

I don't know if I can put into words the severity of having the fate of someone's life in your own hands, especially your own mother's. I never thought we'd be in that position. I never thought about being put in a situation where I would have to make such a terrible decision. I'm the kind of person that stresses at a restaurant because I don't know if I want breakfast or lunch, and here I was trying to decide if my mother gets to live? After discussing it, my family decided that we didn't want her to be in pain anymore. Her entire life had been nothing but pain. It was a constant struggle to get from one painful obstacle to another, and it had to stop at some point. I kept thinking about her moaning, the moaning I had become accustomed to, and realized that it had to stop. Wanting my mother by my side was not worth making her go through so much pain; I thought it was selfish of me to think that way. Once the decision was made, papers were signed and we decided to have the machines turned off. A priest soon came to my mother's room to give her the last rites. It was all happening so quickly. Right before they turned off the machines, I asked my siblings if they were going to be in the room with her. None of them wanted to be there; I didn't want to either. I understood my siblings were experiencing severe heartbreak and none of us could handle it, but at the same time, I didn't want her dying without at least one of us present. She deserved that. I remembered those words when she asked me to not return to Los Angeles: "Cristela, I got better because you were here with me. Please, don't go back. Stay here with me. I need you here with me."

I wasn't sure if being with her when the machines were turned off was going to traumatize me or leave a scar, and honestly, there was no time to think about that. I realized that this moment was about her, only her. I realized that the only way to honor the journey my mom had made was to be with her in that last moment.

I will say, I was surprised that, out of my siblings, I was the only one who decided to be with her when she took her last breath. I always thought that me being the baby of the family would be my excuse to get out of dealing with the heavy stuff, but it turns out that in that moment, I was the only one capable of handling it. It's funny because my mom dying made me realize that strength doesn't necessarily come with gender or age. On that day, I forced myself to have the strength to face my biggest fear: saying goodbye to the woman who didn't have much but still gave us everything.

Then the moment came. I tried to walk into the room and be as close to her as I could. I made it as far as the door. Every ounce of strength I thought I had disappeared. Every step I tried to take into that room made me feel a pain that I had never felt before. I can tell you that even now, fifteen years after she passed, I have never felt pain like the kind I did in that moment. I kept thinking, *What if my mother is a miracle? What if she is one of those rare cases when they turn off the machines and she doesn't die?* My mother had established herself as someone that could make the impossible happen time and again. What if this was on par with everything else in her life? I *knew* that moment was going to hurt. I didn't know the exact amount of pain . . . but I stayed with her. I thought I *had* to be there with her. She had been there when I took my first breath; it was only right that I would be there when she took her last.

They turned off the machines. The beeping started slowing down. Beep, beep,

Courtesy of Natalia Alonzo

I made my mom take these pictures with me at a Kmart photo booth in McAllen, Texas. She never liked taking pictures, but I always wanted to take pictures with her.

beep . . . then a minute later . . . beep . . . beep . . . beep . . . then
another minute later . . . beep . . . . beep . . .

Then nothing.

I fell to the ground and remember nothing after that. I was later
told that I had been admitted into the emergency room, where they
ran tests and diagnosed me with a severe case of shock. I lost my
hearing and sight in that moment. People were asking me questions
but I couldn't move or speak. Once I started coming back to my
senses and realized what had just happened, I wailed.

In all honesty, there are a lot of times when I feel like I failed my
mother. This woman managed to somehow raise four children on her
own. She took care of me, but I couldn't take care of her. Yes, I know
it's impractical to think like this, and I imagine that maybe my brain
knows better. I just wish my heart could catch up to my brain. The
thing I think about the most in regard to my mother is that she made
me feel like I let her down. I never got to buy her that brown dream
house she wanted before she died. I made a promise to myself that
I wasn't able to keep and it is something that haunts me to this day.

My family started making funeral plans. We decided to bury our
mother in our hometown of San Juan. We had to make the drive
down to the Rio Grande Valley for the service and the funeral. When
we had to pick what our mother would wear, my sister picked the
dress my mother had chosen to wear to the *quinceañera*, which I
thought was the right choice, especially because it was the last thing
she had chosen. I also thought it was a good idea because (and I hope
it doesn't sound weird) I thought that after my mom died she would
be reunited with her parents and her siblings who had passed away
before her . . . and I wanted her to look pretty for that moment.

I rode with my brothers and listened to "Shape of My Heart" on repeat for the beginning of the road trip. When I realized that from that moment on, I could listen to that CD without hearing my mom moaning in the background, I took my earbuds out and never heard that song again . . . until I started writing this chapter.

I played this song over and over to remind myself of everything I felt during that time because music leaves a fingerprint on our hearts. One of the things I constantly think about is that there will never be that moment where I can look into the audience and see my mother's face and have her know that I pulled off everything I did because of her. I hope that her spirit is somewhere near me at all times. Someone once told me, "Maybe your mom knew it was her time to go because it was the only way she could help you in the way she wanted to." I hope that person is right, because with every big step I take in my life, I want her there with me. I just want her to know that all I want in this life is to make her proud and continue the journey she began decades ago. I want people to know how amazing she was because there are so many people like her in this country. She was an immigrant woman who moved heaven and earth (and once she died, heaven again) so that I could thrive. People like her might go unnoticed and neglected by the majority of the population, but to their children they are their everything. She is part of my future because she helped create my past. I guess it makes sense to talk about the fingerprint that specific Backstreet Boys song left on my heart, since I took the time to explain how my mother helped create the "shape" of my heart . . . like its title.

I took my nephew to Disneyland. He couldn't stop crying because I took him.
This moment was the closest I've ever felt to being a mother.

"AND THE MONEY KEPT ROLLING IN (AND OUT)"
EVITA

This song is from a musical called *Evita*. I fell in love with the movie version of this song, performed by Antonio Banderas. It's got such a peppy feel to it. You know how sometimes you have those go-to songs that just put you in a good mood? It could be in the way the music is arranged or how the lyrics connect to you and make everything feel okay. This was one of those songs for me—and it didn't hurt that Antonio Banderas was a handsome man who could sing.

Speaking of handsome men, I am currently at the age where people start wondering what is wrong with me because I'm not married and don't have any children. It couldn't *possibly* be by choice, so now people have to ask when it's going to happen. I always find that so comical, as if all I've been waiting for is for people to ask me out. *Oh! I'm glad you asked! I've been pining for love but was just waiting for you to ask me that after not seeing me for years! Thank you for your concern!* But the truth is, it just hasn't happened. Regarding marriage, it's not that I'm against it, but I'm not necessarily for it either. It just is what it is. I find it surprising how so many people think that marriage is something that must happen by a certain age, as if I have an expiration date. Guess what: I'm not milk.

To be honest, I haven't dated much and it's because, as I've mentioned before, I was so stifled by my mom, I'm eons behind everyone else in the dating department. In the first four decades of my life, I had only one boyfriend. I am also very old-fashioned, so I don't do the online dating thing, which seems to be quite the norm now. I prefer the idea of meeting someone in real life, and since I live like a hermit, that makes it even harder.

I'll also have people that remind me I can have kids without being married. *Oh, crap! Really? Are you my Yoda? Why are you handing down all this wisdom for free?* Now, the reason why I don't have children is really by choice. I know that there is an antiquated stereotype that women get to a certain age and they just can't seem to sleep because their biological clock keeps going off at all hours of the day. Well, my biological clock ran out of batteries years ago and I seem to have never replaced them. "But you'd make such a great mom!" people say.

I try to explain to people that, in a weird way, I have already been a mother. While I didn't give birth to my sister's three children, I felt like they were my own because I helped raise them: two boys, one girl. I lived with them for years. I helped them with homework and school projects. I would chaperone their school trips. I helped them with their extracurricular activities. People at their schools used to think I was a teenage mother because they always saw me with them. Meanwhile, my sister and her husband had full-time jobs with commutes that took up a chunk of time and childcare was expensive. They needed my help and I wanted to help, especially their eldest son, Sergio. I have spent the most time with Sergio and I love him like he's my own. He's always needed more attention than the others because Sergio is special needs. Having to take care of someone that is special needs can be tricky. In our area, special education programs were scarce and, therefore, could be expensive and usually included wait lists. I always figured that if I helped raise Sergio, at least we knew he was being taken care of by someone that he could trust and feel comfortable with.

Over time, Sergio and I would bond over music, more than I did with his siblings. His brother and I would bond over rap, but Sergio seemed to like a lot of different genres like I did. He would always be near me as I cleaned up around the house because he had fun learning the songs I played. I always liked when he showed an interest in them because he would try to sing the songs with me and he always sounded great. The song "And the Money Kept Rolling In (and Out)" was one of those songs. I used to watch *Evita* all the time. Since I couldn't afford to go see live shows, I would rely on movie versions of musicals shown on TV, or I'd rent a copy of a taped Broadway show from the public library. Not having money was not going to stop me from being immersed in that music.

I think the reason I loved when Sergio would get into a song is because I realized at an early age that music was a way that he could express himself. I thought this was special because Sergio oftentimes struggled, quite literally, to express himself. When he was a baby, he was diagnosed with Klinefelter syndrome, a condition that affects males born with two or more extra X chromosomes. Once he was diagnosed, we learned that symptoms of the syndrome included problems with speech and language development. By the way, I should add that now as an adult, Sergio still struggles with words, but he is also bilingual; he speaks both English and Spanish.

I remember when my sister brought Sergio down to visit for the first time. She and her husband were living in Houston and would occasionally drive down to visit us and her husband's family in Mexico. He was a tiny baby. She carried him into the house and I stared down at his face and thought he was the most beautiful thing I had ever seen. My mom grabbed him and held him for a while, staring at her first grandson ever. She tried making him laugh and was so nurturing and loving to him that I couldn't help but look at her and think, *Oh, so you're actually capable of feeling those things, just not with your own kids.* I guess nurturing skips a generation in her family? I was eleven when he was born. I was terrified of holding him. What if I dropped him? I was sitting down and held him in my arms, and for that moment, I remember thinking life was perfect.

My sister was going to be in town for several days and my mom and I were going to help her with the baby. I quickly learned how to do things like change diapers, prepare the bottles for him, and make sure to burp him after meals. I was a child playing house, but with a real baby. My sister and I ended up going to Blockbuster and renting the *Batman* movie with Michael Keaton and Jack Nicholson. It was a new release back then and we rented it as much as we could. We became obsessed with that movie. We would watch it over and over when we were with Sergio. These were sweet, simple times where we were all so happy to have been blessed with that baby.

Sergio was a quiet baby, and rarely cried. It wasn't till later that my sister started noticing that, as he got older, he was having trouble sitting up by himself and speaking. It was then that she took him to a specialist and eventually discovered he had Klinefelter syndrome. My sister told my mother and me about it and, to be honest, we had trouble understanding what that all meant. We weren't a family that was very educated about anything medical. She explained to us they thought Sergio would require more attention to help with his development. I still didn't understand what was happening; I was twelve years old.

Once Sergio began to speak, it was hard for me to understand what he was saying. I couldn't make out all of his words. Eventually, the specialist thought it would be beneficial for him to learn sign language to help him communicate with his parents. I learned to sign as well because, at the age of thirteen, I started going to Dallas in the summer when I was out of school to help take care of him and another baby (my nephew David) my sister had just had. I needed to be able to talk to him. The words he used most were: *milk*, *Mom*, *Dad*, *socks*, and *shoes*.

The kids eventually got older. My sister had her third child, a girl named Stephanie, and as the kids grew up, so did my duties to help with them; that's when I dropped out of college. They were in elementary school at the time. Sergio didn't go to the same school as his brother and sister because he had been enrolled at another school with a special education program. Each day I picked him up from school felt like I was going into the final round of a game show because I never knew if the teacher was going to tell me he'd had a good or bad day. Sometimes Sergio would throw terrible tantrums and disrupt the class. There were times he couldn't control himself, but there were also times that I knew he was doing it just to do it. That's the thing I had learned about him because I was with him for so long. I used to discipline him and he would rarely get frustrated and throw a tantrum. He used to do that with his father all the time because his father would let him get away with it, but with his mom and me, it was a different story.

I always thought it was important to talk to Sergio like a regular kid, meaning I didn't want to coddle him. I wanted him to know that I thought of him like his brother and sister. Yes, he was special needs, and trust me, there were times when things would get tough, but the same can be true for most people. When I picked him up from school and the teacher told me he had been bad, we would get into the car and I would ask him if he was faking it. If he was, he would say yes. One thing about Sergio is that the kid has never been a liar. We would get home and I would make him something to eat, and if he had been faking it, I would tell him he couldn't watch TV for a bit.

Those years, when the kids were in elementary and junior high, were some of the best times I ever had. There was that block of time between when I would pick them up from school and when their parents got home from work that we would all hang out together in the living room and just watch TV or listen to music. It was always the best part of my day because I always thought of it as *my* time with them. I felt like it was my time to teach them about things I didn't think they would otherwise be exposed to, like musicals. I was the only one they knew who loved theater. I think everyone in my family tried figuring out where I picked it up, as if Broadway was the same thing as doing drugs. "WHO TAUGHT YOU HOW TO DO THIS?" I used to love when I would teach the kids new songs from musicals because Sergio would go and tell his mom, and my sister would always say, "Cris, why do you keep doing this?!" Because it made me giggle.

I always kept up with what was playing on Broadway. I couldn't afford to see the shows, but I could afford the albums of the cast recordings. There was something wonderful about listening to the albums because I could imagine what the show would look like in my mind. It was also during this time that I discovered the internet. Some people had been using it for years, but I had just been introduced to it. I discovered chat rooms and would go online to talk to people because, in reality, I was lonely. While I absolutely loved taking care of the children, I didn't have any friends to hang out with or any interaction with people that didn't live in my sister's house.

I ended up finding a Broadway chat room where people would log on and talk about musicals. It ended up being my go-to when I had free time. I had found a spot where fellow Broadway nerds would gather to talk about albums and shows they had just gotten into. It was exactly what I was looking for because I was craving conversation about something I loved. Now, remember when I mentioned earlier that I've always felt like I was decades behind everyone in the dating department? This is a perfect example of that. During this time, I had no idea that people were using chat rooms to try to meet other people to hook up. The idea was so foreign to me and, honestly, I think I was kind of naïve that it never occurred to me that people were using the internet to date. Remember, this was back in the late nineties and the internet wasn't as evolved as it is now. Back then, when someone wanted to find out more about you, they would ask you, "A/S/L?," which means "age, sex, location." That was how a lot of people said hello. Occasionally I would get someone who tried hooking up with me in the Broadway chat room and I would have none of it. I would instantly say no and tell them I was solely in the chat room to talk about Broadway, nothing more.

I think that's why I ended up teaching the kids about Broadway. I yearned for conversation about this thing I loved and they were the ones I had the most human interaction with on a daily basis. So, sorry, kids, but you were going to learn who Fosse was whether you wanted to or not!

The first musical I taught them about was *Ragtime*, a wonderful show that told the story of an African American couple and European immigrants, along with stories about affluent figures at the beginning of the twentieth century. To be honest, I was drawn to the show because of the African American couple more than anything else, because the character named Sarah was originally played by none other than Audra McDonald, who has one of the most amazing voices to ever exist. I am lucky to be alive at the same time as her. CAN YOU TELL I'M A FAN? Her love was a character named Coalhouse Walker, Jr., played by Brian Stokes Mitchell. Both of these voices together made me have those moments where every time I heard their songs and someone started talking near me, I wanted to tell them to shut up and "feel things with me."

When the cast recording was released, I knew I wanted to buy it—which was a big deal because, back then, there was no way to go online and just buy one song without buying the entire album like you can now. There was no way to sample chunks of songs to make sure you liked it. If you wanted to buy an album, you had to just take the leap and hope that more than a couple songs were good. This rang true with Broadway musicals because a lot of them were double CDs, so when you invested in buying them, you were actually willing to spend more money than for a regular CD. I bought the cast recording and started playing it around the house as I cleaned. I was instantly hooked.

Now, while I had originally purchased the *Ragtime* CDs for Audra McDonald, I found myself playing a song from the show called "Gliding" over and over nonstop. This is a song in which an immigrant father, from a Jewish shtetl in Eastern Europe, who has immigrated to America, comforts his daughter by singing about ice-skating. I noticed one day that Sergio took a liking to it and I started singing it to him. There was a part of the song where I sang and I'd tell him to close his eyes. He would do so and smile. It happened every time I sang it to him. He would soon start asking me to sing the "Close Your Eyes" song and I would. It was our first special song. In this song, the same immigrant father attempts to comfort his daughter by giving her something he made. The chorus of the song talks about gliding, and when that part would come up, I would grab Sergio and dance with him across the living room. He used to squeal because he liked it so much. Toward the end of the song, the immigrant father has made a gift he's planning to give to his daughter. Someone approaches him and asks to buy the gift. The father sells it in order to pay for food and shelter. The next day he realizes he's found the thing that will ensure a future for himself and his daughter.

I told Sergio about that part of the song. I told him about immigrants and explained to him that his own father was an immigrant of Mexico and that he was doing the same thing as the man in the song. His father had a flooring business and he was doing the best he could to make sure that Sergio was taken care of. He loved hearing that.

After *Ragtime*, I wanted to see what other musical I could show him to see if this genre was something he was interested in. I couldn't think of one because I loved so many, I didn't know how to pick. One day, my sister and I were on the couch watching TV and started watching a movie called *Mr. Holland's Opus*. We had no idea what it was but we decided to leave the channel there. Part of the storyline is that this music teacher, Mr. Holland (played by Richard Dreyfuss), is married and has a deaf child. Mr. Holland thinks his son is incapable of sharing something that he loves so much because he can't hear the music. There's a scene in the movie where Mr. Holland finally understands that he was wrong and decides to make amends. There's a concert at the school and Mr. Holland decides to sing "Beautiful Boy (Darling Boy)" by John Lennon to his son, Cole. Up until now, he had made no effort to really learn sign language to communicate with his son, but during the song as he sings, he signs along so his son can see. I couldn't stop crying. At this point, Sergio was so much older than when he had first learned sign language to communicate with us, but to me, he was still my baby boy.

A couple of days later, we were eating and I asked him if he remembered some of the signs he used to use when he was younger, and he immediately started doing the signs for *Mom*, *Dad*, and *milk*. I wish I could describe those moments accurately, but I feel as if the right words to capture them don't exist yet. In those instances, I feel as if I'm removed from myself. I feel light, as if those moments are so pure that they live separately from other memories I've created.

There was a day when Sergio came home from the park we lived next to and he was very upset. A kid had been mean to him. This was something that I had to deal with every now and then. Kids would say crappy things to him and not understand that he was special needs. That day, he came in and started telling me about the boy who had bullied him. He was angry and started crying. I hated when someone made him feel that way. I wished I could have taken away that pain from him, shielded him from it. I was trying to explain to him that he had done nothing wrong and that sometimes kids got mean when they didn't understand something, because it was easier than them letting people know they didn't know something.

I told him I wanted him to sit on the couch because I was going to play a song for him. He sat on the couch and had no clue what was happening. I played the song and the first line I sang contained the words *Close your eyes.* Sergio closed his eyes and started giggling. Then I realized that he probably thought I was going to sing the song from *Ragtime.* I stopped singing and explained to him that I was going to sing a different song to him and he needed to look at me while I did it. He opened his eyes and I started singing again.

I did the scene from the movie *Mr. Holland's Opus* where he signs "Beautiful Boy (Darling Boy)" to his son. I had been memorizing it and had learned how to sign it to sing it to Sergio at some point. I figured I knew when that moment would be and, lo and behold, I was right. I sang the song and signed the words. Once he realized that the line that said "beautiful boy" would repeat, he started joining in with me, singing along and doing the sign for *boy.* I hugged him afterward and told him I would always try and protect him.

Now let's get to the part where I get to stare at Antonio Banderas for multiple hours nonstop. There was a cable network that started showing the movie *Evita* pretty frequently. I was very excited because it wasn't often that I would get to catch a movie musical on a regularly scheduled lineup. I hadn't seen the movie version yet, but the fact that it starred Antonio Banderas, Jonathan Pryce, and Madonna? Well, I was intrigued. I was already very familiar with Jonathan Pryce. He had played the original Engineer in the musical *Miss Saigon* and I used to own a documentary of the making of the musical on VHS, so I was all in for Banderas and Pryce. And, of course, I wanted to know what Madonna would be like as Evita.

I really liked the movie and I do think it was because of Antonio Banderas. He brought a liveliness and a sharpness to the performance of "And the Money Kept Rolling In (and Out)." It just made me feel happy, even though it was about people embezzling money. (People stealing money from other people makes me want to do jazz hands; we all have our quirks.) There was one thing that stood out to me also that made me really love the song. It was that I liked that Antonio Banderas had an accent singing the song and he looked like someone that would play that role. I didn't get to see a lot of brown-skinned people on TV with accents getting to have such a vital role in a movie musical.

I used to watch the movie over and over. For a while, it seemed as if the channel that was playing it would show it at the same time of day, which coincided perfectly with me having just gotten home from picking up the kids at school. All three kids would watch it with me as they ate, and when "And the Money Kept Rolling In" came on, Sergio and I would start dancing. Sergio has always loved to dance. One of his favorite go-to dance moves is the "Walk Like an Egyptian" dance from the Bangles video. He will do that move with any song he hears. Rap? Heavy metal? He breaks it out. *Evita* is set in Argentina during the 1930s to 1950s and in this particular part of the movie, there are scenes of poor villagers getting electricity for the first time, getting access to clean water . . . But if you looked to the side of the television, you'd see Sergio walking like an Egyptian to the song. It was perfection.

Now, back then, Sergio didn't know Antonio Banderas's name, so he would call him "Che" because that was the name of his character. I ended up getting the soundtrack to the movie and would play it around the house, and Sergio would squeal, "Che! That's the Che song! Cris, do you hear it?" He would start humming along to it and would sing out the few words he knew.

Eventually, I ended up moving to Los Angeles to try to pursue my dreams, but came back in 2002 when my mother got sick. When I moved back in with the family, the kids were a little older. My nephew David and niece, Stephanie, were busy doing extracurricular activities while Sergio was obsessed with video games. Luckily, he and I had the same taste in games and spent a lot of time talking about Super Mario Bros.

That second part of my life when I went back to help with the family was yet another very lonely time for me, except it was worse because I found myself in the exact same spot I had been in years earlier. I went into a default mode, doing the same thing I used to do when I first lived with my sister. I talked to no one and focused solely on taking care of the family.

One day, Sergio heard me playing the "Che" song and he got excited and, almost like clockwork, started doing the same squeal and saying the same things he used to say, only now he was maybe four years older, but other than that, it was like time hadn't passed. He started singing along with it like he used to. I remember that moment so specifically because at that time he didn't know how much happiness he brought me. I tried to hide how sad and lonely I felt. I would smile, crack jokes, and laugh as I usually did, but inside, I was really depressed. In that moment, though, his smile and his laugh, as he remembered the time I first taught him about the musical, made me feel as if my sacrifices had been worth it. It was a reminder of how much I loved that kid and how his happiness was one of the few things I cared about.

Courtesy of Julie Alonzo

Sergio and me at our yearly tradition of dancing at the Special Olympics Summer Games. He's showing off his medal because that's what you do when you're great.

My mother's death hit Sergio very hard because he had not dealt with death before and he and his grandmother had been very close. He would come to me and start crying, telling me he missed "Ama." This is one of those times I was afraid of how to deal with him because it's one of those things that don't come with manuals. I could learn how to change a diaper. I could read about his condition and learn what to possibly expect, but one thing you can't learn is how to deal with comforting a child about death. His mother did a great job during that time and I'd like to think I did my best as well. I think that Sergio used to come to me a lot after my mother's death because he connected me with her, since I was the one at home with her all day. Every time he would cry, I would hug him and tell him that it was okay to be sad and cry, but he also had to remember that his grandmother was now in a place where she could always look after him. That used to make him feel good. He would repeat it after I'd say it. "Ama is watching, right?" I would tell him that she loved him so much, I didn't know how she couldn't be.

I make myself available to him whenever he needs me. I have always dropped things and gone to him when he's needed something. An example of that was back in 2016; my sister and I had been talking, catching up on what was going on. I told her I was going to Washington, DC, soon to go to the White House. I was super excited because I was going to meet President Obama. As a kid, I could've never imagined that I would ever have the kind of life where I would end up meeting the president of the United States, and this was obviously something I was extremely excited about, especially because of who I was meeting. I was going to get to meet the first black president of the United States. I cried the day he won the office. I remember seeing it on TV, not expecting to cry, and the moment he came out with his family, I lost it. It was such a huge moment to see a family of color make history like that, and the fact that it happened in my lifetime? I was overwhelmed.

My sister then mentioned that Sergio had a bocce tournament in Bryan, Texas, but she and her husband couldn't take him because they were both working and couldn't get time off. Now, one thing you need to know about Sergio is that he's been playing bocce for years. He likes it a lot and I try to really indulge him in things when he takes a liking to them because he rarely takes a liking to such specific things. I asked her when it was and I looked at my calendar. The bocce tournament was taking place while I was in Washington. I immediately started to see if there was any way I could pull off going. I didn't want to mention to my sister that I was even trying to make a trip to Texas possible unless I knew it was a go. I searched online and realized the only way to make this possible was if I went straight to the airport from the White House. I wasn't sure what time the White House event would end; I was just hoping I would have time to meet the president and then go. I offered to fly down, drive him three hours to the tournament, and stay overnight with him at a hotel. My sister loved that I offered and I changed my flight and booked a trip to Dallas.

I remember the day of the event. I got ready and put on a dress I had bought on clearance because even though I was meeting President Obama, I did not have Obama money. I should mention that this was not my first time at the White House. The first time I went was to speak at an event celebrating five years of DACA (Deferred Action for Childhood Arrivals), which was absolutely the most perfect way to go to the White House for the first time because I have been a supporter of DACA for years. I walked around, taking in every inch of every wall. I kept thinking what a big deal this would've been to my mother, to know that one of her children was at the White House and was going to meet the president. At the same time I was taking in that I was standing inside the White House, there was also part of me that was thinking, *Let's get this show on the road! I got a plane to catch!*

I was eventually ushered into a room with a small group of people that were going to meet President Obama as well. I waited and started getting anxious because it wasn't until I got into that room that I started feeling all kinds of emotions. I remember thinking it was taking longer than I expected, which made me nervous about missing my flight. It was the last one leaving to Dallas for the day, so if I missed it, I missed it. I kept thinking I had to get to Dallas that night to make sure Sergio got to bocce. Then I saw Joe Biden in the room. I had no idea he was going to be there. Then I saw Obama. *Barack Hussein Obama* was standing near me and it was then I had an epiphany. *Oh my Lord, I'm meeting the president!* We exchanged words and I took a picture with Obama and Biden. I walked out of that room wondering if that had really happened and I thought to myself, *You can think about all that on the way to the airport because you have a plane to get on!* I left the White House like Cinderella leaving the ball, but instead of leaving a glass slipper, I had broken a glass ceiling. This girl had come from nothing to achieving something she didn't even know was possible. I met the president because of what I had accomplished. That was amazing . . . Now let's get me to Texas!

I sat on the plane that night, still reeling over what had just happened and excited that I could pull it off *and* make the Dallas leg of my trip. In a few hours, I would go from Barack to Sergio.

The next day, I picked up Sergio and got directions to where we were going and details about the tournament. We had a three-hour road trip to do and I was afraid of getting stuck in traffic, so we left as soon as we could. Once in the car, Sergio and I began talking. Once you get him started, he doesn't stop. He will talk about everything. We started talking about YouTube videos he had been watching, what music he'd been listening to, and everything else was video game related. I usually let him go on and on about what he wants in the car because the thing about Sergio on road trips is that he hasn't changed since he was a baby. He will fall asleep in a second because he gets lulled to sleep by the motion of the car. Within minutes, he was out.

We ended up getting to Bryan early, so I checked into our hotel room. We hung out a bit until we had to report to the field and qualify for finals that would take place the next day. The day was hot and sunny, and then it started pouring rain. We were in the rental car, waiting to see if the rain would go away soon to resume the bocce. While we were in the car, Sergio told me that he had seen my favorite movie ever. I was intrigued because I really don't have a favorite movie, but according to him I did, and he knew which one it was. When I asked him to reveal it, he said: *Evita.*

This moment in the car happened in 2016. I had first watched the movie with him in 2000. Yet he remembered it and started talking about Che. I know it might not be a big deal for someone to remember that they used to watch something with you years prior, but this moment was a big deal to me because it meant that he remembered it fondly. Here was Sergio, an adult male who sometimes struggled with words, who got fed up and threw tantrums, who sometimes had trouble thinking about what he wanted to say . . . and he was talking about watching *Evita*. He remembered the songs. He remembered the dancing. He remembered the singing . . . all of it.

Soon after, the rain let up and we went back to our bocce and were done for the day. We returned the next day and finished up. Sergio said he was tired and couldn't wait to go home. After the finals, he got his ribbon and we left. I always ask him how he feels about how he did and he'll always tell you he doesn't care if he wins a medal or a ribbon, he just wants to go eat. This is how I know Sergio and I are related because I think the exact same thing.

We stopped to eat and then got on the road. I told him that I knew he was going to fall asleep soon, so I was going to play some music for him until he passed out. I played the "And the Money Kept Rolling In (and Out)" song and his eyes got huge. He started saying, "Cris! That's the song! That's the song," and I started singing it, and just as if no time had passed, he started doing what he always did. He started humming and singing out the words he knew. He said it was the "Che" song. After the song ended, he fell right asleep.

This is something I found interesting about his reaction. I realized how great it was to have a movie version of the musical *Evita* for him to learn about Broadway. When I first shared this show with him, I couldn't afford to take him to any show, so I did the best I could. He loved *Ragtime*, but he's never seen the musical, so he doesn't really understand what is happening visually at that point in the story. At least with *Evita*, he had a visual reference. I also liked the idea that whenever he catches *Evita* playing on TV, he will think of me because, again, it's my "favorite movie."

Once we got to his house, I dropped him off and hung out with my sister for a bit before I went to the hotel. She asked me how the trip had gone and I told her it was great. Sergio and I had a lot of time to hang out, we had fun, and most important, he got to play bocce. She asked me how the White House event had gone and I remember, for a second, forgetting that I had actually done that because I was just so happy Sergio had a great trip. Who knew my nephew could make me forget that I had met the first African American president of the United States?

Sergio has been involved in Special Olympics for years now, which means that I have been an active member as well. The events he competes in vary from year to year. Whatever he does, I'm there for it. It's a tradition that I fly down to Texas every year for the Special Olympics Summer Games held over Memorial Day weekend. I rent a car and drive him and my sister to and from his events. One of my favorite parts of the Summer Games has always been the dance they have on Saturday nights for the athletes and their families. Every year I go, and every year I dance with Sergio and his friends until he gets tired and wants to go to Olive Garden. And yes, of course, he walks like an Egyptian at the dance because you have to give the crowd what it wants.

Sergio is one of the best teachers I've ever had in my life. Being able to see moments of joy and happiness through his eyes is different from anyone else in my life. When he gets excited about something, there is just this pure burst of love that makes you believe in anything he's saying. When he gets excited, he just exudes this energy, so much so that he's almost shaking and he has to hug me and say, "I love you, Cris. So much." He reminds me to try to feel joy.

Sometimes I'll listen to "And the Money Kept Rolling In" on repeat and think about how two of my biggest loves, Broadway and Sergio, coincided. It's funny that Sergio calls "And the Money Kept Rolling In" the "Che" song because I like to call it "Sergio's song." I listen to the peppy song and think of so many memories I have of spending time with him. Like when I had to take him to get vaccinated and chase him in a parking lot because he refused to go inside to the doctor's office or how I had to take him to get glasses and he kept bumping into everything because he had his pupils dilated. I guess when I think of those things, it makes me realize that those moments are reasons why I don't have that biological clock telling me to have kids. In a weird way, I feel like I already have them.

"IT WAS A GOOD DAY"
ICE CUBE

I got writer's block writing this chapter. I had been invited to a NASCAR race and decided to go. Ice Cube was there. I took it as a sign to finish the chapter.

A callback to the title of the song . . . There's a lyric that talks about seeing the Goodyear Blimp, and right after I met him, it was in the sky!

started getting really into action movies because I used to see the same movies my brothers saw and they were all about anything that went BOOM! I used to like watching them because of the reaction of my eldest brother, Ruben. If there was a scene where something big happened, he would say, "Ooooh . . ." and try to high-five us. He still loves to high-five and has a cute way of doing it. He sticks his tongue to the side of his mouth and raises his hand. I always high-five him. My other brother, Eloy, *never* has. It's become a running joke. Anytime Ruben thinks something is cool, he raises his hand and I high-five him; he goes to my brother and gets the cold shoulder. It's been over three decades of this.

Everyone in my family loved action movies, except my sister. Julie loved romantic comedies. She was the quintessential teen girl, and speaking of quintessential teen girls, I was thirteen at the time and definitely not one of them. I used to wear my brothers' clothes without telling them because I liked their baggy fit. I didn't wear makeup, I was into rap and hip-hop and loved sports. I was a tomboy.

One Christmas my mother decided that she wanted Ruben and me to drive her up to Dallas to spend the holiday with my sister and her kids. I didn't mind that at all. I loved driving up to Dallas from San Juan because it was a nine-hour journey and I got to see big buildings along the way. The only tall building we had nearby was the big bank in downtown McAllen. When we drove up to Dallas, we would drive through big cities like San Antonio and Austin. I'd get to see downtown areas filled with huge buildings.

Eloy had moved up to Dallas a couple of years prior, and I was looking forward to seeing him because I didn't get to talk to him very much once he moved.

Christmas was never a big gift-giving holiday when we were growing up, mainly because there was no money with which to buy gifts. We didn't really do the Santa Claus thing because my mom had grown up in Mexico and was more familiar with the Three Wise Men instead of Santa and you didn't celebrate the Three Wise Men until January 6 (which is also my birthday, so my birthday was never celebrated either). The concept of gifts was rare for us, but everything changed when my sister had kids and, suddenly, my family went into Christmas overdrive. When my mom and I knew we were going to Dallas for the holidays, we went to El Centro Mall in Pharr, Texas. The best way to describe that mall would be to imagine the kind of stores that would sell ninja swords along with Hello Kitty merchandise. Now, multiply that by ten, throw in a Montgomery Ward, and that was El Centro Mall. There was a toy store outlet at the mall where we'd buy as many toys for the kids as we could afford for Christmas. We liked going to that mall because it was cheap and we were broke. My mom and I used to walk the aisles at the Dollar Store as if it were a Nordstrom, picking up items and evaluating their worth. "It looks like a good nougat roll, but is it worth the dollar? I can get a box of these Little Debbie snacks for a dollar. That could feed us six times."

The drive to Dallas was always the same. We'd start in San Juan and drive for about an hour and forty minutes until we got to Falfurrias. I hated driving through that area because there was a Border Patrol checkpoint there and we never knew what might be in store. I never understood why it was there, considering that it was almost a hundred miles away from the border. It was only recently that I learned there's a law that makes that completely normal (even though it still doesn't make sense to me). My mother and brother had their resident alien cards so we weren't worried about that; it was about getting a nice or rude border patrol agent. Most of our encounters were pleasant, but you'd also get the guys (we rarely got a female officer) who would be incredibly rude for no reason. Sometimes they'd pull us over to ask us more questions. I hated when those questions were for me. Being at the age where you don't have an ID sucked for a kid like me living in a border town because I was used to the Border Patrol asking me questions about what school I went to, what the name of my teacher was, or what activities I liked to do for fun. They would ask me questions like that to make sure I hadn't rehearsed the answers. Once we got through Falfurrias, we'd end up stopping for gas around San Antonio or maybe Austin, depending on the rental car we had and how good the mileage was. We'd pick up some food to eat and keep going until we got to Dallas.

That year, when we reached Dallas, Eloy told me something that caught me by surprise. He wanted to take me for a drive because he wanted to give me something for Christmas. I couldn't understand. I didn't get Christmas gifts. We ended up going to a record store, walked inside, and my brother said, "Okay. For Christmas, I'm going to let you pick five albums of anything you want." I almost felt like I had to look for a translator because I could not understand what he was saying. I could have *any* five albums I wanted? I couldn't think; there was so much pressure! I never got to buy the music I liked. I would usually just take ownership of the cassettes my family didn't want anymore. I wish I had known beforehand so I could've come up with a list. I started going through the aisles looking for anything I could remember that I loved. It was overwhelming. What if I picked my five and, on the way back to my sister's apartment, I remembered the one I really wanted?

The first one I picked was *The Beatles: 1962–1966*, also known as the "Red Album." When I've mentioned this to people, a lot of times they'll ask why I chose that one. It was because it was the way they had been introduced to the world. The tracks on this album were more of the bubblegum sound known in pop music. The harmonies sounded cool. I loved all of them, but I especially loved "We Can Work It Out." That remains one of my favorites because of the tempo changes it has. When the song reaches the middle, it slows down . . . I can feel what the song is about. They *can* work it out. There is a struggle between when the relationship is great and when it's bad.

Before I could make the rest of my choices, I had to ask my brother if the Beatles album counted as two of my choices because it was a double cassette. He said no. [Whispers and raises fist in air.] *Yes!*

The next one I picked up was Billy Joel's *Greatest Hits Volume I and II* (that is the iconic album with the black-and-white picture of Billy). I figured since I was allowed to get double cassettes, I would get the ones I wanted the most. I was going to make Ruben play this one in the car back home.

The third choice was *The Muppets Take Manhattan* soundtrack because it combined two of my loves: Broadway and the Muppets. This movie was amazing. The range in the musical numbers was fantastic. A song like "Saying Goodbye" could move you to tears, but then another one like "Somebody's Getting Married" could have you riled up and ready to celebrate.

The fourth choice was a cassette single of 4 Non Blondes' "What's Up?," which I bought accidentally because I grabbed it by mistake instead of what I thought I was grabbing (which I can never remember). I ended up liking the song a lot, but I always felt like I wasted a choice because it was a single instead of a full cassette.

The fifth (and last) choice I made was Ice Cube's *The Predator*. I didn't really know other songs from the album, but Ice Cube's "It Was a Good Day" was on it and that was all I needed. I loved that song. Rap wasn't something readily available in my hometown, at least not to me. It was so different from anything I had heard. But as rap became more mainstream, the more I got to hear it.

I left that store hugging my cassettes as if they were my children. They were mine. I had my own music. Anytime I was able to have something new that belonged to only me was special; it was a big deal. The fact that I was able to get not one but five different albums was unheard of, and I had gotten them for Christmas. For the first time in my life, I thought that I was finally feeling like other kids got to feel every year of their lives when they got more than one gift.

I was always looking for music that really spoke to me on a deep level, but now I was craving it. My mom had that music in Spanish. For her, that kind of music was called *corridos*. A *corrido* was a song that told a story, like a ballad. Some of them talked about relevant social issues, like poverty or oppression. Many of the songs were about the life of a person from beginning to end. For my mom, these songs were truth-tellers. A lot of times when we'd clean the house, she'd put on a Mexican radio station that would play *corridos* a lot. The lyrics to the songs painted a picture like we were listening to stories on the radio. I'd take the plastic doilies my mom loved off our furniture to dust the dirt from the tabletops as I heard a verse talking about a cowboy who killed a snake to have food to eat. The song would describe the poverty he lived in and how he was fighting for what was right. My mother would say she loved listening to *corridos* because it was reality set to music. I wanted to find my own version of *corridos*.

The truth was, I was starving for a deeper connection to the world I was living in. I was in search of a reality that would merely acknowledge my existence. I was trying to find the people like me in the world of music, TV, and film. They didn't have to look like me; I was looking for people that could speak to things I knew, even if I had to grasp at straws to find them. I had already surrendered to the notion that people who looked like me were really only allowed to sing or act in Spanish, because the only time I would consistently see them was in Mexican pop culture. What a sobering thought to have at thirteen. I just wanted to find a piece of a culture where I felt included because it made me feel like my life mattered. Then I found it: rap and hip-hop. They would become my version of my mom's *corridos* because the rap I ended up gravitating toward served the same purpose my mom had described in the songs she liked: it was reality set to music.

My love of rap started in an interesting way. As a teenager, I used to have a little white AM/FM cassette player my mom bought me at Montgomery Ward. I used to bust it out after school while I did homework in junior high. At this point, CDs were really taking over the music industry, but I was still rocking the cassettes because I was used to having to wait for the "new technology" to become more affordable for my family. I'd come home from school and sit at the kitchen table with my little cassette player next to me. One of my favorite things to do back then was record songs off the radio onto blank cassette tapes so I could learn the lyrics to them before anyone else. I wanted to show off that I knew the words because in those days there was no internet; you really had to put some effort into learning a song. Sometimes if you were lucky, you could find the lyrics in a magazine or they'd come with the album, but a lot of times (especially if the songs were new) you had to figure them out on your own and you were considered so cool if you knew them before anyone else.

There was a song that became huge in 1993 called "Informer" from a Canadian reggae musician named Snow. I couldn't go anywhere without hearing that song. It was on heavy rotation on the radio, and the music video was shown all day on MTV. The pace of the lyrics confused me and made it really difficult for me to learn them. All I could kind of sing was the chorus, "Informer . . . [blah blah blah blah blah blah, insert a lot of words here] . . ." The song was so tricky to learn that MTV had to start playing a version of the music video that had the lyrics showing at the bottom of the screen while the song played. I recorded the music video with my VCR and also off the radio and got to work, trying to decipher what was being said because I was convinced that people at my school would think I was super cool if I figured it out.

It took me about a week to learn it. One day, somebody played the song during lunch and I sang the words along with it and the people eating around me looked at me really surprised. A girl asked me how I knew the words and I told her I had painstakingly memorized them. She was surprised and got a friend of hers to hear me, and that friend got another friend to come over, asking me questions about how I had done it . . . as if I had found a cure for a disease or something. One of the girls asked me if I could write the lyrics to the song and offered to pay me for it. I thought she was crazy, but, hey, I was *not* going to turn down money. She offered me five dollars. The next day, I gave her the lyrics and I put the money in my pocket. After that, other students started asking me for lyrics. I would tell them it was five dollars; they would pay it. I used to handwrite the lyrics in a notebook with pencil so that if I made a mistake, I could erase it easily. I personally didn't understand why people didn't just share my notebook paper with friends, but, hey, it meant money for me, so what did I care?

Eventually I started a business at school where I would sell students lyrics to all kinds of songs that were hard to learn or just really new. If there was a song you wanted to learn the words to, I was the go-to person. It didn't matter if I knew the words or not. The students would ask me if I knew the words to a song and I would always say yes because I didn't want to lose the business. If I didn't know the song, I would tell them it would take me a couple of days to get them the words because I had a lot of homework, when the truth was, I didn't know the song. When that happened, I would come home from school and take out my little cassette player and wait to see if the song came on our local radio station, B104, to record it on a cassette tape. Simultaneously, I'd watch MTV to see if there was a music video I could record off the TV. I would get to work transcribing the words as quickly as I could. Days later, I'd give the student the lyrics and they'd give me my money. Yes, I know that sounds ridiculous, but I was making a good amount of money. I never got an allowance because, as my mom would say, "I allow you to live here. That's your allowance." A song like "Whoomp! (There It Is)" would come out and become a hit not only for Tag Team (the group that released it) but also for me. I realized quickly the songs I would sell the most copies of lyrics to were the ones that had a fast tempo where the words would shoot out quickly. I didn't know if that style had a name, but what I knew was that it was becoming popular.

Then one day, I heard Ice Cube's "It Was a Good Day." My life changed forever. It was a song I noticed a lot of other students at my school flocked to, not just me. They wanted to know the words to it and, honestly, it was the hardest song I had to transcribe because I was unfamiliar with a lot of the terms Ice Cube used in it, so I hoped I was getting them right.

There have been a few times in my life when I hear a song that I know will be important to me, whether I know exactly why at the time or not. This song was one of them. It started with a laid-back vibe (from the Isley Brothers' "Footsteps in the Dark") and immediately broke into Ice Cube describing what a good day would be to him from beginning to end. What I thought was so great about it was how that specific day seemed somewhat mundane as he explained that nothing bad happened and he just got to live his life. That was what made it a good day to him. The kicker was that after describing the entire day, the very last line of the song is him basically implying that it's crazy for him to imagine that a day like that could actually exist for him.

Before I continue, I guess I should explain that since I lived a pretty sheltered life, when I first started getting into rap and hip-hop, I didn't know it had bad words in it. Since I didn't have much access to rap music, I didn't realize the versions I was watching on MTV were not the real versions of the songs. I had no idea that two versions of the same song could exist: the clean and the explicit one. I learned the songs off the TV, so I only knew the clean versions of them. But to tell you the truth, I didn't really even notice the bad words nor did the fact that Ice Cube talked about hooking up with someone to have sex in the song even register with me because I was drawn more to the actual theme of the song. I wasn't allowed to say bad words at home, and I definitely wasn't having sex, so I always thought of it as that was part of what made Ice Cube, Ice Cube. Just because I knew things existed didn't mean that I would immediately be interested in doing them. I mean, if I liked the song "Memory" from *Cats*, that didn't mean I wanted to become a singing cat. Just like that thinking, I merely appreciated the art that Ice Cube had put into that song.

It made me feel like I "got it" on a totally different level. No, I didn't live exactly like him, but my neighborhood wasn't great and I was currently in junior high at a time when I started noticing some kids I grew up with were veering off onto different paths. A few of the kids I used to play with a couple of years earlier were now telling me they were getting jumped into a gang. The high school I was going to the next year had decided to stop letting the students use lockers because of a fear that kids were bringing weapons or drugs onto the campus. Some of my friends were starting to smoke weed and drink. My mom was trying her hardest to keep me from going down what she called "the wrong path," but at times, it was difficult to escape it. Yes, I was a nerd, but I also found myself dealing with the environment I was living in. I had to get into fights with girls to defend myself, sometimes over the dumbest things, like sports. I once had the crap beaten out of me because my class had beaten another girl's class in a volleyball game and I had scored the most points. After PE class, this girl came over to me during lunch and just started punching and kicking me. I was not going to go down without a fight, so I started kicking and punching the hell out of her as she grabbed my hair and kept kicking me. The moment I saw the principal approach, I stopped hitting her and fell to the ground because I wanted the principal to think I never fought back. She got suspended and I went back to class.

Hearing a song like "It Was a Good Day" made me feel like I wasn't the only one that was living the kind of life I didn't normally see on TV. It made me want to imagine what a good day would be for me.

If I had to write about what a good day for me would've been back at that time, it would have to start with me waking up at 9:30 a.m., because that meant I got to oversleep. My mom used to expect me to be awake by no later than 9:00 a.m., and even that was late. She had been raised keeping farmer's hours, so her thinking was that she was indulging us kids by letting us sleep till then. After that,

I would have breakfast! It didn't matter what I'd eat, I just normally didn't get to eat it. Food was sparse, so I didn't eat as much in the summer as I did during the school year. When I was a little kid, I would sometimes get white spots on my face from malnutrition in the summer.

After breakfast, in my hypothetical good day, I would get to play or read a book and not have to help my mom clean the house. She used to make us clean (sweeping, mopping, dusting) every day and would inspect to see how good our work was. I used to love reading books and would've loved to have a morning where I could just sit and read. After that, my good day would include being able to go to the mall and buy one thing that was name brand. ONE THING. I didn't care if it was a key chain or socks (even one sock), I just wanted to know what it felt like to own the same things that my friends wore, instead of having to be ridiculed by people for wearing my "poor people" clothes. At this point in my good day, I would want to eat lunch even if I wasn't hungry. I would want to go out, maybe to a fancy place like Red Lobster, which I've only been to once in my life, because the only place we ever went to was Furr's, a buffet-style restaurant that to this day I *still* take my family to when I'm in Texas. After that, I would go see a movie with friends. I rarely got to go to the movies and when I did, I would only go because my siblings took me. I would've loved to have seen what it was like to hang out with friends, maybe even spend the night at one of their houses for these sleepovers I heard so much about. After the movie, I'd get to have dinner. Having three meals in one day back then would've sounded like the premise of a science-fiction movie to me. Was this something that people really did on a daily basis?

At the end of my version of this good day, I would walk into my room, strewn with posters of people I liked hanging on the wall, and close the door. I would lie on my own bed and play music as I got sleepy. This is the part of my version of the song that would elicit a reaction like Ice Cube's at the end of the song when he says, "Hey, wait, wait a minute, fool, stop the shit. What the fuck am I thinking about?" Because aside from having three meals a day, not having to help my mom out, and getting to spend time with friends outside of school, the idea of having my own room was when I knew I had reached the point of fantasy in my good day. Other than the front and back doors, the house I grew up in didn't have any other doors, so there was no space in the house where you could be by yourself. Everyone in my house always saw everyone else's movements, so the mere idea of having a bedroom door to close was ridiculous (yet magical) to me. I wasn't allowed to ever hang up a poster or display anything that would indicate I had any kind of likes or interests because, again, our entire house was a communal space and none of us had a space that belonged to just us. The closest thing we had to a poster was a picture of Jesus Christ that my mom hung in the living room. We all had to live in a house that was devoid of any trace that would imply that any of us had a personality.

I know that when Ice Cube was writing his words, he wasn't writing them specifically for me, but the idea of him having a day that was so uneventful made me realize how special that kind of day would be to me. It also made me realize there were people living like I was. Thinking about the beauty of a day without any worries was something one could only dream about.

This song served as a portal into a world I didn't know anything about. I thought rap was this new thing that had just started and was about to take over the world. I started watching *Yo! MTV Raps* a lot and would get my rap knowledge from that show. I'd hear rap on the radio, but only if the song was a huge hit because we had one radio station (B104) that would only play the big hits, which meant they'd rotate about ten songs over and over for months on end. I went to the library and looked up rap to learn about the background. I went to bookstores and read rap articles in magazines (I had no money to buy them). It was only after researching that I realized rap wasn't a new thing. In fact, it had been around for decades at that point. This was one of the things that used to frustrate me the most about living in a tiny town on the US–Mexico border. It was so hard at times to have access to things that a lot of the country was experiencing in real time. It would make me wonder if the things I was getting into were still relevant to the "real" world. I realized that I had a lot of catching up to do with this world I had just discovered. There were so many basic facts I had to learn. I had no idea Ice Cube had been in a group called NWA or that one of my other "new" favorite rappers, Dr. Dre, had been part of it too. I was working backward to learn some of the history of this genre I really liked, while also trying to immerse myself in new stuff that was coming out.

It's also important I mention that no one in my family cussed. In fact, I'm the one that cusses the most, always have. I didn't cuss at home, but at school . . . I cussed like I was being graded on it. My siblings, on the other hand, hardly ever do. On a rare occasion when I've heard them go off, I usually freak out for a bit because it feels as if I just heard Winnie-the-Pooh call me a slut; I don't know how to react. I never said a bad word near my mother, though. I would've felt terrible if I had. My mother had raised us to be respectful toward adults, and by her standards, that meant not saying bad words in front of them. (PS: It doesn't bother me anymore, by the way.)

I remember when I played the Ice Cube cassette my brother had bought me for the first time, and realized that the album had so many bad words: THAT was how I found out rap had bad words in it. I had accidentally (but thankfully) bought the explicit version and I loved it. Unfortunately, my mom walked by when I was listening to it and I got scared because I thought she'd get mad at me. "And what is that?" she asked, but in Spanish (*¿Y qué es eso?*). My mom couldn't speak English, but she knew the bad words. Side note: You ever notice that when people know a couple of words of a foreign language, it's usually the bad ones?

While it did surprise the hell out of my mother, I was surprised she didn't tell me to stop listening to it and walked away once I told her it was just a song I liked. This is something I didn't understand at the moment but would look back and appreciate about her. My mom didn't actually care what I listened to or what I watched in regard to it being "vulgar" or "violent" or anything because it didn't affect me as a person. My mom never understood why people on the news would complain about how a video game or an album could drive people to do things. Occasionally when we'd see stories like this, and I translated what was going on, she would say, "You play those games and listen to the music and you don't want to do those things. You like the game with the plumber [she was referencing Super Mario] and I don't see you fixing things around the house . . ." I appreciated my mom understanding that what I liked helped define me as a person but didn't define my actions. It also made me understand that while I thought I knew her, the truth was, there was a part of my mother that always surprised me. I had assumed a devout Catholic, Mexican woman would forbid me to listen to rap because of the bad words.

I loved "It Was a Good Day" so much that I got into a fight over it in eighth grade. I was in drama class and this guy who was really into grunge rock started talking about how rap was a fad and would eventually become obsolete.

When I heard that, I immediately asked him to explain himself. He said rap was like boy band music. People liked it because it was different, but in the end, it wasn't going to last. I told him he was wrong. Rap and hip-hop were not going anywhere and, in fact, we would become exposed to more of it. I told him "It Was a Good Day" was a great example of how huge rap was becoming because that song was the one students asked me to give them the lyrics to the most. We got into a fight about it and the teacher broke it up. I knew this guy was wrong. It only made sense that, in two years, this same guy would become the closest ally to my high school bully. Looking back at this, I realize this argument might've been this villain's origin story.

Throughout my life, this song has been the one I play when I feel that I have had a good day. It's a song I play when I'm driving around my neighborhood and have a moment when it hits me that I actually live in Los Angeles. Thirteen years of living here and it still doesn't get old to me. It can come out of nowhere. There could be a nice day where the sky is clear and I make one turn and see the Hollywood Hills looking down at me. It all looks so beautiful. I can't believe that not only have I been able to survive living in the city, I've been able to thrive in it. It serves as a reminder of how far I've come. From growing up and trying to survive in my tiny town to living in one of the biggest cities in the country and not having to worry about how I'll find food. My good days never have to be amazing; at times it just means that it was a normal day that sparks a special feeling about it out of nowhere.

The dynamic of my family was not average. You had parents and children living under one roof, but there were also other relatives that served different purposes, like me. I was "the aunt" and, yes, I am well aware that many people have aunts. The role I play in my family is a different kind of aunt. My job in the family was to be a second mother to my sister's kids, and help raise them.

I found that to be the same with a lot of the immigrant families I grew up with. I think in part this aunt role was a fairly common one I grew up seeing a lot of due to the archaic views of gender roles many people in my neighborhood were taught. The women were taught we were the ones responsible for looking after the children, even if they didn't belong to us. It goes back to the idea that women are supposed to be "the homemakers" while the men are "the everything else" of the family. The roles were apparent when my brother-in-law's family would come over to hang out on the weekends when I was living with him and my sister. The women sat around the kitchen and gossiped while they cooked or ate and the men were outside drinking. The kids would run around inside the house and wouldn't dare bother the men. The only time the kids went outside with their fathers was when their mothers wanted them to do something and they didn't want to listen to them. They'd go outside because they knew their fathers would go against their mothers' wishes and they would get what they wanted, because again, women were seen as the submissive ones. If I had a choice, I would've picked to be outside drinking beers with the men, but there was no choice for me. I couldn't drink a beer because the women couldn't drink alcohol with the men. Then who would look after the children?

I am thankful I was there for my nephews and niece, but there was always a piece of me that wondered if they were ever aware of what I sacrificed to be there for them. There have been moments when one of them has asked me why I'm not married or why I live alone. I always say the same thing: "I guess it just hasn't happened for me yet." What I wish I could say is, "I made a choice years ago that your happiness and well-being meant more to me than my own. I wanted you to have a shot at a future I couldn't have, and that made me stick around. I stayed because your mother helped raise me. I helped raise you, and hopefully me being here means that we can break the cycle of that kind of sacrifice and you can go and live your lives, whatever that may be." But again, I just say, "I guess it just hasn't happened for me yet."

I want to make it clear that I have absolutely no regrets about how things happened for me. It's not as if I didn't eventually end up chasing after my dream; I just had to put it on hold. I am very grateful to have been able to serve my family in the same way they watched over me as a kid. I think the struggles I went through with them have made me appreciate everything I've gotten on a different level because I am well aware of what had to happen for me to get those opportunities. Looking back, I remember how I just wanted a sign that felt like it was all worth it because sometimes when I was by myself, it was hard to see if it was. As the aunt, I didn't get the hugs and kisses that a kid gives their parents. I just hoped that one day I would get a sign that made me feel like what I sacrificed didn't go unnoticed. Eventually I did.

So, the year is 2010 and my nephew David is graduating high school.

David is great. When he was a kid, he was obsessed with peanut butter and jelly sandwiches. He thought I made the best ones and would always ask me to make him some to eat. He's the kind of guy that could eat the same thing every day and never get bored of it. We both collected sneakers and loved rap (we still do), so even when I moved away to Los Angeles, we would stay connected by telling each other about what sneakers we were getting and what rapper we were into.

The day of his graduation, he asked me if I would mind driving him to the ceremony. It was taking place at a college that was an hour away from where he lived. I was really flattered that he would want me to drive him because I assumed he would want to drive himself there or go there with friends. I told him I would. During the graduation ceremony, I felt like *my* child was graduating. I have been present for all of my nephews' and niece's most important moments of their lives and it's always the same overwhelming feeling that washes over me. I look at them and feel such pride for everything they're doing. I wish my mother (their grandmother) was there to see how her sacrifices made those moments possible. I look at their faces and remember them as babies. The love I have for them is something I can't explain. If I had to shorten my life to lengthen theirs, I would in a heartbeat, without question.

After the graduation ceremony ended and we had all taken the obligatory family photos where no one looks comfortable, we walked back to our cars because we had to go and do our mandatory celebratory dinner at Olive Garden. I got into my nephew's car and remember looking at him as he sat down. It was a milestone and I was there with him. I felt love. He lowered the windows (his AC didn't work) and said he wanted to play a song while we drove away, and without him knowing my history with it, he decided to play Ice Cube's "It Was a Good Day." He thanked me for driving him to his graduation and told me he was very happy I was there with him. The moment the song started playing, I smiled and tried to hold back the tears I was feeling. I remember the sun hitting the car and blinding me through the rearview mirror, which I had to adjust as I made my way out of the parking lot. It was a magical moment when I felt like maybe, just maybe, that was the sign I had been looking for. David wasn't someone who told you how he felt.

It had all been worth it. The years I had devoted my time to them had not only been worth it, it had been necessary. Now, as adults, the kids reminisce about things I used to do for them and it makes me feel so good that they remember. I carried out the promise I made to my mother back when I was a child, and still do to this day. I am there for my family whenever they need me. I will do whatever I can for them to give them the things my brothers, sister, and I couldn't have when we were younger, because it takes a village to raise a child. In our family, it literally was a village. The village in Mexico that our mother was from helped shaped my family into what it became.

UPDATE: While writing this book, I was really feeling stressed and decided to accept an invite from NASCAR to attend one of their races to distract myself for a bit. At the race, I ended up bumping into Ice Cube himself and taking a picture with him as the Good-year Blimp flew over us, just like how he wrote about it in the song. I couldn't stop laughing like an idiot, thinking, *How much more obvious of a sign could I get that I need to write this book? I'm literally having a "good day," standing with the man who wrote THE song about it.* As I walked away from him, I thought, *I can't believe today was* that *good of a day!*

"LOSE YOURSELF"
EMINEM

The new reina of comedy.

This is a selfie I took based on the original artwork the network wanted to use for my show. I begged them to remove the *quinceañera*-style tiara and the Spanglish. I wanted the show to be seen like any other sitcom.

This is the chapter where I teach everyone how to be famous—but first let me talk about "Lose Yourself." This song is one of my favorite songs of all time, and it is by Eminem, who wrote it for his movie *8 Mile*, which was based on his life growing up in Detroit. I've said this time and again: I am not saying that I had a similar childhood to the rappers I loved listening to, but I did listen to them because they seemed familiar to me.

The song starts with a gritty sound, as if it's on vinyl. Then a quick guitar kicks in as Eminem starts asking a question about what you would do if you had ONE chance to seize everything you've ever wanted. Would you go after it or would you let it slip? It's also one of the questions I've always asked myself. What would I do if I had only one shot to make it? Although I had been chasing my dream my entire life, I rarely thought about what would happen if I actually attained it.

The truth is, I struggle with really bad anxiety and even worse social anxiety. I know it might be hard to believe, but I have a really hard time dealing with people. I panic a lot, and always have. There's not a day that passes when I don't regret everything I've said because I question everything about myself. In fact, I hate being in front of crowds, which I know makes no sense considering what I do for a living. I love acting, I love stand-up, I love writing . . . I love the way I feel when I get to do it. Every time I am onstage, I feel like I am home because I am living my dream. All the same, I get terrified every time I go up there. I have frequent nervous breakdowns and panic attacks because I am scared of seeing people. I never think I'm good enough and always think that people will find out that I'm not very good.

In a way, I think the fact that I'm so hard on myself and never think I'm good enough has helped me in my career because I try to hold really high standards for myself, meaning I'm very picky about what I do. However, I'm also incredibly fearless because I've got nothing to lose.

Okay, so this is the part where I tell you that the first line of this chapter is a lie: I'm not really famous and I'm sure my version of success is completely different from everybody else's. I'm at that point where a handful of people might know who I am, but I still get asked if I work at Target when I'm there shopping. I consider myself successful because I can pay my bills doing what I love. I do get asked a lot about how I was able to do things, how I got my TV show, how I got to do this or that, and I never know what to respond with because I honestly have no idea how any of it happened. It was never planned. I've never really gone into detail about what I've gone through and I figured maybe I'd write about it so that people would know that it took me years to get to where I am. It wasn't a random stroke of luck. It was never giving up, and I'm still far from over.

I've already written about my love of theater, but I haven't really explained my jump from doing stand-up to getting a TV show, so let me start from there. I think my family thought I was done chasing after my acting thing after my mom died. It was kind of like "Well, you moved away but ended up moving back because you didn't 'make' it," which couldn't have been further from the truth. I was always seen as the one in the family who could stop her life and help them when times were tough, but I wasn't ready to give up on my dream. How could I give up on my lifelong dream if I hadn't spent a lifetime chasing after it? That's one thing I've never understood about dreams. So many times, I meet people who say, "I'm going to give myself until I'm [insert age here], and if nothing happens, I'll do something else." I always want to tell them they should go to their backup plan now, then, because I always felt like this dream I wanted to pursue was my job. The job was to chase the dream and, if I had to, I could always have a day job to support the chasing of this dream, but overall, it was *always* about my dream.

I had too much riding on it. I had invested too much time. Every time someone asks me what I would be doing if I wasn't doing stand-up or any kind of acting, I always respond with "I have no idea. I don't know how to do anything else with my life." There was never an option of me *not* doing it in some kind of capacity. I know it seems extreme, but really, this thing has lived within me my entire life. I couldn't see myself doing anything else.

One thing I have noticed is that while my dream has always been the same, throughout the years it has also taken on different versions of itself. The first thing I wanted to be when I was a little girl was president of the United States. People told me I was dumb for wanting that and that I didn't have a chance. Four years later, I fell in love with Broadway and dreamed of being onstage doing musicals and plays, and again, people told me I didn't have a chance. I never understood why people said this to me; looking back, I have to say, it still infuriates me. Why on earth would anyone tell a child they are limited to what they can accomplish? Maybe it was because most of the people in my neighborhood were poor and that made them think that my dreams seemed comical because they were so foreign to them? What I believe those people failed to understand is that sometimes you can try to suppress a dream, but if it really lives within you, the faith and belief in yourself will always beat out anyone who says no to the dream.

So, before I knew stand-up was a job, I tried to get into theater. I'd audition for shows, and I booked a couple of them but quickly hit a ceiling. When I was eighteen, a voice teacher told me that, as a Latina, I could shoot to be cast in *West Side Story* or *A Chorus Line*. This was back in the nineties. When a teacher tells you that you will hit the peak of your career after two shows, it can crush you. Luckily for me (being sarcastic), I didn't have the chance to wallow in my feelings because, soon after, I had to stop chasing after my Broadway dream because of family obligations.

Eventually, I ended up moving away to go back to try to chase my dream again . . . At least that's what I thought I was going to do. I roamed from St. Louis to New York City, trying to figure out what to do next, but again, that try was quickly squashed when my mother called to tell me the doctor told her she was sick. Once again, I had to stop everything I was doing, move back to Texas, and now help take care of her. Okay, putting dream on the back burner . . . again.

During this time, I couldn't really do anything to pursue my dream because I was living back in my hometown of San Juan. There wasn't a lot of Hollywood business going on there. I ended up working as a server for a chain restaurant that I would rather not name, but let me just say that it's an Australian-themed steakhouse. The owners were lovely people who wrote their own birthday song with verses that implied we had to sing it in an Australian accent. I always wanted to remind them that we lived in a border town right next to Mexico. No matter how hard we tried to do the accent, our customers would probably remember that we weren't in Australia. My mother was happy that I was home and had stopped trying to do "whatever it is I was trying to do." Little did she know, I wasn't done yet.

I remained by her side until her last breath. Soon after that, I didn't know what to do with my life. I needed a job in the worst way. I ended up responding to a help-wanted ad in a Dallas paper from a business that was looking for someone to answer phones and do office work.

When I got to the place to fill out an application, I discovered the job was at a comedy club. I instantly wanted that job. I had loved watching stand-up growing up. My brothers and I loved it, though I had no idea that it was a real job people could make a living at. So many great stand-up comedians made it seem as if all they were doing was saying things that had just come to their minds, so I had no idea the work that went into crafting a set. Everyone in my family had a history of working jobs that demanded slowly killing your body, ranging from double shifts at a restaurant to construction to working in fields for very little money. I couldn't believe that stand-up comedy was a job because it just seemed fun and made people feel good through laughter.

I ended up getting the job and became the office manager. The first comic who worked the club after I got hired was Mitch Hedberg. I stayed and watched his set and couldn't stop laughing. He was brilliant. I started staying to watch the comics every week, loving the fact that I had access to come to the shows for free because I worked there. I started slowly befriending some of the comics, not in a "Hey, we're best friends now" kind of way, but if they came to the club more than once, we would say hi and maybe have a beer.

Once I got to know some of them, a handful started telling me I was funny. I told a small group of them that I had lived in Los Angeles, had tried to pursue acting, and now lived in Dallas. I mentioned I had moved back to take care of my mom and how I had just stayed there. We would then start talking about Los Angeles. Some of the conversations made me miss California. It made me miss what I had been trying to do. It made me miss the struggles because I was struggling for a good reason: to try to chase the dream. After a couple of stand-up comedians who I was a fan of told me I should try to do stand-up, it stayed in my mind. Was I dumb for considering it? Would I be any good at it? The more I thought of it, the more it called to me. If I wanted a real chance, I would have to create that chance for myself. I realized that stand-up was that thing. I could make people laugh with words I had written. I finally came to this epiphany that if I was *ever* going to have the chance to perform, to be in anything, I would have to make the opportunity happen for myself. It would be the only way.

I started doing stand-up in Dallas. There was a comic named Dean Lewis who taught classes at the club I worked at. He would come in to teach while I was wrapping up business things for the day, so we would cross paths and start talking about stand-up. I knew his class ended with a graduation show at my club, so I ended up taking his class to get some kind of idea of how it worked. My first stand-up set ever was Labor Day 2003.

I really started getting into stand-up. I liked performing onstage, I loved writing the jokes. It really became something I looked forward to doing all the time. I ended up meeting my first (and only, so far) boyfriend, Steve, in stand-up. He was also a comic, which I liked because he knew what it was about. I was in my mid-twenties when we started dating and it just kinda happened. We hung out one night after we had done an open mic and we didn't stop hanging out for the next eleven years. Since we broke up, we've remained very close. He's one of my best friends.

Just because I worked in a comedy club didn't mean that I got all this stage time there. In fact, it was quite the opposite. I had to go and do the open mics like everyone else because the club saw me as the office manager, not a comic. I'd get off of work at the club around five o'clock and try to hit spots I could find to work on my material. There were people who noticed how quickly at ease I was onstage, and that was true, but it was because no one knew that I had a theater background. It was about six months into doing stand-up that I was at the club about to leave my shift for the day. I left my notebook on the bar while I went to tell the box office worker something. When I came back, the stand-up comedian who was headlining that week (and selling out) was reading my notebook. I got instantly offended and took it out of his hands. He asked me whose notebook that was and I said it was mine. He said he thought I was funny and asked me to do a guest spot that night at his show. I said no.

I know, I know . . . Why would anyone say no, right? Isn't this what comics want? A shot? Why would you say no to a shot? But I was too new in the stand-up world and I didn't think I was ready to do a guest set at the comedy club where I worked. People remember first impressions. I thought about it and thought that if it was meant to be, my chance would come when it was the right time. So I thanked him and said no.

I was really getting into a stride with my stand-up. Well, as much as you can get for being brand spanking new. I would frequent an open mic in Dallas at the Backdoor Comedy Club, a local club run by two Dallas comics, Linda and Jan. What I liked about this club was that they made you work clean, so I started doing stand-up really clean. The idea behind this was that you always wanted to be able to do a set on late-night TV, so you had to have the ability to work clean.

A year passed and the same comic who had asked me to do a guest spot came back into town and remembered me. He asked me if I was still doing stand-up and I said yes. He asked me if I wanted to do a guest spot that night and I said yes. By this time, I had been doing stand-up for a year and a half and felt comfortable doing five minutes. That night I did well enough that the comic asked me to open for him in San Antonio the next week, then El Paso, then Austin. Once in Austin, I thanked him for letting me work the weeks in Texas and wished him well. He asked me to leave my job at the comedy club and become one of his openers full-time. I had no idea what to do.

I was conflicted because our styles were different and I wasn't sure if I wanted to do that. A lot of the comics told me I was stupid if I didn't take him up on the offer. This was my chance to have my

move to Los Angeles paid for and to work full-time doing stand-up.
I decided to take a chance and go for it. I moved to Los Angeles and
went on the road with him for the next two and a half years.

Life wasn't great during that time. I was the only woman on the
road and it was tough. I wasn't the only opener the comic had and I
ended up sparring with a couple of them. One in particular liked to take
jokes from other comics and pass them off as his own. I took that very
seriously because I didn't do that. I would call him out on it but realized
that he was never going to listen to me, so after a while, I stopped saying
anything. I started getting depressed because I wasn't doing the stand-
up that I wanted to be doing. I was part of a circus and I hated myself
for it. I felt like I had sold out. I had to hide a lot of who and what I was.
For example, I've always been a geek, a nerd. I loved playing Scrabble
and I had a handheld version of it in which you played against a computer. I loved that game. Very early on the tour, I was playing with this
game and the guys started making so much fun of me for using it. They
were relentless, they just kept making fun of me. Look, I was used to the
vibe where everyone made fun of one another. The busting-balls aspect
of hanging out with comics is totally understood, and trust me, I like
taking part in it myself. The thing that started feeling weird was when
it seemed to just flip a switch and become cruel. I realized that in order
for them to stop, I had to stop showing what I was into. I had to really
withhold a lot of who I was and become more like them. I started drinking a lot during that time to make me forget about what I was doing.
Days started to run together, but I still wasn't getting paid enough to
be able to leave the road. I would help sell merchandise for the comic
and would help set it all up. By the way, the other openers? They never
had to do that. Never had to lift a finger, but I did. Before the show, I
would put my iPod on and listen to a playlist I had for before the show.

The last song I would hear before I went onstage was "Lose Your-self." I had to play that song because I was terrified of going out on-stage. I wasn't doing jokes like the kind I wanted to do. I had made myself a version of something I wasn't, just to be able to get by work-ing with these guys. I used to play that song because it reminded me that this was my shot, my ONE shot to do what I wanted to do, and I couldn't throw it away. I'd play it every single day, every time I was about to walk onstage. I kept telling myself that my love of this dream was bigger than my fear of the people.

Then it happened. One day I woke up to see that the comic I opened for went viral and for all the wrong reasons. He and another comic had gotten into it at a comedy club and my boss had been accused of stealing jokes. Within a day or two, I found myself in the middle of a scandal. I had never used my boss's name to get ahead—in fact, I always tried to get things on my own—but during this time, people knew I opened for him, and instantly, I was seen as the plague. Nobody wanted to touch me because of my connection with my boss. That was the bottom line. I didn't know what to do. I worked with him for a couple more months, and one night in down-town Atlanta, I thought to myself, *What the hell am I doing? I hate where I am right now. I can't stay here. I have to save myself.* I was out drinking with the tour manager, and that night I decided I'd had it. I hated myself so much. I hated what I had become. I knew that if I was going to have any chance at saving myself, I was going to have to leave the bad place. That night, I went down the row and told everyone from that tour bus off, one by one. I told them all how I felt about them, got on a plane, and never spoke to them again.

That was in 2008. When I walked away, I was so proud of myself and so scared. I didn't know what I was going to do next with my life, but I knew that in order for me to have a fighting chance, I had to try to save myself. I fell into a deep depression for the next two years. I spent my days in bed, crying. My boyfriend at the time (yes, still the same one I had met in Dallas) took care of me. Getting out of bed was a big deal for me. I couldn't get any work. The few times I could get a set, I always begged the bookers of the shows to not mention that I opened for my old boss and they still would include it in my intros, so I would walk up to a booing crowd. I had no idea when it would end.

After a while, a friend of mine introduced me to a college agent. The agent was looking for new comics to submit for NACA (the National Association for Campus Activities), the organization that books acts to perform at colleges across the country. He told me that if I submitted a five-minute set and a check to cover the submission, he would send it in. I figured I'd take a shot. I had nothing to lose. Within a couple months, I found out I had been picked to showcase at a NACA in Wisconsin. Working the college circuit is how a lot of people get their start (if they get lucky), especially stand-up comics. If you get booked, you travel across the country performing at schools that are celebrating freshman orientations, homecomings, graduations, anything you could think of. I wasn't really sure if I was going to be good at any of it, but I figured this was the first glimpse of hope I had felt in years, so I had to push forward. I went to the showcase and, surprisingly enough, ended up booking a lot of shows. I can't remember how many exactly, but the college agent said I had booked the most out of anyone, and I thought, *Hell. Maybe I will be able to make it through this depressive lull?* Knowing that I booked all of these college gigs was a great thing until I realized I had to have money coming in to get to these shows. It's deceiving because it looks like you can make money in the college market, and trust me, once you build up to it, you can, but for me, starting out was painful.

When I first started booking colleges, I was making about a thousand dollars a night. Sounds great, right? It is . . . except I wasn't working every night and I had to use that money to get to the school. Travel, I learned quickly, wasn't included. Some of the colleges were in the middle of nowhere and I had to fly into the closest airport I could find, but soon realized I could save a couple hundred bucks if I flew into a larger airport and rented a car to drive to the school. There were times when I would break even getting to the college or even owed money from my trips because I also had to pay my agent a commission.

Pretty soon, and for years to come, I began touring by myself in rental cars across the country. I played all throughout Wisconsin, Iowa, Illinois, North Carolina. I was lonely. I had no one to talk to. I would call my boyfriend, but back then (and mind you, this was 2011 to 2014) there were many chunks of the country that I didn't have cellular service in. Sometimes I would pull off to the side of the road and start bawling, wondering what the point of it was. The unfortunate/fortunate thing was that I was becoming really popular in the college circuit, so I was busy and could pay bills, but I couldn't really break even.

In 2012, life was pretty bad for me. My boyfriend and I were broke, even though I was working my butt off doing these college gigs. We were trying to make it work, but I told him there was no point. I thought we should move back to Texas. I had given it my all, we both had, but it wasn't working. It wasn't enough. He and I decided to drive to Texas to visit family for the holidays (and for me to possibly tell my family I was giving up) when I got a call from my college agent. I had been accepted to NACA Nationals in Charlotte, North Carolina. That specific convention was the big one because so many schools from all over the country would attend it. I told him I didn't have money to go to the national convention; I was completely broke. He said he thought it was worthwhile. I talked it over with my boyfriend and we decided to let it ride. We already had nothing; how much more of nothing could we have? I cashed in all my miles to get a plane ticket and I used award points for a rental car and a hotel room. I was going to give it one more college try (which I had dropped out of, so maybe I should use a different phrase).

I had been picked to emcee a showcase, which meant that instead of doing only a five-minute set, I also had to introduce acts after I did my set. It meant that I had to do more time. I was terrified because I had so much riding on this. This moment *was* the Eminem song. This was my last shot. If it didn't work, I was done. I popped in the song and waited for the showcase to start. It was in a big venue. I went onstage and introduced myself and did my set, then introduced the next performer. This went back and forth for the entire show, and at the end of the showcase, I reminded everyone what booth I was at so they could come and see me. You see, after the showcase, the schools would visit you at the booth your college agent was at and give you slips of paper if they wanted to book you. It was a marketplace, and after every showcase, it was open for an hour to give schools enough time to find the performers they wanted.

After the showcase, I headed over to the marketplace a little late because I had to go to the bathroom. As I walked in, I saw a long line of students waiting. I couldn't imagine who it was for, and when I got to my booth, I realized it was for me! The kids were lined up to see me. *What?* I couldn't believe it. I was shocked. School after school was coming over and giving my agent these slips of paper saying they wanted me to perform at their campus. What was happening? I couldn't understand it. After the marketplace hour was done, my agent told me he thought I should come over to the next two market-places that were scheduled later in the day because he thought more schools would want to meet me; and I did just that. Now, remember, I have really bad social anxiety, and being around so many students was freaking me out. I kept having to walk away and try to compose myself because I couldn't tell anyone what I was feeling. I had no idea I had anxiety back then. For the rest of the day, I was a little celebrity at that convention. Everywhere I went, people wanted to stop and say hello and take pictures with me.

That night, my agent told me he wanted me to stay another day to meet more students. I told him I couldn't because I didn't have the $150 to pay to change my flight. He said he thought it would be worth it, so I called Steve and told him. He said that if my college agent thought it was worth it, maybe I should do it. We borrowed the money from his parents and I paid to change my flight. That night, Steve and I calculated that if I could book nine college gigs, we could get by and not have to move back to Texas. All I wanted was *nine*.

The next day, I walked into the convention center and imme-diately noticed people were high-fiving me. They had just had the meetings where schools would determine who they wanted to book. If more schools within a certain area were interested in the same per-son, they got a lower rate for the comedian because so many schools wanted to book that performer. I had no idea what was happen-ing until I found my agent. That is the moment he told me that I had booked *131* schools for the upcoming school year. I remember hearing him say that but not understanding it. I heard the number, but it sounded foreign to me. Maybe it was because I was hoping I would hear the number *nine* somewhere in that sentence, but hadn't. I think my agent noticed that I wasn't as excited as him and he asked me to do the math on that much work. I still didn't understand, but I knew I had to call Steve to tell him what was going on. I was standing in the middle of an empty hallway.

I'll always remember that moment. He answered the phone. He had been waiting to hear if I had hit the magic number nine. I told him what my agent had told me about the schools and the phone went silent. I had no idea what happened. I asked if he was there and he was crying and then I started to cry. We were talking about how that meant we didn't have to move back to Texas; we could stay in Los Angeles and keep working on our goals. I think I needed to have him say those words to me because, in that moment, I remember sinking to the ground, crying on the floor, and thinking that something wonderful had just happened. I rarely felt that way, but right then and there, I felt like it was going to be okay.

The year that followed booking those colleges was ridiculous and unexpected. When I was a younger comic, I wanted things and was always so crushed when I didn't get them. It wasn't until I got older that I realized the things I wanted and didn't get were never mine to begin with. I wanted to focus on keeping my dream simple. I have friends who say they want to be rich and famous. Good for them. I used to try to think like that, but I realized that wasn't who I was. I kept wondering, if their goal was to be rich and famous, how much fame and how much wealth was going to be enough? At what level would they feel they had succeeded?

The next big thing that happened to me was changing agencies. My college agent was let go from the agency I was with, and when that happened, I didn't know what was going to become of me. I didn't have support from anyone there. My manager at the time told me not to worry. He was going to send out emails to see if any of the agents he knew wanted to meet with me. I was nervous. What if no one wanted to meet with me? Five minutes later . . . he got the first email back from an agent who I ended up signing with. At the signing meeting, I met with her and a room full of agents who wanted to help with my career. I remember sitting there in a conference room, not knowing exactly what to do. I started telling them a little bit about myself. I told them about growing up in an abandoned diner, being poor, my mom dying, all the greatest hits, and they just sat there listening. Right then and there, an agent named Eric Rovner mentioned a producer he thought I should meet and pitch my life to as a possible TV show.

This is the part where a lot of people might have been really excited—but I was terrified. I had no idea what I was doing. I hadn't graduated college. I wasn't a known name. I had no clue why anyone would think I was capable of doing this, but . . . I did it. That's one thing I'll say for myself. Most of the opportunities I have had come my way have terrified me to the point of extreme panic attacks, but regardless of that, I still take the terrified leap. I do it because, despite the fear that washes over my body, the love of my dream always seems to take over. I went in and met with the producer and told her about my life. I broke down my stand-up and talked about how it focused a lot on my family and how I had grown up. I didn't think it would lead to anything. I have never had any confidence. I kept thinking to myself, *Why me? Who would want to see me on TV?*

It turned out Conan O'Brien did, actually.

Right after I signed with the new agency, I got my first late-night spot. I was going to do stand-up on Conan's show. I had submitted a set to the booker and he called to let me know I was going to be on it. He had no notes. I was to deliver the set I had submitted the way I had submitted it. At this point, I had been doing stand-up for a decade. There's a saying that goes: It takes ten years to become an overnight success. Well, I wasn't sure about the overnight success part, but it had taken me ten years. I remember doing that set and having it go great. I also remember being so nervous that when I said good night, I mispronounced my own name because I had forgotten it. I always thought I had a difficult name to pronounce. It turns out it's so difficult that even I don't know how to say it.

The producer I had met with saw my Conan set, and soon after, I ended up getting a development deal, which meant that someone thought maybe my life was interesting enough to make into a TV show. I could not believe it.

Things were going well for me and I was having trouble accepting it because things had rarely gone well for me. I wasn't sure what I was doing; I was scared. I listened to "Lose Yourself" a lot during that time in my life. I kept thinking this was my one shot. Everything I had done up to now led to this point of my life. What was I going to do? Was I going to waste it or was I going to take advantage of it? I would think of every struggle, every ounce of pain I have felt, and it pushed me to not quit. I remember thinking to myself how I had to wait until my mother died to actually get my shot because, while she was still alive, she would always take top priority. Now that she was no longer around, I could go after the life I previously had to stop dead in its tracks. I kept thinking to myself that my mother had come to this country and raised a family by herself as an undocumented immigrant for years before she became a permanent resident so that I could be in the position I was currently in. All of the struggles were for this time of my life I had been waiting for. I was not going to let this chance go to waste. I was going to do whatever I could to make it happen. I was going to make the most of my shot.

I was co-creating my show with a writer I had met and liked. We had both been writing the script together on the few days I would be home from doing the college gigs. I was working all the time. We had pitched the show to a network that bought it. We had written an outline and were sent off to write a script for a potential pilot. We submitted the script and waited.

We didn't get picked up to pilot. It was heartbreaking, but I felt happy that we had gotten that far. I had to move on and go back to focusing solely on my stand-up, so I did a weekend of shows in San Antonio. When I landed in Texas, I saw I had missed phone calls from the producer. I called her back and we talked about an idea she had. She wanted to shoot the script we wrote as a pilot to show the network what the show could be. She didn't believe they really understood the comedy as it was written, so why not show them? When we had sold the show to the network, it had come with a penalty, which meant that if the network, for some reason, decided not to shoot a pilot, the studio that owned my show would get a lump sum of money.

The producer said she had a plan but knew it was a long shot. She was going to see if she could convince the studio to let us have that money to use to shoot a pilot. First of all, for those who might be unaware, a TV pilot is not cheap to make. It easily costs much more than a million dollars for just one. We didn't have anywhere near that money; we had about a third of it. If the producer could pull off this Hail Mary, we were going to have to make miracles happen . . . but we did.

I don't know how she did it, but she did it. She got the studio to give us the penalty money. We had weeks to put a pilot together and shoot it. We auditioned people and found a cast. Interestingly enough, there was a moment during the casting process that made me feel uncomfortable. Looking back, I should've seen it as something I would have to deal with while the show was on air. I had sat in on every audition because I wanted the casting to be as perfect as possible. I remember this one specific time right after someone had left the audition room, I was sitting between the producer and the writer I had partnered up with. The casting director was speaking and used the word *sycophant*. She was going to continue her thought but decided to stop, look at me, and ask, "Do you know what the word *sycophant* means?" I looked at her, nodded, and said, "Yes, I do. Why did you think I didn't?" She didn't ask the producer or the writer in the room, just me. I'd like to say I was surprised, but living a lifetime of moments like that, you get used to it, which I think is frustrating and sad.

We needed a set to serve as the backdrop of the house my family would live in and we couldn't afford to build it, so the producer had a brilliant idea. She had a show on the air that was based around a family, so she decided to use that show's set for our own. She asked the crew to help out and move the set around to make it look a little different and, boom, we "borrowed" my home. The other show she produced was still in production, so we were unable to rehearse on the set till the very end, right before we shot the pilot on that same stage.

The day of the shoot came and I was terrified. I kept wondering what the hell I was doing. I had a panic attack, but I knew I had no choice but to go ahead with it. I knew it was a long shot, but, hey, it was a shot. I had nothing to lose. They had already said no to me. What could they do? Tell me no again, but louder than the first time? The moment had come. The actress playing my mother (Terri Hoyos) started and it was my cue to come in and say my first line. It got a laugh. I don't know if I can describe how I felt in that moment.

I had so many things coming together at once. My love for television coinciding with my love of performing connected, and for that second, I felt like I had never felt before. I felt complete. I felt hopeful. I felt nothing but love.

The next day, I had to leave the country to go on a stand-up tour in Canada. I would be gone for two weeks. I figured that I, along with the producers, had done everything we could to show what the sitcom could be. There was nothing left for me to do but wait. Who knew how long it would take: a couple days, a week, a couple of weeks? I had no idea. I tried to put it past me and focus on the tour.

Turns out, I had to wait only a couple of days to hear something. Now, we had been told that no one had money to test the show in front of audiences. That's when they gather people to get their reactions to characters, the story . . . well, basically everything. This is when they figure out if the show has any appeal. The phone call I got was from the producer telling me the studio had suddenly found money to test the show and I had tested higher than any other character in seasons. I had no idea what that meant. The producer had to explain to me that it meant the audience had thought I was likable. Well, that was a good sign.

Soon after those great results, the network suddenly found money to test my show too. Isn't it crazy the luck I had that suddenly, mysterious money kept popping up? The show tested positively for the network too. All of a sudden, it looked as if the long shot became the little engine that could. My sitcom had gone from a no to a possible reality. I couldn't believe it. For the next couple of weeks, I waited to see if the show would get picked up. Every day, I would wake up and read the articles online of what shows weren't moving forward and which ones were still contenders. Every day, I saw mine was still hanging in there. Before you knew it, the time had come for the last decisions before the networks had to go to New York City to announce their lineups for the next fall season. That last day, I got a phone call from the producer. The network had decided to pick up the show. My show was going to be on TV. The first thought that came to my mind was that this was the phone call I had always wanted to make to my mother. The phone call where I finally showed her what I had been striving for since I was a kid. It was a call I couldn't make. She wasn't alive. I sat down and cried for a minute. I just kept thinking, *We did it.*

With that phone call, I had made TV history. I was the first Latina to star in, write, and produce her own network TV show. There had been other women who had gotten their chance to star in their shows, but I was writing mine as well. It was then I realized that, unfortunately, despite it being 2014, it still hadn't been done by anyone else.

I went to New York by myself, which really bugged me. Well, let me correct that. The producers and the writer I had partnered with were going, but I wanted the cast there, too, because they were such an important part of the whole thing. I always wanted my show to be considered an ensemble show. The idea to name my show after me was not mine. I always believed in having the show be a group effort. Why? Because I knew that not everyone was going to like my character—that's just unrealistic. If we wanted to have a great show, every single character on that show had to be likable to people; they had to appeal to different people. I couldn't understand why I wasn't allowed to celebrate that moment with the entire cast.

My trip to New York for the network upfronts was when I first started having to deal with problems I wasn't prepared for. Upfronts was an event that I saw as my television *quinceañera*. It was my first time being introduced to the industry. And this time, I didn't have a team of people to help me get ready to make my "debut." I didn't have a stylist or anyone to help with hair and makeup. I had to figure it out. Oh, I guess I should mention at this point that I was completely broke and hadn't been paid one cent for developing the TV show. I can't explain to you the irony I felt flying cross-country in first class with a dress I had bought online at J.Crew that I was planning on returning when I got back from New York because I needed the money to pay bills. The dress was navy blue and low-cut, a complete departure for me, but I figured that moment was different from anything else in my life, so why shouldn't my outfit be as well? My managers at the time found hair and makeup for me in New York that fortunately had small windows of time to help me get ready. FYI: I still use the same person for my hair to this day.

The day of the announcement, I had to go up onstage with everyone else that had a new or returning show coming that fall. I was the only person on that stage by herself. *Fresh Off the Boat* and *Black-ish* had been picked up along with my show, but mine was the only one that had just one person representing it. I was terrified. As usual, per my anxiety, I had a panic attack before the presentation and I had no one there to help me. The moment I came out, I tried to stay onstage for as little time as I had to, and the moment I could, I ran off.

That night, the network had a party I had to go to. I didn't want to. Parties have never been my thing, but it was required I go.

At the network party, I got a text from my producer telling me that someone really important wanted to meet me and I was expected to go to another party. Basically, the universe was telling me, "Hey, remember how you freaked out a little while ago? Well, we're going to do a sequel of that. You're welcome." I tried to get out of it, but I had to go. It was required.

I hopped into an Uber and went to the other party. Once I got there, I realized the party had already been going for a while. People were having a really good time and most of the people I passed were tipsy. So, before I continue with this story, I have to admit that I am getting very nervous about telling it. I'm writing about panic attacks while I feel one coming on. I have never spoken about this in public and I have to admit right now, I don't know how well I'm going to tell it. This is something I still try to deal with in therapy, so I apologize if I can't go into complete detail. The moment I walked into the party and saw people tipsy, I tried to look for my producer so I could say hello and leave as soon as possible. I hadn't been drinking and it's not that fun when you're the sober one at a party where the majority seems to be loving life. I ended up spotting her in the corner of the room. Great. I had to walk through the entire party to make my way to her. As I tried to reach that corner, two men who were high up on the food chain came up to me and started making remarks about my boobs because my dress was low-cut. I remember one of them saying, "Where have you been hiding those?" That made other men come over and start trying to get handsy. I was the only woman I noticed they were doing this to.

My producer saw what was happening and came over to save me. She grabbed me by the hand and told the men to stop. She took me to meet the person that wanted to meet me. It was another woman who was somewhat connected to my show and I hadn't met yet. She worked with the two drunk men I had been dealing with. I said a quick hello and before you knew it, the men had made their way to where I was to keep trying to have conversations with my boobs. My producer once again told them to stop and ushered me away from them. We walked back to the entrance of the party. I bumped into a male agent from my agency. We told him what had happened and he felt bad. I told him I wanted to leave and go back to my hotel room, but he told me that a small group of people were heading out to another place and he invited me to go with him so that we could end my night on a high note. I didn't want to do that, but my producer thought it would be more helpful to not go straight to my hotel room, where I would be alone and feel bad. I caved in and went off with them to go to another bar. For the rest of the evening, I tried to forget what happened, but I couldn't. I kept blaming myself for wearing that dress. If only it hadn't been so low-cut, I could have avoided this. Looking back, I must say the thought of that makes me cringe. I instantly blamed myself, not the men in question. It was what I had learned through my surroundings my entire life. I now know that I was wrong in believing that, but that night, it was all I could think of.

The next day, I ended up telling my managers at the time what had happened and one of them was instantly livid. He wanted to make a big deal about it. But I didn't. I had never been in this position before and I didn't know what to do. I was afraid that if I brought it up, I would be labeled as difficult and my show would struggle. I also thought I would be messing things up for other Latinas. That's an interesting thing that I have had trouble understanding. In my career, I've always wanted to represent myself, but I found that if I did something, a lot of people would assume that *all* Latinas did it that way. As if I were a mascot for a specific demographic: The Fighting Latina. Part of my thinking (whether it was right or wrong) was that if I was seen as difficult, it would be hard for other Latinas to get opportunities. My managers told me they would not do anything and I flew back home to Los Angeles.

I remember that flight didn't have access to the internet, so I had no access to anyone. When I landed in Los Angeles, I had a couple of voicemails. When I listened to them, I realized that the manager that had gotten upset had said something to a higher-up and it had become an issue. As I said, this incident involved executives who were high up on the food chain. I remember getting angry with my manager because he hadn't respected my wishes, and, honestly, because I didn't want to deal with all of this. Actually, let me correct myself. I *couldn't* deal with all of this. Mentally, I was far from being okay. My manager apologized but said it was important to let someone, this female higher-up, know what had happened because she was a woman and would understand. He told me that this woman wanted to talk to me and would call me at home. I did not want to have that phone call and started panicking while I waited for it because I didn't know how to handle it.

When the phone rang and I picked it up, there was the female executive on the phone telling me she had heard what had happened to me and felt bad. She was very apologetic and understanding. She asked me to tell her what happened and I broke down the story with greater detail. Here's the thing that I thought was strange, though. This woman had been at that party I went to. She was the one I was beckoned to go and meet. I had told her what had happened right after it occurred that night. I didn't know why she was asking me other than the fact that my manager had brought it up. I had told her how I felt in that moment. She then began apologizing to me for the men's behavior and started in about how "boys will be boys" and she understood how I felt. Then she told me about how she knew where I was coming from because she was a woman as well and we both were part of "the sisterhood" in an industry where women had to fight to get ahead. She said all the right words. Then she said the wrong ones. She asked me not to make a big deal about anything that had happened and I realized that the sisterhood talk was her setting me up to ask me to stay silent and not publicly say anything. She said she would get one of the men to apologize to me for what he had done. *Oh, wow, a whole ONE man? Don't spoil me!* There was a moment in that phone call where I felt like I was nothing. There was no honest concern from that woman other than that she knew I could be an issue. Business meant more to her than how I felt. Unfortunately, that was an overall theme I would have to deal with for the year my show was on the air . . .

Things started well on my show. Everyone seemed to get along. I was excited about getting it started. Including myself, there were eleven writers, four of which were Latino. I should mention that those four Latino writers were ones I had personally picked. Then one of the first problems came up. I had to go into a meeting and discuss the marketing of the show. I went into the network and sat in a room where they revealed the "artwork" for my show. It was a picture of me, looking up. Photoshopped on my head was a tiara with eight points, each of which had a letter that spelled out my name: Cristela. The tagline at the bottom of the poster read "Meet the new 'reina' of comedy." I looked at it and thought it had to be a joke. They couldn't be serious, right? Well, guess what? They were. I was terrified. I didn't say anything in the meeting because I didn't know the protocol of how to approach this, so I waited till after I left to talk to the producer of the show, who had also been there with me.

I couldn't understand why the poster had to be so stereotypical. The first thing I told the producer was that I couldn't have that image be the artwork because I was afraid it wasn't something that uplifted the Latino community. I wanted my people to know that I was trying to be honest with my truth and not exploit what we are. The president of the network at the time couldn't understand my problem with the artwork and kept pushing for it, but I kept pushing back. I kept thinking, *What is the point of telling my story if it's already become a caricature from the get-go?* I would rather not do the show than have people think I didn't respect the story I was trying to tell—MY story. After weeks, the network changed the artwork and that was a win for me. I never thought it would be so hard to get that win.

Then I realized the artwork wasn't going to be the only thing I would have to fight for. I had been pitched an idea the network had about talking bus benches they would install in predominantly Latino neighborhoods. The idea was that people would sit down to wait for the bus and I would say something "funny" about them sitting on me and tell them to watch my show. Bus benches. That was their idea of getting the word out. Is this a good time to mention that my show NEVER got a billboard? Not ONE billboard, but . . . I was getting offered bus benches, so that was good enough, right? I hear bus benches are the new billboards! I said no to that too. Then a bigger problem came up. The fact that I spoke Spanish was going to be the biggest fight I would have, and one that I would lose. The network wanted me to do more Spanish interviews than English to promote my show. They thought it was a great way to get Latinos to watch my show. I was trying to explain to them that, once again, my show was in English and I thought focusing on interviews in English would be beneficial. I thought it was strange they thought speaking Spanish was the only way to get people to understand what the show was about. Did they not see that I was Latina and spoke English or didn't they realize I wasn't the only one who was capable of having such a gift?

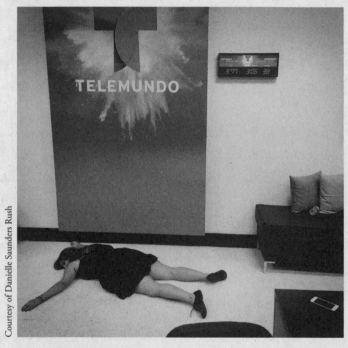

On this day, I did over twenty interviews to promote my show, most of them in Spanish after the network found out I spoke Spanish. This was the last interview of the day.

Let me be clear: I was not saying I refused to speak Spanish. I think the more people you can talk to, the better. My problem was that once I started seeing the culmination of the bus bench idea they had, along with the *quinceañera* artwork and now the string of Spanish-language interviews that were outnumbering the English ones, I wondered what on earth they thought my show was going to be.

My show ended up getting picked up for a full season of twenty-two episodes. While filming, my day consisted of going to rehearsals onstage with the cast, getting notes from the studio and network, and then going into the writers' room to work on the script with everyone else. I was exhausted, but it was a good kind of exhausted. As the season continued, I started noticing I was starting to have problems with people on my show. Sometimes one of them would pitch something that I thought had been overdone by other shows or just thought that it was so outside my character that it didn't make sense, and they didn't like it. I didn't care. I really wanted to focus on the quality of the show more than anything else. As the year progressed, I started talking to the producer of the show about the problems I was having with someone that at one point seemed to be supportive and that I saw as a partner. I was given a card of a therapist to go talk to about my problems. That didn't make sense, but okay. Then the executives kept asking us what we could do to get the ratings up. I kept suggesting they try a novel idea like advertising, but no one paid attention. I ended up getting an idea that I thought would give me free airtime to promote the show. I was going to book myself on *The View*.

I had already done the show once as a guest, and the producers had taken a liking to me, so I figured that I could go on *The View*, hang out with the ladies, and get eyeballs to my time slot. I ended up getting booked to do the show on a week my sitcom was on hiatus. I flew cross-country and did a couple of episodes. I had a great time and I loved the women on the show during that time. You had Rosie Perez, Rosie O'Donnell, Nicole Wallace, Whoopi Goldberg, and Joy Behar. I considered myself very lucky to grace the table with them because I thought all of them were great. They were kind and the episodes were easy to do. After that week, I was asked to come back to host *The View* during the next hiatus week I had. I was hesitant to do it because I was afraid that it would keep me away from the writing of the show. This show was about my life. Shouldn't I be around to write for that? I ultimately decided to go host *The View* because I knew it was for the good of the show.

For the next number of months, hosting *The View* became my part-time job. I would shoot episodes for my show, fly to New York and host for a week. I was slowly becoming a fixture on the show. I was getting a lot of love from the fans. Every time I went to New York, I started noticing that I was getting recognized more. People knew my name. They would stop me on the street and say hi, but . . . it was for *The View*, not from watching my show. They didn't know my show even existed. I remember getting to the point where I was worried that the network would cancel my show in order to have me jump over to *The View*. I didn't want to do the talk show on a full-time basis. I wanted to work on my sitcom. I feared the worst and it was slowly coming my way.

I remember the week I thought my sitcom was dead. I wasn't talking to two of the writers and they were trying to run my show without me. It was a hiatus week and again I had to go host *The View*. That specific week, one of the storylines from the show was that for some reason we would find out that one of our characters who seemed superficial all season long really had a special gift of a photographic memory and was secretly really smart. What? First of all, I had always wanted that character to be very smart. Intelligence doesn't only come from reading books. I believed that one could be smart in different areas. I always said my character in the sitcom and this specific character would be like Elphaba and Glinda from the musical *Wicked*, two smart women from different worlds who end up really caring about each other in an unlikely friendship. I was against the photographic memory thing. Let's do it like we would in real life. Let's get to know what this character is really good at and teach her that she's capable of so much more than what she had been given up to that point instead of suddenly making her an overnight genius. This is how I approached my show, which really goes back to the question Eminem makes at the beginning of "Lose Yourself." If you had one shot, would you let it slip? For me, having a sitcom on TV was the peak of my dream at that point. I had been the underdog and had won. I knew that this might never happen again. The future is uncertain and I had to take advantage of what was happening in the moment. One day, I was in the writers' room and one of the writers had mouthed off at me because he didn't like a note I gave. I took a moment to explain to him that this show had MY name on it, not his. If this was the only chance I got, I *had* to try to make the best of it because once the show was canceled, he could move on and write on another show. I, on the other hand, would have to answer questions about this show for years to come. *That* was why I wanted things done a certain way. For me, this show was not about churning out stories for the sake of filling the time slot. For me, this show was about making sure that people who connected with the show knew that it was trying to be as authentic as I was in real life.

While I was in New York, I kept asking for a copy of the script for me to read and give notes, but they wouldn't send it to me. Finally, on Thursday, I took a flight back to Los Angeles and as I got on the plane, an email popped in. It was the script I had been asking for. I was landing in Los Angeles in the evening and had a table read early the next morning. I sat down and started reading the script. And there, within a couple of pages, was the specific thing I had said

I didn't want. The character was suddenly brilliant and we didn't know why. I emailed them right away and told them how I felt because my flight didn't have internet, so I would have to stew on the plane for hours. During that flight, I was alone in my thoughts. I started thinking about the past year and the things that had happened against my will, like how two writers I really liked were fired from my show despite me not wanting them fired. Or how I had mentioned what happened to me at upfronts to the writers' room one day and one of the male writers instantly said about the male executives, "I don't know. They've always been nice to me . . ." Which is a nice way of saying they really didn't believe me at all. The more I sat there on the plane, the more I knew I had to do something drastic. I had tried talking about the problems I had, but no one was listening to me. I figured there was only one way to do it.

When I landed, I had replies to my email expressing that they heard what I was saying (they didn't) and telling me we would address my notes after the table read. That is what people had started telling me on a regular basis. Nothing was changing. The table read started and I thought, *Well, here I go.* I proceeded to throw the table read on purpose. I tanked it. I read the lines with the disdain I had for them. Everyone knew what I was doing. Afterward, everyone was upset at what I had done. It's funny how when people get treated with the same disregard they give others, they're suddenly offended. I told them why I had done it. I talked to the producers and they said they didn't know that things were so broken. I don't know how they missed it because I was pretty clear about it, but okay. We had a meeting with writers I had problems with and the second show-runner we had, who was absolutely amazing and I loved. In that meeting, I brought up what I thought was a great point about my

show. I had just gotten back from hosting *The View* for a week, something that at that point I had been doing for months, and I pointed
out that they really seemed to like me a lot over there. They liked my
point of view, they liked what I said and how I said it. I was valued
there. Why was it that I wasn't getting that same treatment in my
sitcom if the show was based on my life? I had gotten the TV show
because of my stand-up, which was focused a lot on my upbringing
and family. Why was the thing that got me the TV show not enough
for the TV show? When I was allowed to be myself, people liked what
I was doing. Why wasn't I getting the respect for saying that my show
had to be more like my stand-up and myself?

Things didn't improve after that. At that point, I was waiting
for the show to end the season. I figured if by some chance it got a
second season, there would be so many changes to it, but I also wondered, if my show was canceled, how long was the network going
to wait to call and offer me a job on *The View*? Well, the show got
canceled and I got an answer to my question. Between getting told
that my show was done and getting notice about *The View* . . . there
was a gap of about fifteen minutes. I was getting an offer to become
a permanent host on *The View*. It took me seconds to decide that my
answer was no.

No one could understand why I didn't want to take that offer.
How on earth could I say no to that? I would be on TV every week-
day. I would move to New York City and make money! I could
become famous!! More exclamation marks!!! I told my agents that
I didn't want to do the show because I wasn't done telling my story.
The sitcom hadn't gone the way I wanted it to. I didn't have the support I needed and was told I would get. A talk show was not what I
wanted to do. But . . . but . . . I could be big! I couldn't make people

understand that my goal in this career was not to become rich and famous; it was to be able to do what I wanted to do, to say what I wanted to say in a way that felt true to me and my experience. I wanted to be happy living the dream I had chased since I was a child, and I was only going to say yes to things that felt right.

People kept coming back and asking me if I wanted to reconsider. I didn't. I realized then what a rarity it was for someone to say no to something that others would jump at. I just knew I wouldn't be happy having that job full-time, and as someone who struggled with depression, I knew that inserting myself into a situation like that wasn't good for me. I couldn't explain it well, but after multiple times of getting asked, they moved on and got someone else.

Now that I had no job and no idea what to do next, the network reached out and said they were interested in me developing another show for them. I said no. Again, you might ask why I said no to that. BUT THIS IS WHAT YOU WANTED! YOU WEREN'T DONE TELLING YOUR STORY . . . SO GO TELL YOUR STORY! I didn't want to develop another show. I told my agents, "I don't want to do it. They had the show with the story I wanted to tell. They didn't want that." People kept suggesting I come up with another show just to get me back on TV and I kept trying to explain to them that I would only try to create another TV show if the story was something that I felt had to be told. I didn't want to just concoct an idea that my heart wasn't into because I didn't want people to forget who I was. It just wasn't my style. The thinking behind all of this for me is that when I was a kid, I would watch amazing shows that had heart. They would make you laugh but also make you care. I loved those shows. I always believed that in order for me to make something similar, it would have to have heart because the audience knows when your heart is not in it.

I went back on the road and returned to doing stand-up. I had put it on hold during my sitcom because I wanted to focus on the show. I personally don't think I can do my best work when I try to split my time between two very distinct yet similar worlds. I was so concerned with giving people a stand-up show that was worth the ticket price, I only wanted to go back on the road when I was sure I could give them a solid show. I used my shows as a way to thank people who were fans of the show for having watched it. I would do my set and close the show by thanking them for helping my dream come true. Every time I would mention the show, the audience would clap so loudly and lose it. They would yell that they wanted me to bring it back, but there was no way I could, and now looking back years later, I realize I wouldn't have wanted to bring it back if it meant working with certain people.

Then something interesting happened. I got approached by a TV veteran to meet with him and talk television. I had no idea what the meeting was about but I had to say yes; he was TV royalty. I went to his office and had about a three-hour meeting. We talked about everything. I sat there thinking, *I used to watch his shows religiously and now I can't believe I'm talking to him in person.* We got along wonderfully. He had a wicked sense of humor. He mentioned that he was working on a reboot of one of his famous TV shows and told me more about what he was thinking. I thought it sounded interesting . . . and somewhat similar to what I had been trying to achieve with my sitcom. We chatted about it and we both agreed that in order for a show to succeed, it needed heart. I ended up leaving the meeting. The next day, my agent called me and asked me what I had thought about how it had gone. I told him I was a huge fan of this person and thought it was really cool that I got to meet him. He asked me if I was interested in doing the reboot with the TV veteran.

I told him I would call him back because I had to think about it. I eventually ended up saying no to the offer later that day. My agent asked me why and I was honest with him. I was afraid that I would make the reboot too similar to my sitcom without even being aware of it. I didn't want to do that because I didn't want people to think that I could only write that one version of life. I had already been fighting against being pigeonholed with so many people that I was afraid of doing that myself. I told my agent that the next thing I came back to TV with (if I ever did) had to be completely different than what my show had been. I wanted to go live life and have things to talk about. I wanted to go do stand-up and connect with people on the road so I could see what they were thinking. In the end, the right person for the job got that job. It was never mine to begin with.

At this point, people are wondering what the hell I'm thinking. How and why am I shunning everything being offered to me? I had been approached to develop my own talk show and had turned it down. I had said no to *The View*. I didn't want to develop a new show because I didn't feel like I had anything to say. The truth is, I didn't know what I was looking for, but I was sure of what I didn't want. I didn't want to not be happy. I wanted this lifelong dream to bring me joy, and I knew that when I wanted to say yes to something, I would know to say yes.

It was then that Pixar came knocking on my door. They were working on the new *Cars* movie for the franchise and they wanted me to voice a character named Cruz Ramirez. She wasn't a big part, but I liked the character. I imagined her spunky and fun. I said yes to them because the idea of doing voiceover intrigued me. I started flying up to Pixar to do the sessions, and slowly realized that, as time passed by, the character of Cruz Ramirez was getting bigger and bigger. It eventually became the co-lead of the movie along with the character Lightning McQueen. I would tell Pixar stories during breaks and lunch about my doubts growing up, about the struggle of fighting to be seen as a real person like everyone else. Then I realized that slowly the script was implementing themes from my own life that Cruz could struggle with too. Oh! This story showed the heart of Cruz. It's the kind of thing I looked for in stories. It made me so proud to bring her to life. When the movie was released, I got so many messages from people saying how much they loved the Cruz Ramirez character because she was a great role model for their kids. It made me happy. My time with Pixar reassured me that listening to my gut was the best thing I could do.

Between 2017 and 2019, I have been pretty silent on the work front by choice. After my first stand-up special was released, I decided to take a break from stand-up. I also didn't feel like it was time for me to do anything related to the entertainment industry. The 2016 election had just passed and a lot of people in my community weren't doing well. There were feelings of fear and sadness. I didn't feel right trying to make a living at the time because, overall, I wanted to make sure everyone was okay. Instead of working, I decided to spend my time going across the country and checking in to see how different parts of my community were doing. I had no idea how the dust would settle and I figured that my top priority was to make sure I did everything I could so that people knew we were going to be okay.

During that time, people would send me messages online. If they liked me, they would send me encouraging messages telling me not to give up and that I would catch a break soon. If they hated me, they would tell me the reason no one wanted to hire me was because

I was such a bitch. What I find funny in both instances is that people seem to be incapable of thinking that the reason I'm not around is intentional. During my "break from life," I have aligned myself with amazing organizations that focus on lower-income neighborhoods, immigration issues, and health care. I felt it was necessary to do so because something inside me told me to do it. It helped me immensely. It made me realize how important that kind of work is to me, as much as the entertainment side. I took a break to save my life, literally, from diabetes. I took a break so that I could be sure that when I wanted to go back to it, I would approach it with the same love and excitement I had for it since day one.

What I've learned throughout my journey so far is that money and fame don't make me happy. Trying to be true to myself and my instincts is what brings me joy, and I believe that following that will lead me to success. I'm ready to go back to work like I used to. I'm actually really excited about it. I'm a different person now. I know so much more than I did years ago. Sometimes the downs in your life teach you to realize what the ups are.

A lifelong dream has the word *lifelong* connected to it because that's how long the dream takes. There is no end to a dream, just a continuation. I guess I'm saying that if you say yes to happiness, I believe you will always be successful. I really ask the question at the beginning of "Lose Yourself" constantly, about what I would do if I had *one* chance to get everything I've ever wanted. Would I go after it or would I let it slip? Answer: Sometimes I have to do both because all the nos will get me closer to a yes.

"LIVIN' LA VIDA LOCA"
RICKY MARTIN

The last picture Byron and I ever took, at the trivia night where we were accused of cheating because we were way too smart for our own good.

This is the part of my life where I become a chola and get a part-time job to buy my first lowrider, thus the song I have chosen for this chapter. I didn't pick that way of life; that way of life chose me.

I'm kidding: I was never a chola, nor did I have a lowrider. I just wrote that because this is the story of the life of a Latina and I feel like people expect those things to happen at some point. I didn't grow up with the lowrider culture, though I do appreciate it. The cars are gorgeous and the truth is, they are part of the culture. There is no denying it, nor should we try to. I think it's important to celebrate all parts of a world that bring people joy within the community. The closest I've ever gotten to becoming a chola is knowing, without having to look it up, that in Scrabble, that word would be worth nine points.

I love words. Always have, always will. I was the kid who used to get excited when my school would have spelling bees because I used to win them, though I stopped competing in the fifth grade after a freak word accident. I had won the local Scripps spelling bee and went on to regionals. Here's a fun fact: What some people are unaware of is that every year, the spelling bee hands out a book of words they'll use so kids can study it. I was given a book and told to memorize the words, and boy, did I ever learn those words.

When I told my brother Eloy I had made it, he decided he was going to help me and become my spelling bee coach, like we were in the movie *Rocky*. I was Rocky, and my brother was Mickey. He'd have me chase after a chicken to help my speed. In the end, I lost the spelling bee to whoever was the equivalent of Mr. T because, apparently, I spent more time working out than I did learning to spell the words. Truth was, my brother *did* become my coach, and for a couple months, I was in extreme word training.

My brother Eloy has served as one of the most important teachers throughout my entire life. Whatever he deemed an important skill, he would take it upon himself to make sure I learned it. He taught me how to play baseball because he was coaching a Little League team and wanted me to join it, so I did. I'm actually pretty good at baseball, to the point that when I've thrown a ball to guys, they've made remarks about it. You know, the usual "You throw pretty good for a girl." (I never exactly understood what they meant by that. If I was a girl and I was throwing pretty good, doesn't that mean that girls can throw? I always imagined that what they meant by that was that they expected me to give birth and bake a cake before I did anything.) My brother taught me how to play sports and also taught me a lot of academic stuff. He bought me a program to learn French when I was a kid and would make me do book reports in the summer "for fun" so I could keep learning while other kids were out playing.

For months, I prepared for the spelling bee. Every day after school (and on weekends), I would sit at the kitchen table and study words from the Scripps book. At the end of my study session, Eloy would quiz me. When the day of the competition came, I went off to represent my school, but when I arrived, I learned something terrible. I had gotten the wrong book of words to study—the previous year's book. I was unprepared and started freaking out. I ended up not doing well and was eliminated within the early rounds. I lost misspelling a word that I have since refused to learn how to spell correctly. The word was *jerriatrix, geriutricks*? I wasn't lying when I said I never learned to spell it right. The word was *geriatrics* (I had to look it up to write it here). It's like being a runner and reliving a fall at the Olympics. I walked away from the spelling bee world and never looked back.

I still love words so much that my idea of a perfect hangout is sitting around with a couple beers and playing Scrabble. I *love* Scrabble. So much so that I was a member of the National Scrabble Association many moons ago. I never competed in the national championships; I signed up to read up about tips and what was happening in the world of words. (And yes, you're right. I *am* cool for doing that!) The best times I've ever had playing Scrabble is with my friend Byron Demond Jefferson. We met in college at freshman orientation. Byron would not only become my Scrabble soul mate; he'd become one of my best friends ever.

As part of orientation, we had to go to a mandatory lecture about safe sex. I didn't want to go because I was a virgin and so far away from being sexually active, I felt like I was going to a real estate course at the Learning Annex; the info might serve me one day but not today. The lecture took place in the school's cafeteria. We had to pick any seat and I (as I normally do) picked a seat away from people. I figured people would come and sit near me, and I was just trying to hold off on doing the obligatory small talk with people until I absolutely had to. I *hate* small talk. It's not real; it's a placeholder for depth. Do we really have to comment about the color of the sky? We see it.

When the talk began, I noticed that no one in the room looked comfortable. The guy leading the discussion stood like he was posing for a catalog in an effort to be cool to the students. The university I attended used to be a church and, if I'm not mistaken, my dorm room was in a building that used to be a convent, so it felt weird for me to get a sex talk there knowing its past. The talk seemed to last forever; I had no clue where it was leading . . . and then we were each given a banana.

I wasn't sure what the banana was for. I figured they were either going to tell us that if we were going to have sex, we had to eat something before for longevity *or* they were about to discuss fetishes. Who knew? Then they handed each of us a condom and we were told we were going to learn about contraception by putting the condom on the banana. Um, why did I have to put a condom on a banana? Was this guy teaching me how to eat safely? I was all for teaching about safe sex, but there was something odd about having to put a condom on a banana in front of a group of other awkward teenagers who had just been dropped off at college to live on their own. I mean, the week before, I had bought a stuffed animal and now here I was, stuffing a banana into a condom. My, my, how times had changed.

The guy leading the lecture started giving us directions on what to do with the condom. It was laughable. He was giving directions like "Take it out of the wrapper." Um, yes. I hadn't slept with anyone yet but I had opened a package of Pop-Tarts before. I knew how opening packages worked. I looked around and noticed some of the other students had already wrapped the condom around the banana while I was trying to listen to the instructions to make sure I was doing it right. I felt like I was putting shelves together and struggling to read the instruction manual. When I got to the part where I actually had to roll the condom on the banana, I couldn't do it. Not because I was struggling with some moral code of any kind; I literally could not roll the condom on the banana. I didn't want to ask for help because I was embarrassed; it seemed like I was the only one struggling. I kept tugging at the condom, trying to make it fit on the banana—and then it happened. The banana exploded in my hands. I had tried squeezing it so much, the banana peel burst open and mushed up on my fingers. Now I was even *more* embarrassed. That's when I heard a laugh and a guy ask, "Are you a virgin?" I looked up and there was Byron. I was mortified and said, "How could you tell?" We both got to the point of tears from all the laughter. He moved closer to me and said he figured he'd sit with me since we were some of the only people in the room who weren't white. He was black, I was Latina. We started making fun of the whole thing, saying that if we were doing the safe sex talk, we would have devoted a section to what Boyz II Men songs people should play and in what order. We kept hanging out for a bit. He was from Missouri and had grown up in a town a couple of hours away. I told him I was from Texas. We both lived a few floors away from each other in the same dorm. He told me he had a car and offered to give me a ride when I needed it and we went our separate ways.

A couple of weeks later, I was walking back to my room from the library when I bumped into Byron. We had assumed we would've seen each other since freshman orientation, but hadn't. We asked each other how we were and both of us were okay but could be doing better. He told me he was going to a store and asked me if I wanted to tag along. I hadn't been off campus since I had gotten there, so I said yes. I got in his car and we ended up spending the entire day together. I went with him to run errands and we discovered that we had the same taste in music. He popped in CDs for us to sing to. We ended our night at a Target, in the toy department. We were walking by the board game section and we both mentioned we liked Scrabble. Then we each had to take a moment to warn the other that we each *really* liked Scrabble. It turned out we were both *obsessed*. We decided to split the cost of the game and share custody of it (remember, we were broke college kids). That night, we played our first game and we instantly proclaimed, like little kids would, that we would be Scrabble soul mates for the rest of our lives.

Our Scrabble games became a routine thing. We weren't big partiers, we just liked hanging out with each other, but when it came to playing Scrabble, we were out for blood. We'd pass each other on campus and trash-talk each other, saying things like "Oh, is that the guy I beat spelling 'jazz' on a triple word? 'CAUSE I THINK IT IS!" He'd say something back like "Is this coming from a girl who tries to pass her Mexican words into the game as words that count?" It was hilarious to have this beef between us. We'd act so serious that people sometimes thought we didn't like each other, but that was our running joke. The idea that these two big word nerds would yell Scrabble insults at each other made our day.

The longer we knew each other, the closer we got. We started spending so much time together, our Scrabble sessions became more frequent and longer. Sometimes we would play one game that could last all night because when it was our turn, we didn't only consider it our turn to place a word on the board; it was also like it was our turn to talk about things we wanted to accomplish. Byron called these our "world domination chats." There wasn't a lot of diversity at the college we attended. We used to say that when we hung out together, we were the "college brochure" portion of whatever room we went into. We joked that when one of us would say, "Brochure," we would pose like we were students in the college brochure, holding up a sandwich with one hand and pointing at it with the other, smiling unrealistically and way too big and saying things like "If you come here, you *too* could hold a sandwich like this!"

We used to spend so much time together, people asked if we were dating, but no, our friendship was nothing like that. It was a connection we shared as two people who knew what we wanted to accomplish in our lives but had no clue how to pull it off. We were both people of color who were big nerds, but also had bursts of coolness. You see, we didn't need anyone to tell us we were cool; we had so much fun with each other, we knew we *were* cool. We could show up to any place and know we'd have fun together because we *made* our own fun.

We became known for our Scrabble games. We even had a theme song for them. Two years after we started playing, Enrique Iglesias had a huge radio hit called "Bailamos," and we changed the words to it so it became about our games: "Scrabblamos." When either one of us wanted to play, we would sing our version of the song to the other and wait for the other to chime in. If we both started singing, a game was about to bust open:

Tonight, we craft
The perfect word to get us the most points
We take the tiles
That's seven points if we use the word moist
We're gonna hope for the J
We'll be all right with a K
Nothing can stop us tonight . . .

Scrabblamos! Let the letters take you over . . .
Scrabblamos, te quiero*'s not allowed*
Scrabblamos, te quiero*'s not in English*
¡Te quiero!

Those years of my life taught me so much. I grew up so fast in such a short amount of time. Maybe most of us do. I learned so much about things I didn't understand, like race. I know, it sounds simple, because obviously I am Latina and a lot of other people in this country are not, so how could I not understand race? Well, it's because I didn't grow up in a very diverse place.

My freshman year, I was working as an usher at the regional theater, which was based on our campus. I was showing this older white couple to their seats and joked around with them while they made their way down. Once they were seated, the man said, "Thank you for your help. You know, you're very pretty for a black girl." *Um, I'm sorry. I didn't catch that, what did you just say? Can you repeat that again, because I apparently had my "DID YOU JUST REALLY SAY THAT?" hearing aids on and I KNOW I just didn't hear you say what you really said.*

Look, I had brushes with people saying things to me. It wasn't completely new, but it was the first time I remember figuring out that people who seemed nice could be racist too. Most of the time when you saw a racist depicted in TV or film, they were mean and bitter. They loved to be vocal about how much they don't like a certain minority. I wasn't used to seeing seemingly nice people so comfortable in their ignorance, they'd throw out those kind of statements as if they were giving me a compliment. I remember staring at this couple for a bit and turning around and walking away. I was taken aback; I didn't know how to respond. I told Byron about it that night. He chuckled and said, "Yeah, that sounds about right in these parts . . ."

Byron was the first person that I got to talk to about my culture. We were playing Scrabble and he asked me about my background. He knew my family was from Mexico, but he wanted to know more. He said he noticed that I never talked about being Latino and asked me why. I had never been asked that before. I thought about it and realized that since I had grown up in a Latino neighborhood, I never really thought about *where* I came from because everyone I grew up with had such similar backgrounds. He told me I should think about what made me different because our differences could also be our strengths. I loved that about our friendship. We were teaching ourselves so much about life all while spelling out words on a board.

Another big lesson I learned in that time is when I had friends come out to me and tell me they were gay. Byron came out to me in a Scrabble game. He didn't know how to tell me. It was not because he felt uncomfortable or anything, he just said that he felt weird bringing it up while playing a board game. I reminded him that our deepest talks had always happened while we "Scrabblamos'd," so it made sense. After he came out to me, he asked me how I felt. I remember looking at him and asking him, "Does you being gay change how you feel about Scrabble?" He laughed. I told him I obviously still loved him and would be there to support him.

What I loved about my friendship with Byron was that he was my first "adult" friend. I had met him in college, but since we didn't have any classes together, we had to make an effort to be friends. I laugh when I think of some of the moments we had where I look back and think, *Only a real friend would do that,* like this one time when I had hooked up with this guy and woke up at the guy's apartment. First of all, let me tell you that the fact that I had hooked up with a guy was super rare for me because I usually freaked out whenever I knew I would end up possibly making out with a guy, especially if I knew it would lead to more. I was in my twenties but felt as if I had no clue what I was doing and the guys would notice that. The best way I can describe it is that I felt anything sexual was like a set of IKEA instructions to me in that I had seen pictures of how it was supposed to look like, but it didn't come with literal instructions, so sometimes I wasn't sure if I was doing it right.

I had gotten so drunk the night before, I didn't know where I was. I remember waking up, looking at this dude, and thinking, *What the hell did I do last night?* I got up slowly from the bed, trying not to disturb the guy (he was still asleep), and made my way to the bathroom to call Byron. When he answered, I told him what had happened and he could not stop laughing at me. I asked him if he could come and pick me up because I didn't have a car back then (I was taking a bus everywhere). He said yes and asked me for directions. That's when I realized how hungover I was and didn't recognize the neighborhood at all. He laughed even more as he asked, "Okay. Are you near a window? Tell me what you see outside." I looked out and replied, "Byron, I see a bunch of trees. Do you know where that is?" He started laughing even harder. That's when I heard the guy I had hooked up with moving around. I told Byron I was going to figure out what had happened and would call him back later. The guy I hooked up with was a friend of a friend. I pretended I totally knew where I was and said I had to leave because I was going to be late for something. He offered to drive me home, but honestly, I just wanted to get out of there and told him I'd catch the bus. OH MAN, I WAS SO AWKWARD! (I love that I say that in past tense like I'm not anymore.)

Once I left the guy's place, I walked blocks to get far away from his apartment so that he wouldn't notice I was lost and then I called Byron back. I told him the intersection I was standing at so he could come and get me. When he showed up, I tried to open the car door, but it was locked. He rolled down the window and said, "You can't come in yet. I need to laugh at you for another minute." And yes, he did exactly that. That day, I felt like Byron had truly saved me.

Even after I dropped out of college, we stayed in touch. That's when you know you have a real friendship, when you both work to stay in each other's lives. We used to spend hours on the phone talking, and this was at a time when long-distance calling was still a thing. For those of you who are unfamiliar, long-distance calls were a relevant thing before cell phones were the norm. Phone companies used to charge you per minute if you made calls outside of what was considered your local area. I rarely allowed myself to use long-distance calling, so if I did, that person *had* to matter to me. It used to be that if I liked someone a lot and asked them where they lived, and it was out of my area, I would dismiss them and say, "I would love to know you better, but it's going to cost me way too much money." But Byron was worth it.

Here's something that might be news to anyone who knows me, but the most important people in my life end up getting their own theme song assigned to them. It's not something I do intentionally, it's just something that happens because music is so important to me and so are these people; it's organic. Byron's theme song was "Livin' La Vida Loca." Every time we were together, he'd play the song and start dancing for me at random points in our hangouts. It always made me laugh so hard, on such a ridiculous level, I'd reach the point of tears.

"Livin' La Vida Loca" is a song from Puerto Rican gorgeousness Ricky Martin. For some people, that hit was the first time they would become familiar with him. For others (like me), that song was a refresher course on him because, at that point, Ricky Martin had already had a career that many would envy . . . and he had done it as a child. Before releasing this mega-hit, Ricky Martin was a little boy who stole the hearts of many as a member of the boy band Menudo. For those of you who are unfamiliar, you're either too young to remember them, or you lived under a rock and I hope the rent there was cheap. Aside from the boy band, Ricky Martin also had stints on soap operas in both the United States and Mexico. In the United States, he played Miguel Morez on *General Hospital* and in Mexico he played Pablo Muriel in a telenovela called *Alcanzar una estrella II*. The Mexican soap opera was actually a sequel to a telenovela that starred two pop stars and was so successful they decided to make *another* one. A rarity in its kind. The premise of the sequel was that there was a national search to create a new pop music group with both men and women, and Ricky Martin's character was chosen. The sequel was successful as well, to the point that they decided to have the fictional band from the telenovela actually become a real band that would release an album and tour. The group was called Muñecos de Papel, which in English translates to Paper Dolls.

Ricky Martin exploded into American pop culture again in 1999 with "Livin' La Vida Loca." The song is a collaboration of lyrics and energy. Seriously, it's got such pep, I can't imagine being sad listening to it. You could be at a funeral and once those horns start at the beginning, there would be an instant dance party around the coffin. It took the world by storm. That emotion was the same feeling I got every time Byron was near me.

When I think about the experiences I've shared with Byron, I'm reminded of a simpler time. It was a part of my life when I had fun and didn't think about work so much. I was raised to be a workhorse. My mom worked double shifts at the restaurant, which led to her children working a lot as well. Some of the best memories of my life were with Byron. The nights that would feel like we had just started only after realizing we had been together all night. The talks about our hopes and dreams as we sat and drank beer. The Scrabble . . . oh my, *all* the Scrabble. It's funny how sometimes the most important people in your life enter in the most unexpected moments.

We didn't physically see each other for years because we were both broke and traveling was not cheap, but we still kept in touch. Within the next few years, I had moved back to Texas from LA, lost my mother, gotten a DUI, started doing stand-up, and eventually began touring the country by myself doing shows at colleges. When I started touring on a regular basis, I ended up planning visits to spend time with Byron every time I was near St. Louis. Even when I was still pretty broke I managed to stretch a penny to see him because it was important. I would book a big hotel room and he would come over and spend the night with me so we could have a Scrabble marathon. We'd buy beers and drink them as we caught up. He's the kind of friend who even if years passed without seeing him, the moment we met up again, it was as if time had frozen and we would pick up right where we left off.

The last time I was in St. Louis was years ago. I told him I was going to be in town and we started plotting. The night I was arriving he was supposed to do a trivia night with friends to help raise money for St. Louis Pride. We made plans for me to pick him up from work. He was bartending/serving at an Italian restaurant. When we saw each other, we immediately started making up strategies because he and I both wanted to mop the floor with the competition. Once we got to trivia night, we sat next to each other and started playing. We were doing okay. I thought we'd do better, but some of the questions were harder than we had expected. Then we got to a round where there were thirty company logos and I knew all of them. I told him we were going to kill that round and we did. We killed it so much that we were actually accused of cheating. People wanted to know how we knew all the logos, especially because there were logos from Canadian and Mexican companies. I explained to them that I had spent a lot of my childhood in Mexico and that I was a comedian who toured Canada and that's why I was familiar with them. They didn't believe me, but there was no proof we had cheated, so they did nothing. For the rest of the night, other tables looked at us with shady eyes. Byron and I laughed together and started saying, "Be so good they think you cheated" for the rest of the night.

After that visit, Byron and I started playing games of Words with Friends (the Scrabble-adjacent app). We were both getting busier with our lives but were now staying connected online. What I found ironic was that social media made you far less social. We didn't have those long phone calls like we used to have; now we texted. We "liked" each other's statuses but didn't really tell each other *why*. Technology was causing us to become less connected, but we were really trying to keep it going. Who knew this more convenient technology would make us feel less connected to each other?

Throughout the years, we would keep in touch less, but it never felt like our friendship had ended. Again, he was the kind of friend whom I could go years without seeing and pick up right from the conversation we had with each other years prior.

But then, in 2016, I got a message from him that I never expected to get.

Byron had cancer.

In September 2016, Byron found a lump on his neck that ended up being non-Hodgkin's lymphoma. Even when he told me, we talked about how he was going to beat it. He had to. Byron was a strong person and he was not going to let cancer get him down. I asked him if he needed anything, but he told me he was fine. I told him if he needed anything to let me know. He said he would. He was getting treatments and seemed to be doing well. At one point, I got a text from him saying he was feeling better, and that made me so happy. I told him he had to get better because we still had to go on our World Domination Tour. He got serious for a moment and told me I was already on the World Domination Tour. I had my own show named after me on TV; I was doing *big* things. I told him if that was the case, he had to get better so he could jump on the train with me. He said he was proud of me for having gone out to do the plans we had made. I said I would've never had the vision if I hadn't gotten his pep talks about it in college. We told each other we loved each other and I told him I had to plan a trip to see him soon. I just wanted him to let me know when he was well enough to see me. He said he would.

That following summer, in July 2017, I had flown to Montreal to do the Just for Laughs comedy festival. It's a festival I've done every summer for years. That year, I was going to tape a set for the Howie Mandel Gala that was going to air in the United States. I usually stay in the hotel where most of the other comedians stay, but that year, I felt like going rogue. I asked for a quiet hotel room away from the parties and got just that. It was farther away from the theater I was taping the special for, but I liked being away from the noise. (I had finally gotten to the age where the sound of people having fun was considered *noise*.) The day I had to do the special, I had made plans to have breakfast with my agent at a diner we go to every year called Beauty's Luncheonette. I was getting ready to head out when I got the news. Byron had lost his battle to cancer.

For a second, I thought it was a joke. I was hoping it was a joke. It *had* to be a joke. It wasn't. I hadn't been prepared to lose Byron. I had experienced death years before, with my mother. This felt different because I didn't have that final moment with him like I did with her. I was in Montreal; not even in the same country as him. In a weird way, even though he was sick, I didn't think dying was a real option because it was Byron. He could beat anything. I burst into tears and canceled breakfast with my agent, but I couldn't cancel this special I was taping. I had to do it. I spent the rest of the day sitting by myself in the quiet hotel room I had asked for, with my loud crying being the only sound you could hear coming from my room. I went to Byron's Facebook page, hoping it had all been a misunderstanding, but once I saw the ongoing posts with condolences, I knew it was real.

As people started finding out about Byron, I began getting messages asking me if I had heard the news. The thing that I wasn't expecting that completely destroyed me were messages I got from some of Byron's close friends in St. Louis who reached out to me to tell me how much Byron had loved me and how proud he had been of me. I didn't know how I was supposed to function that day while processing everything. Hours passed and I had to make my way to the theater. That was when my *other* best friend from college, Eddie, texted me to check in and see how I was doing. We talked about how great Byron was on my walk to the theater. I laughed as we reminisced about a road trip Byron and I had done from St. Louis to Champaign, Illinois, to visit Eddie while he was doing summer stock there. At the time, it was exactly what I needed.

Once I got to the theater, I quickly realized it was the last place I wanted to be. My agent, Stacy, was there and couldn't have been sweeter and more supportive. She was trying to get me through this. It's a weird feeling to feel so somber in a big crowd while everyone else is having fun and happy to be there. At that exact moment, I felt as if sadness were running through my veins. When it was my turn to do the set, I told my agent that I wanted to leave the building the moment it was over. I walked out onstage, did my portion of the special, but was not present at all. I finished the set, and as soon as I walked offstage, I started bawling.

In the following weeks, I cried a lot. I tried attending Byron's funeral, but ended up not going. I couldn't cancel work that I had set up and part of me felt relieved because, honestly, I wasn't sure I could handle it. I couldn't deal with it. I couldn't do it.

I have to admit that one thing from Byron's passing made me furious. When he passed away, he had been crowdsourcing to help pay for his treatments. I had no idea. It made me furious because when my mom was dying, she had no health insurance and we couldn't afford to pay for her treatments either. The idea that someone must ask people for help to live is infuriating. How on earth can we live in a country that deems itself "great" if we can't take care of ourselves when we get sick?

Byron's death scared me. We were the same age. He was young. It's weird how so many of us think that when someone dies. "They were so young . . . ," as if death had a minimum age requirement. I thought about his life, about his death, and figured that I would have to continue doing our World Domination Tour by myself, and if I was going to do that, I was going to have to make sure I was okay. I decided to go to the doctor for a checkup.

Up to that point, I had only had two physicals in my life. I grew up without health insurance and could only go to the doctor if I was really sick because doctors were expensive. I was never taught that health was a priority because medical attention wasn't accessible. I always thought going to the doctor was for the rich. I ended up finally getting health insurance when I got my TV show on the air. It was the only way I was able to afford it. Even once I had health insurance, I had no clue how to use it and was embarrassed to ask people for help. The idea of taking care of my health was completely foreign to me, but I figured that Byron's death was a sign that I should get a checkup, so I started looking for doctors.

I found doctors in my neighborhood online and emailed them, but didn't hear back from any of them. After a couple of weeks, I was finally able to get one doctor to see me: a gynecologist. I figured I'd go and get checked out while I found a primary care physician for a physical. I was really nervous about going to the doctor because I was terrified of them—and of needles. I was worried the doctors would have to draw blood and I was preparing for it like you could've done a montage of me training for a big karate fight. I walked over to the doctor, hoping for good news but, at the same time, figuring I had everything wrong with me because I hadn't been checked out in a *long* time. When I got there, I did the obligatory weigh-in, but not before taking off my earrings, removing my car keys, and throwing away the mint I had in my mouth because EVERY OUNCE COUNTS! I had to take a urine sample and once I was done with that, I waited for the doctor to come in and see me.

I hate waiting for the doctor. The room is cold and sterile. You have posters of medical stuff hanging on the walls. My friend Steve says, "Do they hang those up in case the doctors forget how to be a doctor?" Very true. Once the doctor came in, she told me she wasn't going to do a checkup. They had looked over my urine sample and she had found something that alarmed her. I had protein in my urine, which made her feel I could be not only diabetic but extremely diabetic. She told me she wanted to draw blood and have me come back the next day because there was an endocrinologist who worked out of that same office and it was important that I see her immediately.

I walked home from that appointment and so many things started popping into my mind. I had no idea what was happening. How diabetic was I that I was finding out the news from a gynecologist? The vagina doctor told me my vagina had high sugar? I didn't even know what an endocrinologist was, though the next day, I went back to meet one. She drew more blood from me. I hated needles and dreaded it, but I also hated and dreaded death, so I sucked it up and got pricked again. She asked me if I had any basic diabetic symptoms like an excessive thirst or having to go to the bathroom a lot. I told her I've always been a big water drinker, so I hadn't noticed excessive thirst. I went to the bathroom a lot, but I figured it was from all the water I drank. I didn't feel anything strange. She ran some tests and told me that we had to wait for the results to come back in a couple of days, but after having seen that I had protein in my urine, she was convinced I was diabetic. We needed to get the test results back to know just *how* diabetic I was. What on earth was happening to me? I had gone from going to the gynecologist to get a checkup to suddenly being told I had diabetes. The urgency the doctor had was alarming to me, too, because I didn't feel sick.

The next couple of days I did what most people do. I spent hours online self-diagnosing myself, assuming I had the worst of everything I was reading. When the results were in, I was terrified to hear them. Then the doctor started saying big words I couldn't understand and I had to constantly ask her to stop and explain what she was saying. Turns out, I was diabetic and had been for a long, long time. She explained that a normal glucose level for people with diabetes could range from 80 to 130 mg/dl. I was at 500 mg/dl. The protein from the urine showed that my doctor's hunch had been correct. There had been permanent damage to my kidneys. I had high blood pressure and cholesterol too, but she wasn't going to focus on that yet. I had a severe vitamin D deficiency as well that she was concerned about because what I had in my body was almost nonexistent. She told me our first priority was to try to get my sugar under control because the numbers I was showing in my results were a medical emergency. She told me we had to save my life.

For the next months, I told only a handful of people what was happening with me; only my siblings and a couple of friends knew. I became kind of a recluse. I didn't want to talk to or see anyone. I was put on medication to see if pills could work in lowering my levels and started experiencing side effects. Sometimes they'd get so severe that I eventually stopped leaving my apartment because I didn't want to deal with getting sick while I was out in public. I started working out and changing my diet. It's funny how some people can say they want to lose weight and get in shape but don't. I used to do that. I would say I wanted to lose weight and would go buy the obligatory workout clothes, but would throw in junk food, and eventually the yoga pants I bought to work out in would become my "eating potato chips" pants. I also found it hard to lose weight because there was "never enough time" for me to work out. It's weird how when a doctor told me I had to "save my life," I suddenly found time and made the effort to work out and lose weight.

I wanted to get in shape without making a formal announcement telling people what I was doing because, honestly, I wasn't sure what was going to happen to me. I used to be a big runner when I was younger, but I knew I didn't want to go back to running. I came up with a thing I call "wogging," which is a half-jog, half-walk. I decided to walk everywhere within a two-mile radius of my apartment. If I had to run errands, I would jog to the place I needed to go, do the errand, and walk back home. I bought a tracker to record my steps and started learning what I could and couldn't eat. I was really overwhelmed with all the information I was getting. I didn't know how to process any of it. I had gone from being completely ignorant in regards to my health to suddenly trying to become an expert about my body. One thing I was certain about was that if I was going to get in shape, I wanted to do it on my own because I knew, at some point, I would have to tell people about my changes and I wanted to be able to say I had done it without getting a trainer, or having someone cook my meals or get food delivered. I wanted to show that I could make a change because I realized that if I was going through this, how many others were too? I had grown up poor and didn't have access to doctors. I wasn't taught about eating healthy because when you grow up not having enough to eat, you don't take a minute to ask, "Do you have vegetables instead of this? Trying to lower those numbers, you know." You just eat whatever you can get your hands on. A thing that I also found myself struggling with was an increasing fear I was getting toward food. I was scared to eat certain things because I wasn't sure how I would react to them. I didn't want to spike my sugar because I was terrified that I was going to kill myself. The good thing about it is that I'm a pretty dull eater who can eat the same thing every day for a while, so once I knew something was good for me, I'd eat it for a week.

Luckily, the medication started helping my blood sugar numbers. I went from averaging a 500 for my glucose down to 300 within weeks. With food and exercise, in a couple of months I lowered it down to the low to mid-hundreds. I started getting into my wogging and now average about six or seven miles a day. The incentive to keep working out was to keep living. That's a hell of an incentive. I started losing weight from all of the changes I was making. It wasn't something I was trying to do. I wasn't trying to lose weight. I'll admit, I liked that I was finally fitting into clothes I kept buying for "the day I lose weight." I was just trying to get healthy.

People on social media started noticing physical changes in me. I started getting compliments on how "good" I was looking, but I was also getting a lot of criticism from people who were telling me I was "going Hollywood." It's interesting to see how bold strangers are in telling other strangers what they think of them online. Strangers kept telling me I was losing too much weight, as if I were getting too thin. I'd respond with "I'm getting healthy, not losing weight for looks. I'm not feeling well and will stop losing weight when the doctor tells me it's enough."

Who knew that the idea of possibly dying could be the best diet ever? They should really advertise diets like that. "TRY THE NEW 'GRIM REAPER DIET'! You can eat whatever you want that won't kill you! It's THAT easy!" When the doctor told me I was a medical emergency, I got scared. When she said she was glad we caught it in time, it was terrifying because I couldn't help but think, *What if I hadn't?* What if I hadn't gone to the doctor? More important, what would've happened if I hadn't been able to afford to go to the doctor? My mother died at the age of fifty-seven from things that were so easily treatable but had worsened from the lack of money to take care of herself. You would think that my mother dying from not going to the doctor would've made me want to become more diligent with my health, but I wasn't doing enough.

Overall, my health is improving, but I will admit that (for now), I still get sick. To be honest, there have been a couple of moments when I've felt so bad it made me cry out of fear. There was a time, months ago, when I woke up in the middle of the night to go to the bathroom. I remember walking into the bathroom, and next thing I knew, I was on the floor. When I woke up, everything was pitch-black. I didn't know where I was. I couldn't move. It took me a while to realize that I had passed out in my apartment and was lying on the bathroom floor. I don't know how long I had been on the floor, but I know it was long enough for the left side of my body to be completely numb from having all of my weight on it. I felt so weak that it took me a while to get up. I picked up my right arm and grabbed for my left arm to see how much feeling I had in it. Not much. I then grabbed onto the cabinet door underneath the sink and tried to lift my body. I struggled, but little by little, I eventually got myself up and walked back to my bed. I can't exactly explain how I felt. The best description would be to say that, mentally, I felt like I wasn't present in the moment. I was struggling to move and all I wanted was to get to my bed. I was having trouble breathing and felt like I was trying to stop myself from blacking out. I eventually got myself to bed and passed out again instantly.

The next day, I told two of my closest friends what had happened. I checked my blood sugar and saw it was extremely low, the lowest I had ever had it. My glucose was at around 45, which is a big difference from the 500 number I had when I was first diagnosed. I had a hard time accepting that now I had to keep an eye on my glucose getting too high or too low. My friends asked me why I hadn't called them or why I hadn't gone to the hospital. I was trying to explain to them that, in that precise moment, the thought of getting help hadn't crossed my mind. I hadn't been capable of making any kind of decision in that moment. The only thing I had wanted was to get to the bed. I felt it was the only option I had. I was feeling so weak that I just wanted to muster enough strength to get to the bed and just have whatever was going to happen, happen.

I had never felt like that before. It scared me and made me think about my life. I live alone and don't really talk to a lot of people on a daily basis. If anything happened, how long would it take for anyone to notice? That day made me realize I had to plan things, just in case. I'm not trying to exaggerate or come off as melodramatic. I just became aware that I am an adult and need to do adult things, like make sure my affairs are in order. I want to make sure my family is taken care of. I owe that to them. My number one priority in my life is to make sure they are okay because of the promise I had made to my mother when I was a kid that I would take care of them. I also needed to make sure that a couple of my friends had access to my apartment in case they had to come over in an emergency because I wasn't sure if I would pass out without notice again in my apartment.

SPOILER ALERT: I obviously haven't died. I have lowered my numbers. My doctor told me I was out of the dangerous part of my diabetes and could now focus on other things like my blood pressure, cholesterol, and so on.

I feel like I should take a minute to explain that I know I'm talking about this like it happened a long while ago and I have everything under control, but all of this is still very new to me. I found out I had type 2 diabetes in late August 2017. I'm intentionally trying to talk about it without being so medically factual and throwing out terms that might make me sound like I know what I'm talking about because I really don't have a clue. I'm still confused and trying to figure things out and make sense of everything, and I hope that people who maybe grew up like me, with no money and no health insurance, know that I get that it's overwhelming and frustrating, but it's absolutely doable to understand it and do something about it. It can be challenging but is also life-saving.

The changes I have gone through since then have been a crash course in taking care of myself. I keep listening to Tupac's "Changes." In case you're unfamiliar with Tupac, a lot of his songs talk about problems that decades later are still relevant in society. There's a part of the song where he talks about how we have to eat better, we have to take care of each other and change how we do things because "the old ways weren't working." That is where I find myself now . . . changing because my old ways "weren't working." I'm determined to not let diabetes get the best of me. I'm determined to take care of myself because I still have a lot left to do.

You would think that after my mother passed, I would have taken better care of myself, especially since I was with her when she died, but her death oddly didn't affect me as much as Byron's. Again, maybe it's the fact that we were the same age; I'm not sure. Byron was such an important part of my transition from childhood to adulthood. Our friendship was different from most of the other ones I've had. In every Scrabble game we played in our almost twenty-year-old friendship, we allowed ourselves to be vulnerable with each other in a way that we couldn't be with others.

I struggle when I hear "Living La Vida Loca" pop up on the radio now. Sometimes it makes me cry, other times it makes me laugh. I laugh when I imagine Byron standing in front of me dancing the entire song and pointing to me when Ricky Martin sings "Her skin's the color of mocha" while gyrating his hips like Elvis to make me laugh, but I cry knowing there are no more "Scrabblamos!" moments to be had. I don't know if I can bring myself to play Scrabble again. It doesn't feel right to do so without him. Maybe that will change down the line, but as of now, the game is a part of my past.

Throughout my challenge of getting my diabetes under control, I find myself constantly thinking about him. I think about that day he picked me up in the middle of nowhere after I hooked up with that guy in St. Louis years ago. I think about him locking me out of his car so he could laugh at me for being so stupid. I think about how I felt when he came to my rescue and "saved" me that day. Then I realize that, years later, Byron has saved me again, for a second time. If he hadn't died, I don't know what could've happened to me. In his death, Byron saved my life because that's the kind of thing a best friend does, especially him. In our long friendship, Byron constantly taught me how to live, both literally and figuratively.

> *Our World Domination Tour is still happening. Every time I get to do something I could've never imagined, I imagine you there beside me. Every time I prick my finger to test my blood, I think of you. You saved me and, for that, I l-o-v-e you, Byron (and for those keeping track, love would be an eight-point word in Scrabble).*

My dear friend and mentor Dolores Huerta and me, the day after the 2016 election. She teaches me lessons; I try to pass them on so others know her wisdom too.

"WE THE PEOPLE"
A TRIBE CALLED QUEST

I was a Republican when I was in fourth grade, so it makes absolute sense that the last chapter in my book is about "We the People," a song by A Tribe Called Quest from their last album, *We Got It from Here . . . Thank You 4 Your Service*, because when you think "Republican kid," you think of Q-Tip, Ali Shaheed Muhammad, Jarobi White, and Phife Dawg.

Okay, so let me explain my GOP history. It was an election year and my fourth-grade teacher, Mrs. Edwards, wanted to teach my class about the election process. One day, she announced that she was putting small slips of paper in a bowl and we had to pick one. When it was my turn, I reached into the bowl and picked a paper that read "Republican." The kids in my class were confused by the words written. *Democrat* and *Republican*. What were those words?

My teacher explained to us that the country was having an election to vote for the next president and, during the school year, she was going to teach us about the process by making us become a part of it.

She was a great teacher. She used to buy little plastic toys that we could "buy" from her. They were mostly little plastic trinkets. We didn't use real money; we each had our own "bank account" with our own version of Bitcoin. She would reward us for getting good grades or doing good things and "deposit money" into our accounts. We'd accumulate the money and, every now and then, we could "write checks" and buy the trinkets we could afford with the fake money we had. It was pretty brilliant. She wanted us to learn about the concept of money and figured out the best way was to immerse us in it. I learned about budgeting money in fourth grade, which I think put me way ahead of the game of a lot of other children (and adults). I learned more life lessons in that year than I did in any other grade.

On par with her economics lesson for her students, my fourth-grade teacher wanted us to know how the election process worked because she said we were important to it. This was a gifted and talented class, yet none of us had any idea what she was talking about when she said we were important to the election process. She had built up a lesson plan that included dividing the class into two different groups: Republican and Democrat. She didn't include Independents because she wanted us to know about the process from the start, beginning with the primaries, and figured, to keep it simple for us, she should stick with the country's two-party system.

During the school year, we were given assignments like watching CSPAN on TV and reporting back on what the politicians were talking about. I remember being bored out of my mind. I couldn't understand what anyone was talking about. I kept thinking the reason I couldn't understand what they were saying was because I was a child. Little did I know that, as an adult, I would find that at times I still don't know what the politicians are talking about.

Throughout the year, we also had to keep up with what our

candidates were doing. Each student had to pick a candidate to follow in the primary and if our candidate lost, we each had to support
the candidate our designated political party had chosen. This is obviously not how the system works. Sometimes if your candidate loses
the primary, you might not want to support the main candidate the
party chose, but again, for educational purposes, we were told to
support the chosen candidate of the party. We also had our own version of the electoral college for the classroom, so some of the students
(like me) were given the duty of voting for the candidate we thought
was best suited for the job. In our electoral college, we had to explain
why we were voting for the candidate, but the goal in doing that was
to help develop our critical thinking.

I think it's important to mention that I didn't go to a private
school. I say this because I realize what a rarity it is to have these kinds
of lessons taught in any school and I don't want anyone to think that
I was taught this information because of some kind of privilege our
school had. It was a public elementary school in my hometown. We
didn't have enough money for textbooks; we had to share them a lot
of the time. I was just fortunate to have good teachers.

I am grateful for my teacher making us do everything we did
to understand how our political system worked. It was absolutely
foreign to me when we started the school year, but by the end, I was
completely enthralled by it and motivated to become a part of it. I
loved the idea of voting because that meant your voice was heard. I
couldn't wait to vote.

At the end of the school year, my teacher had our class do a little
yearbook so we could all have copies and remember our classmates
and some poignant lesson we had learned. We had to answer a list
of questions she had come up with and she wanted us to give her a

school picture to use for reference. The one question on the list she gave me that I will never forget was "What do you want to be when you grow up?" Without thinking, I wrote down "President of the United States" and turned it in.

Unbeknownst to her, the lessons she taught my class about politics that year spoke to me on a deeper level. I loved politics because I thought the goal of it was to help as many people as it could. I was taught that this country was a "democracy" and when one voted, the more of our voices were heard and the better life could be for more people. As a poor kid living in the hood, I wanted to get out of the kind of life I had. Yes, I was happy. My family laughed a lot, but we were living in poverty. My goal as a kid was to not only get out of poverty and take my family with me . . . it was also to give back and try to help others who were living like me. I thought that politics would be a perfect way for me to help.

The question is: Why would a fourth grader think about helping and giving back at such an early age?

It was because of my mother. My mother, a Mexican immigrant, had taught me to love this country and how important it was to give back to it. It had become her home; it was our home. She was grateful for all it had given us and it was our duty to find a way to repay the country for giving us the life we had.

I never really understood her love of the country and I feel that the reason was partly because I was born here. I am an American. There is a sacrifice and effort that an immigrant makes that someone like me can't completely understand, even if my own mother and oldest brother were born in Mexico. We are all part of the same family, yet my journey was different from theirs. There were five of us in our family: four children and my mother. My parents had separated before I was born and my father was not in the picture; my mom raised us by herself. I grew up in a mixed-status family, meaning that while three of the five were born here, my mother and eldest brother were undocumented and trying to become permanent residents or, as their cards would eventually read, "Resident Alien." I always hated this term because I thought it was misleading. When I thought about aliens, I always thought of life-forms from another planet. I'm a big science-fiction fan and usually the people in those movies and shows would react so extreme to the aliens. People either wanted them dead and would shoot them, or accepted them wholeheartedly and became best friends with them. Then one day, it hit me. I realized the term *alien* was inaccurately depicting what immigrants were because, let's be honest: some people treat E.T. with more kindness than they do our undocumented brothers and sisters.

It took more than a decade for my mother and eldest brother to get their permanent resident status, but after numerous tries and a lot of money gathered for every attempt, they eventually did. My mother was so proud when she got her card. That card represented a freedom that she hadn't felt before and many in the country take for granted. When my mother got her resident alien card, it meant she could finally go back and see her father.

I was a little girl and traveled with her and my sister when she went to see her family for the first time. I remember the trip. It was long. We picked up a bus from McAllen and took it to Reynosa. Once we got there, we had to change to another bus that would take us to Monterrey, Nuevo León. When we arrived in Monterrey, we got a hotel room to spend the night because we had to change buses again the next day. This bus we couldn't miss because it was only available twice a week. We woke up around four in the morning the next day and got on the road. I kept asking my mom if she knew where she was going, since she hadn't been there in decades. She said she knew. She asked me if I could ever forget where my home was and I thought about it and realized, no, I couldn't. Once we passed a town called Saltillo, my mom told me that was the last "big" city we would pass and that we were close. We weren't, but technically she wasn't lying. We had more than three hours left on the bus, but it *was* the last big city we would cross. Once we got near, my mom kept looking out for "the road." Once she realized it was close, she yelled, "*¡Baja!*" so the bus would stop and we could get off it. We ended up getting dropped off in the middle of nowhere as the bus drove away. My mom had my sister and me walk toward a dirt path and said we would have to walk on that road to get to her village. We walked for a couple of miles, all the while noticing my mom having these random nostalgic moments. She started grabbing berries off plants along the road. She told me she used to eat them as a little girl. She kind of skipped. It's as if she had gone back in time to when she was a little girl walking down that path. Meanwhile, my sister, a teenager back then, had overpacked a suitcase that she was struggling to carry because she had no idea she would have to drag it on dirt and rocks. It was hilarious. Once we got to the village, my mom approached someone and they talked. We had shown up unannounced. There was no phone call; no letter to write. She got directions to her sister's house. I had never met my aunt.

Once we reached the house and my mother got to see her sister, she became happy. It was one of the happiest times I had ever seen my mom have. They talked for hours as the sun set and the village turned pitch-black. They started a fire and sat around it, outside under the stars, talking about when they were little kids. I remember that night because it was the first time I saw my mother not be my mother. She was her sister's sister, she was her parents' daughter. She had come home. She was finally able to come back home.

The part I'll never forget is the moment my mom saw her father for the first time in decades. She melted into a little girl when she hugged him. I felt like she was feeling all the same emotions I felt when I hugged her. It was feeling safe in those arms, a feeling that everything would be okay. Even though I was a kid, it hit me that my mom had given up being able to see her family for her children. She was someone's little girl too. She had given up the family she was from to help the family she had made live a better life. Sometimes I wonder why more people don't talk about that part of immigration. The idea that people who come here wanting a better life have to leave their own families behind, not knowing if they'll ever see them again. I couldn't imagine loving your children so much that you'd decide to say goodbye to your own parents and, in a way, become orphans. It doesn't matter how old you are; leaving your parents can be painful. My mother spent decades of her life having no contact with her family because, back then, there was no internet. Once she was in the United States, she couldn't see her family again until she was able to get something that would ensure her return back to her children in the United States.

We spent about a week there. I would go with my aunt to milk cows before the sun set, stepping in cow manure every time because I didn't know where I was going. I went to get water with a cousin of mine. I had to go to the bathroom outside in a bush. That was fun. The best was the day I was squatting in one, relieving myself, and kept getting knocked over by two pigs that left me on the ground with my pants down. Every time I got up, the pigs would come up to me and knock me over. I ended up walking back to my aunt's house with urine spots on my pants, screaming about the pigs that had it in for me. Good times.

When we got back home, I could see my mom was happier than she had been. It was one of those times that I realized how important family could be to people. She had gotten to see her siblings and her dad and it invigorated her soul. Then tragedy struck. She would soon find out through a brother that her father had died. My mom came home from working at the Mexican restaurant that night and cried like a little girl. I started crying because I couldn't make her stop. She told me how lucky she felt that she was able to go home and see him one last time.

Courtesy of Eloy Alonzo

The day my oldest brother, Ruben, became a US citizen. I asked him what it felt like to be a citizen. He said, "Sister, I always was. It just took the US a few decades to figure it out."

Again, let me reiterate: I don't know the struggle of immigrants, even being the child and sibling of them. I grew up in a mixed-status family and I remember the moment I realized that I was privileged. Yes, I grew up below poverty, practically homeless, but I had been born here. That moment happened June 29, 2016, when I went back home to see my eldest brother, Ruben, fulfill the dream our mother had for herself and for him: he became a naturalized citizen.

It took my brother about thirty years to become a citizen since he first came to this country. People don't realize that it can take an extremely long time to become a citizen because there is no line to get in the back of. The time varies based on circumstances; it's a case-by-case basis. I remember when he told me he had been approved but would have to wait for the next naturalization ceremony to take the oath. I don't think I ever told him this, but I cried so much, alone in my apartment. I have a little altar for St. Jude and I thanked him. I saw a picture of my mom and told her he had finally done it. I had to be there to witness it. It was one of the most important moments in my family's history. I wanted to go be with him because I wanted to represent my mother so that he knew that she was there too.

The day of the naturalization ceremony, there was a heat wave, and the morning began with brutal temperatures. We got to the location and hundreds of people were already in line, waiting to enter the building. Ruben wore a suit we bought the day before. Minutes into the line, my brother was sweating in his brand-new suit. I didn't realize how many people were going to be there. The line, which wrapped around the building and into the parking lot, was filled with people ready to become citizens.

A judge came in, sat down, and the ceremony started. Ruben had to sit with the people that were taking the oath, while my other brother, Eloy, and I sat in the back of the room. There were a couple of moments that stood out to me, like when members of the Daughters of the American Revolution came out to teach the soon-to-be American citizens how to correctly fold an American flag and then helped pass out small American flags to everyone taking the oath. We said the Pledge of Allegiance and afterward the judge spoke about how that specific pledge was special to him because the people in that room were making the choice to pledge an allegiance to this country in the grandest way possible: by giving up their citizenship to the country they were born in.

They took the oath and I started crying when it began because people were smiling so much as they said the words. I wasn't ready for it. Then it got way more emotional. We got to the part where the people taking the oath sat down, and as their countries were announced, each person who was from that specific country got to stand up *one last time* for the country they came from before walking out of the room as an American. There were people from so many countries in that room, countries so far away that I wondered how on earth they ended up being naturalized in this south Texas border town. When they listed the countries and people stood up, sometimes it was one person and other times (like when Mexico was called) a huge group of people cheered. The people in that room had decided to become American. Deciding to pledge allegiance to this country as an adult is different than being born in it because you have to not only consciously choose to do so, you have to prove that you're "worthy" of being American.

After the ceremony, we drove to the cemetery where our mother is buried. I took the little US flag that they gave out at the ceremony and placed it on my mom's grave. I told her that my brother had finally done it. He was American, just in time to vote in the next presidential election.

I was worried about the election. The rhetoric that was coming out of one specific candidate (Donald Trump) seemed aggressive in a way I had never seen before. This was the part where aside from trying to get people motivated to vote, I decided to put my faith in people. I figured there was no chance that someone with that kind of rhetoric could thrive. I was sure that he would be quickly dismissed and would be sent packing. He wasn't. He kept lingering on. News networks started focusing on him because he was a ratings gold mine. They showed him nonstop, spewing his hateful words, and I kept thinking, *Why isn't anyone stopping him?* I remember watching a news network that showed the other candidate (Hillary Clinton) giving a speech on the bottom of the screen, muted. They were waiting for Trump to give his own speech and they deemed it more important because God knows what he was going to say. I kept trying to tell myself that it didn't matter. The good people of this country were not going to fail people like me.

I supported Clinton. I thought she was the better of the two candidates. I'm one of those people who tries to vote for the person I consider best of what we have available, regardless of how much I love that person or not. I would tweet about her and get people on social media telling me to go back to my country. I felt tides changing. I WAS in my country.

The day of the 2016 election, I was on a cruise ship in Miami. I was there to moderate a panel at sea with Mexican American activist Dolores Huerta (known for her work in the farmworkers' movement) and African American poet Sonia Sanchez (known for her work in the Black Arts Movement) to discuss their roles and other women of color in the civil rights movement. The coordinators had assumed Clinton was going to win because that's what the polls were saying, so most of the questions I had been given to ask were framed around celebrating women.

I had never been on a ship before and didn't know how anything worked. I went to dinner and was seated in between a guy and a girl who didn't know each other but were hitting on each other. The girl said she was "into magnets and energy" and the guy started asking her so many questions you would've thought she had invented magnets and energy. Toward the end of the meal, things had fizzled between the two potential lovebirds and the guy shifted his focus to me. Let me tell you, nothing feels better than knowing you're the silver medalist of the night. I told him I was leaving. He tagged along and started following me around. He lived in northern California doing something that at the time I thought was really interesting but now I can't remember because the early results of the election were starting to come in. Clinton won a state. And another. Okay. This was promising. Then Trump started winning states and I thought, *Wait a minute. What is happening?*

The later the night got, the harder the guy was trying to make a move. I kept ignoring him because my eyes were fixed on the TV, watching the election results. Hours later, they had projected Trump the winner and I got emotional. I couldn't believe what I was seeing. Surely this wasn't happening. People wouldn't vote for him. I had been taught this country was a melting pot and that there was this dream that existed here where we could ALL thrive. How could he have won? The people he was critical of were the same ones the Statue of Liberty says this country welcomes. "Give me your tired, your poor, your huddled masses yearning to breathe free"—when did those words stop mattering? When did the words lose their power?

I cried a lot that night. I felt let down. I felt like I had no answers. I felt worried. Then I remembered the panel I was moderating and thought, *Oh, none of these questions are relevant now.* I wasn't worried about being unprepared. It actually seemed fitting that the questions were irrelevant now because, when I moderate panels, I don't like having many questions prepared. I like going with the flow and treating panels like interviews. I looked in the mirror and saw my eyes were puffy. That was not good. I did the best I could with my makeup to cover up the fact that I had been bawling until there was a knock on the door. It was the escort who would walk me to the theater for the panel.

I walked into the greenroom and it was full of people. I saw Dolores Huerta and Sonia Sanchez sitting next to each other, talking. I'm friends with Dolores, but introduced myself to Sonia. They saw I had been crying. They asked me what was wrong. I told them I had been crying because of the election results. They both lightly nodded their heads and Dolores said (with a light chuckle), "Ah, this is the first time your country has broken your heart. Trust me. It won't be the last." Those words hit me and, in that moment, I couldn't remember when words seemed so lethal to my soul.

Dolores looked at Sonia and said, "You remember Nixon?" Sonia gave a smile and a small laugh. "Ah, Nixon . . . ," she said. They talked about a time back in 1968 when people felt hope had died. It was when Robert F. Kennedy had been shot. Dolores talked about how hopeful people were back then and how to many it seemed as if hope had died with him. She should know. Dolores Huerta had been standing next to Kennedy at the podium. He had just won the California Democratic presidential primary. He was shot moments later.

She looked at me and said, "It's okay to be sad. Be sad. Cry. Go to sleep. Then wake up and go fight. The fighting never ends because you're sad. The fighting continues BECAUSE you're sad. The work never stops."

Moments later, the panel started and I introduced the ladies. They sat down and we talked about what they had been through in their lives and the first question I asked was for them to treat me as if I were a younger version of both of them. What advice would they give their younger selves in that precise moment we were experiencing?

The women spoke again about their past. Sonia Sanchez told an emotional story about a time a young woman called in for a job interview and after her arrival to the office, she wasn't interviewed because they hadn't realized she was a black woman. Dolores talked about organizing farmworkers with Cesar Chavez and how the movement started at house meetings that she still holds to this day. They had moments when they held hands, comforting themselves when speaking about monumental times that still held such strong emotions for them, and I felt better hearing them. I was seeing these women talk about some of their scars and remembering how an hour earlier they were comforting me about how I felt. I realized that Dolores was right. The fighting *would* continue *because* I was sad. The work would *never* stop.

We were docked in the Bahamas. I had been struggling to get decent Wi-Fi out on the sea and was finally able to talk to Steve back in Los Angeles about everything. He told me I had to download the new A Tribe Called Quest album. I downloaded it while the ship was docked and started playing it.

This album, *We Got It from Here . . . Thank You 4 Your Service*, was one of the ones I listened to from beginning to end without interruption. The second song of the album, "We the People," became my anthem. I played that song nonstop for days and still listen to it every day. The song starts off with a deep bass beat and a siren demanding attention from the get-go. ATCQ used the chorus of the song to address the negative rhetoric by listing the marginalized groups that were not welcomed in this country: African Americans, Mexicans, the poor, Muslim, gays. YES! The chorus talked about what was happening in our country with a feeling of incredulity but also bluntness. This is where a lot of us found ourselves. It made me feel like I wasn't the only one feeling the way I did. "We the People" hit me on so many levels because it speaks about so many different topics that I could relate to. I would get to a line that would make me scream, "YES!" because of the truth it revealed. There's a verse that talks about how street art gets overlooked and how there is no true level playing field. There is no true sense of competition where we can say "the best" wins because people tend to overlook certain communities and their contributions. Therefore, people might be overlooking the best because we don't know they exist (a prime example of that is ATCQ being overlooked for this album by the Grammys).

The album is masterful from beginning to end. It shows how art can be powerful and educate by talking about real issues in a way that cannot be denied. You might not like what they're saying (I do), but that is exactly why it is important that it is being said. *We Got It from Here . . . Thank You 4 Your Service* was the group's first album in eighteen years and a perfect example of how this group's sound can evolve as they mature, yet still keep the honesty that makes you aware of issues while feeling the beat. ATCQ is critical about the current times and they transcend politics. They talk about culture. They talk about race. They talk about social class. No, I take it back: they don't talk about those topics; they *yell* about them. This is what A Tribe Called

Quest has always been able to do and why they are one of the most iconic names in hip-hop. The beats, the sounds combined with the lyrics, told a truth; their truth.

I didn't feel like being very social during the weeks following the election. I'm an introvert at heart anyway; I rarely leave my apartment if I'm not working, but this time I found myself really struggling to think about what I was going to do next. I played the album every day. I would start with "Space Program," the first track, followed by "We the People." Then I'd keep that track on repeat for about an hour because I wanted to learn the lyrics to that song first.

Weeks passed and Thanksgiving came around. I had planned a trip to Hawaii for my family as a thank-you for everything they had done for me. None of us had ever taken a vacation before and I wanted to give them a trip that they would never forget because I thought we had to celebrate that we had come a long way from our childhood. I booked flights for my sister and her kids, my brothers, and me to go to Honolulu. I booked one of the best hotels and got everyone their own room. I booked my sister and my nephew the penthouse because my sister had to share a room with my special needs nephew and I wanted them to have the best view possible. I painstakingly planned the trip for my family. I knew I wasn't going to be able to enjoy myself because I was the coordinator and, frankly, I didn't care. This trip was really meant for them, not for me. They came to Los Angeles, spent the night, and the next day we were off to Hawaii. Since this was the first trip all of us had taken as a family, to be honest, it felt weird because we realized we didn't know how to travel together. I figured it would be exactly what I needed because I love spending time with my family. We laugh so much when we're together. I figured this was a time for me to spend it with my loved ones and press the reset button.

We landed in Honolulu and got to the hotel. I went to everyone's room to make sure it was good enough for them; I wanted everything to be perfect for them. We rested for a little bit but went out for dinner within an hour of landing. Now, my family is not fancy. We are the ones that go to chain restaurants wherever we go because it's a safe choice. We ask one another where we want to go and can never decide, so in the end, we go to places that no one wants to go to because that way, no one wins. It makes no sense, but, hey, it works for us.

We walked over to a chain restaurant that had an hour wait. We had no choice but to wait. We were on the busy tourist street and my sister and niece wanted to go look at stores. There were seven of us waiting for a table, which seemed pointless, so I told them to go look at stuff while I waited. My eldest brother (the new American citizen) and my special needs nephew decided to stay with me.

We had been waiting for a while; I don't know how long because I feel like time slows down when you're waiting for a table. My brother and I were talking about how pretty it was while my nephew had his face buried in the Nintendo DS I had bought him for his birthday, which had been the day before. There were two men who made their way to us. We thought nothing of it. They got closer. Again, we thought nothing of it. Then they asked my brother where he was from. DISCLAIMER: My eldest brother is a sweet guy. You meet him and you can't help but like him. He's a friendly guy who doesn't like to cause anyone any trouble. You ask him for help, he helps. You ask him a question, he answers it. He approaches everyone as a friend. If we lose track of him, it's usually because he started talking to some people and now they're his friends.

My brother didn't answer because I don't think he was really sure if they were talking to him. It was a crowded area and since he didn't know them, he figured maybe they were talking to someone else. They asked him again where he was from. Now my brother knew they were talking to him. He said he was from Texas and the guys responded with "No. Where are you FROM?" My brother didn't understand the question and again said he was from Texas. One of the guys said, "Nah. You're from Mexico." Now it was becoming clear where it was headed; I knew why they had approached us. They started talking about Mexico and cartels to my brother. He wanted none of it. He stayed calm (I think in my life I've seen my brother upset only a couple of times), but the guys didn't. I was watching this and thinking I was going to have to end up doing something, but didn't know what. They kept telling my brother he was from Mexico and kept yelling things about the cartels to him. He finally told them to leave him alone. That was when the men looked at my special needs nephew and got upset at him because they thought his Nintendo DS was a camera and he was recording them being terrible human beings.

This is where I should tell you that my nephew had just turned twenty-five but has the mental capability of about an eighth grader. That is an important detail to this story because of what happened next. One of the men lunged at my nephew and told him to stop recording while trying to take his Nintendo DS away. The moment the man lunged for my nephew, I got in front of my nephew and pushed the stranger away. I told him he could do anything to me but he was not going to touch my nephew. I was NOT going to let anything happen to that kid. I was terrified but had to protect my nephew's life. The guy came after my nephew again and I held my nephew with one arm while trying to push the guy away again. It was all happening so quickly. My brother stepped in, pushed them, and told them they had to leave. They ended up leaving when they saw people were beginning to stare. I looked at my nephew and asked him if he was okay. He started crying and kept asking me, "Why did they do that, Cris? What did I do?"

That was a hard conversation to have. I had helped raise this kid since he was a baby. I was like a second mother to him. I wasn't ready to have this kind of talk and I didn't know it would be one I'd have to have with him. What do you say? I told him he hadn't done anything wrong. I told him he wasn't the one with the problem; they were. He asked me to sit next to him and grabbed my arm. He wouldn't let go. He kept saying he was scared. Throughout dinner, my nephew would occasionally look at me and say, "But I didn't do anything wrong. Right, Cris?"

When I got back from that trip, I was determined to take action. I told my agents that I didn't want to tour with my stand-up. I wanted to take time off from work and focus on trying to help people because I had been in situations like that, but now I was fearful that my nephew was going to have to deal with them and he can't.

I decided that my goal from that point on was to try and help those who needed it. I wanted to be like the little fourth-grade girl I used to be and make helping people a more prominent part of my life. I had already been doing work like giving speeches and doing panels, but I felt I needed to do more. Yes, I decided to start speaking about my own experience and struggles, but I also had to personally go and physically help the communities that needed it as well. I wanted to go live life and share personal experiences with people because one thing I have learned is that while people might not agree with your history, it's impossible for them to erase it. People might not agree with you, but there is no way to deny what happened. By speaking about my own struggles, I let people know more about me and why I want to be so involved. I grew up in a mixed-status household, so immigration reform and the narrative spoken about the undocumented community is important to me. I lost my mother when I was in my early twenties due to lack of health care, and my own life was saved in 2017 by having the "luxury" of being able to afford health care—universal health care is a priority. My eldest nephew has special needs and I have been an active member of the Special Olympics for years because of him, so focusing on people with special needs is part of who I am. My family squatted and was practically homeless for the first seven years of my life, so having affordable housing and more programs for the homeless and those in need is important.

I didn't want to do any of it for attention. I didn't want to go to an event and take a picture on the red carpet and say that I was there to help. And I'm not passing judgment on that. I am just saying that for me, I wanted to do so much more.

One of the battles I instantly found I would have to fight against was cynicism. When I posted about something I was doing, I always got people asking me what the point of it was. The comments seemed to be on repeat:

"The system is broken. It can't be fixed."

"What's the point? No one listens."

"Where's the beef?"

Okay, the last one was a catchphrase from the eighties, but my point remains intact. The cynicism was one thing I was not prepared to fight against and, let me tell you, it's hard because I can be a very negative person myself. Do you know how hard it is for me to *not* be cynical?

When people ask me what the point in even trying is, I always say the same thing: Change is like dieting. You can't expect to lose the weight in a day when it took you years to gain it, but if you make an effort, you can make little changes that amount to a bigger change. The truth is, true change takes a long time. It might not happen in our lifetime, but that doesn't mean we shouldn't try. I am sick and tired of opening my internet browser every day of my life and seeing hateful words fill my screen. I keep thinking, *Is* this *the message we want to send to our future?* Do we really want to tell children that it's pointless right from the start? Because, trust me, kids are listening to everything we're saying; they see our actions. If our future is listening to what we're doing, then maybe we need to make sure that we take action and try to make change. I decided to use my voice, my life . . . to ensure that at the end of my life, I will have known that I helped move the needle. I want to know that I was not only on the right side of history; I was on the right side of empowerment.

Me outside the White House, protesting the family separations.

When I travel, I listen to "We the People" on every flight. When I find myself walking around in cities, I have it playing in my earbuds. When I want to feel empowered, I play it and think about how A Tribe Called Quest wasn't making the album for me, but it sure felt like they did. It energizes me. It reminds me of why I want to do what I want to do.

We are living in a time I never thought I'd see. Nazis are back like bell-bottoms. Blatant racism is running rampant. I'm not saying they ever went away, I'm just surprised by how the ideals have helped empower people once again. Do we not learn from past mistakes? Do we not finish reading the history books?

True change takes a long time and, luckily for us, time is all we have.

I'd like to share a list of things that help me keep going. They serve me; they might serve you as well:

1) If you want to make sure your voice is heard, educate yourself and others. How do we do that? By learning and then teaching others about our rights because YOU HAVE RIGHTS. Don't let anyone tell you that you don't. Make sure the information gets passed around. We cannot make change if we're not informed about WHY we want to make a change.

2) Don't listen to the critics. Anyone who tells you no does not belong on your journey, especially if their argument is just to be cruel and vindictive for no reason. Those feelings are not about you, they're about them.

3) Speak up for people who can't. If you want to help, then do it and know that all help is appreciated. This is something I

cannot emphasize enough. In the past year, I have seen friends organize events and get disappointed when instead of one hundred people, only twenty show up. We need to change our way of thinking and realize that you brought twenty people out. That is a success, NOT a failure.

4) Know that sometimes what is best for everyone isn't what's best for you. Try not to be selfish. Think about others. One of the reasons we are in our current situation is because people thought about their own agendas. We need to understand that sometimes we can't get what we want for good reason. It's like when I hear someone say, "My prayers weren't answered." We forget that, in that case, your prayers were answered, it's just that sometimes the answer is no . . . and that is for a reason.

5) Be kind to each other and check in. Remind each other that we're capable of greatness because, let's face it, the positive is always silenced by the negative and that needs to stop. Tell each other we matter. It might be a reminder for some; others might not have ever been told they matter. Let's remember that everyone is important to someone.

There has been a lot of talk about "Making America Great Again," but the truth is, in order to make it great AGAIN, we have to make it great the first time . . . for everyone. We do that by honoring everyone who has worked to make this country better than what it used to be. By honoring the magic, the heart and soul of every one of its people, and ensuring that we are all treated equally and have a fair shot . . . THAT is how we make America great.

This chapter doesn't have an ending because this part of my life is still happening. I don't know how it ends, but I would like to imagine it will end on a hopeful note. I guess in a way this chapter is like an old-school "To Be Continued . . ." episode where you had to wait a while to see how it ends. I hope it's good because hope is all I have right now.

ATCQ said this was their last album because Phife Dawg died before it was released. I thought it was only fitting to end this book with A Tribe Called Quest because "We the People" made me realize that my quest is about looking for my tribe. To Q-Tip, Ali Shaheed Muhammad, Jarobi White, and Phife Dawg, I want to tell you not to worry.

We, the people, got it from here.

ACKNOWLEDGMENTS

I may have written a book, but I would be a fool to think that I did it on my own. This book exists because of the following people. I am grateful to have you in my life and along with me on this journey.

First of all, I would like to thank my family. Without you, I literally would not have survived. We are the children of an incredible woman that gave us everything she could. I don't know if you know how special you are, but to me, you're everything. To my oldest brother, Ruben, I never met our dad, but I never needed to. You watched over me and moved mountains to make sure that I got a fighting chance at my dream. I love you. To my brother Eloy, thank you for always making me want to strive for more. You taught me not only how to throw a mean baseball, but to question everything, and that knowledge will always trump privilege. Being poor didn't mean that we couldn't compete with the rest of the world. In fact, it was our strength. To my sister, Julie, thank you for taking on the duty of being a second mother when I was a little kid while still being a kid yourself. People don't realize the responsibilities you had were to be the "American" mother to us by filling out paperwork, translating and filling in for our mother when she was incapable of understanding things as we all tried to acclimate to this country.

To my súper friend Emilia, thank you for being there to hear me agonize over everything. You have been there every step of the way with this book, from the moment I pitched the idea, to planning our writing trips where this book was written, to hearing me question myself and always telling me to not stop. I am lucky to have met you. We are each other's fans and support system. I'm glad we are both in this world together, fighting hard to tell our stories.

To my agency, WME, specifically my stand-up agent, Stacy Mark, and literary agent, Mel Berger. WME has helped me attain opportunities I could never have imagined existed and it is because of Stacy Mark. Stacy, I don't know if you realize how special you are to me. You took a chance on me when others wouldn't. Here we are and I can't wait to see where else we go. To Mel Berger, you heard my idea for this book and took it seriously. I can't tell you how much it meant to have someone take me and my idea seriously. You took what I wanted to do and helped set me up with my literary family. Thank you.

To my manager Peter Principato at Artists First, thank you for helping me find myself. You have been vital in the making of this book by helping ensure that my voice is my voice. It's an ongoing project, but I am so grateful to have you, Maggie Haskins, and Brian Dobbins in my corner.

To my publisher, Atria Books, you took a chance on my story. Very few people have trusted me enough to let me do that in my life. You have allowed me to be myself and gave me the most incredible editor ever, Rakesh Satyal. Rakesh, thank you for your words and guidance as I stepped into the literary world, hoping to not make a fool out of myself. You are great.

To my dear and most patriotic, American-loving friend Jose

Antonio Vargas, you and I were writing books at the same time and somehow you beat me to the deadline. You have been there to support me without me having to ask and have become part of my family.

My dear friend Alicia Menendez, I could not have finished this book without your help because you literally saved my life in New York City. I hope you realize how lucky I feel to have you in my life. Your love and support constantly make me ask myself what I did to deserve a friend like you.

And I saved the best for last. To my best friend, Steve Halasz: What can I say? The words *thank you* don't do justice to everything you've done for me. You've been part of my life for fifteen years. You have been there at my lowest points, which makes me want you around for my highest points, because my best moments belong to you too. I would literally not be here today if it wasn't for you. You helped me get here. Thank you.

Cristela Alonzo is a comedian, actor, and producer who made TV and film history twice: in 2014, when she became the first Latina to create, produce, and star in her own network sitcom, *Cristela*, and again in 2017, when she became the first Latina lead in a Disney-Pixar film, *Cars 3*. Alonzo's stand-up special, *Lower Classy*, can currently be streamed on Netflix. In addition to her work in entertainment, Alonzo sits on advisory boards for several organizations, such as People for the American Way, a progressive advocacy group; La Unión del Pueblo Entero (LUPE), founded by Cesar Chavez and Dolores Huerta; and Define America, a nonprofit media and culture organization. She also devotes a large part of her time to being a voice for Latinos, immigrants, the disenfranchised, and the underrepresented. She frequently gives speeches, moderates panels, and helps raise awareness and money for numerous organizations and nonprofits.